Essays on the Trinity

Essays on the Trinity

~

Edited by
Lincoln Harvey

CASCADE *Books* • Eugene, Oregon

ESSAYS ON THE TRINITY

Copyright © 2018 Wipf and Stock Publishers. All rights reserved. Except for brief quotations in critical publications or reviews, no part of this book may be reproduced in any manner without prior written permission from the publisher. Write: Permissions, Wipf and Stock Publishers, 199 W. 8th Ave., Suite 3, Eugene, OR 97401.

Cascade Books
An Imprint of Wipf and Stock Publishers
199 W. 8th Ave., Suite 3
Eugene, OR 97401

www.wipfandstock.com

PAPERBACK ISBN: 978-1-5326-1196-4
HARDCOVER ISBN: 978-1-5326-1198-8
EBOOK ISBN: 978-1-5326-1197-1

Cataloging-in-Publication data:

Names: Harvey, Lincoln, editor

Title: Essays on the trinity / edited by Lincoln Harvey.

Description: Eugene, OR : Cascade Books, 2018 | Includes bibliographical references.

Identifiers: ISBN 978-1-5326-1196-4 (paperback) | ISBN 978-1-5326-1198-8 (hardcover) | ISBN 978-1-5326-1197-1 (ebook)

Subjects: LCSH: Trinity

Classification: LCC BT111.2 E6 2018 (print) | LCC BT111.2 (ebook)

Manufactured in the U.S.A.   07/20/18

Scripture quotations from the ESV® Bible (The Holy Bible, English Standard Version®), copyright © 2001 by Crossway, a publishing ministry of Good News Publishers used by permission. All rights reserved.

Scripture taken from *The Message*. Copyright © 1993, 1994, 1995, 1996, 2000, 2001, 2002. Used by permission of NavPress Publishing Group.

Scripture taken from the New King James Version® (NKJV). Copyright © 1982 by Thomas Nelson. Used by permission. All rights reserved.

Scriptures taken from the Holy Bible, New International Version®, NIV®. Copyright © 1973, 1978, 1984, 2011 by Biblica, Inc.™ Used by permission of Zondervan. All rights reserved worldwide. www.zondervan.com The "NIV" and "New International Version" are trademarks registered in the United States Patent and Trademark Office by Biblica, Inc.™

Scripture quotations from New Revised Standard Version Bible (NRSV), copyright © 1989 National Council of the Churches of Christ in the United States of America. Used by permission. All rights reserved worldwide.

Contents

Contributors | vii
Preface | ix

Essays on the Trinity: Introduction | 1
—Lincoln Harvey—

CHAPTER 1
Choose Ye This Day Whom Ye Will Serve . . . | 14
—Robert W. Jenson—

CHAPTER 2
**"A Semblance More Lucid"?
An Exploration of Trinitarian Space** | 20
—Jeremy Begbie—

CHAPTER 3
Paul the Trinitarian | 36
—Chris Tilling—

CHAPTER 4
That We May Know Him . . . | 63
—Lucy Peppiatt—

CHAPTER 5
The One Divine Nature | 85
—William Hasker—

CHAPTER 6
On Whether or How Far We Can Know God: A Reflection on Epistemology, Language and Trinity in the *Five Theological Orations* of Gregory of Nazianzus | 108
—Claire Louise Wright—

CHAPTER 7
"From His Fullness We Have All Received": Reflections on Divine Agency, Time, and the Experience(s) of Salvation | 125
—Chris E. W. Green—

CHAPTER 8
Restlessly Thinking Relation: Robert Jenson's Theological Uses of Hegel | 140
—Stephen John Wright—

CHAPTER 9
Trinitarian Science? Torrance, Polkinghorne, and McGrath on a Christian Interpretation of the Natural World | 162
—Gijsbert van den Brink—

CHAPTER 10
Trinitarian Prayer: Praying from Slave-Narratives to Son-Narratives | 178
—Julie Canlis—

CHAPTER 11
The Trinity in Paul: From Confession to Ethics | 192
—Douglas A. Campbell—

CHAPTER 12
Bridging the Gap between Piety and the Theology of the Schools: A Working Sketch | 217
—Christoph Schwöbel—

Contributors
Order of Appearance

Lincoln Harvey is Assistant Dean and Lecturer in Systematic Theology at St Mellitus College, London, UK.

Robert W. Jenson was Emeritus Professor of Religion, St. Olaf College, and formerly Senior Scholar for Research at the Center for Theological Inquiry in Princeton, New Jersey, USA.

Jeremy Begbie is Thomas A. Langford Research Professor of Theology at Duke Divinity School, Duke University, Durham, North Carolina, USA.

Chris Tilling is Graduate Tutor and Senior Lecturer in New Testament Studies at St Mellitus College, London, UK.

Lucy Peppiatt is Principal of Westminster Theological Centre, Cheltenham, UK.

William Hasker is Professor Emeritus of Philosophy at Huntington University, Indiana, USA.

Claire Louse Wright is Minister of the Word at Bathurst and Perthville Uniting Churches, New South Wales, Australia.

Chris E. W. Green is Associate Professor of Theology at Pentecostal Theological Seminary, Cleveland, Tennessee, USA.

Stephen John Wright is Lecturer in Christian Theology and Wesley Studies at Nazarene Theological College, Manchester, UK.

Gijsbert van den Brink is Professor of Theology and Science at Vrije Universiteit Amsterdam, Netherlands.

Julie Canlis is a part-time lecturer at Whitworth University, Washington, USA.

Douglas A. Campbell is Professor of New Testament at the Divinity School, Duke University, Durham, North Carolina, USA.

Christoph Schwöbel is Professor of Systematic Theology at the University of Tübingen, Germany. He has recently been appointed to a chair in systematic theology in the School of Divinity at St Andrews University, Scotland, from September 2018.

Preface

On the brink of submitting this manuscript, I heard that Robert W. Jenson had died. Jenson had been the first person I approached with the idea of publishing some contemporary essays on the Trinity. His reply was immediate and decisive, stating his approval for the project and including a beautifully phrased sideswipe at another theologian. (I won't name names, so we all stay on our toes.) He then cheerfully signed off with a greeting and his trademark signature, *Jens*. And that was all I needed. With Jens on board, I knew this project could fly. Without his support, it just wouldn't have happened.

Jenson's essay arrived soon after, and is entitled "Choose Ye This Day Whom Ye Will Serve . . ." As always with Jens, it's a brilliant piece. As always with Jens, you know the one he serves: Jesus is front and center.

The manuscript remains as it was when the news broke. This means it still contains references to Jenson in the present tense, although the list of contributors has been slightly modified and this short preface inserted. The preface is an opportunity to give thanks to the God and Father of our Lord Jesus Christ for the Spirit's work through the remarkable Jens. The book is dedicated to his memory and surrounded with prayers for his beloved Blanche.

May Jens rest in peace and rise in glory.

Essays on the Trinity
Introduction

Lincoln Harvey

To get to grips with the doctrine of the Trinity, the theologian must work their way through a series of technical concepts. The meaning of begetting, spirating, persons, substance, and nature must be grasped, as well as a number of interconnected concepts like *arche*, aseity, *taxis*, perichoresis, and simplicity. These technical terms constitute the tools of the Trinitarian trade. The theologian must learn how to handle them if they are to speak with any precision about God the Father, Son, and Holy Spirit.

To learn how to use these technical concepts, the theologian must study the work of other theologians. They will likely wrestle with the writings of Athanasius and the Cappadocians, for instance, examining the way these early theologians used the various concepts in the run up to the councils of Nicaea and Constantinople. Of course, the theologian quickly discovers that the technical terms didn't drop out of the sky—doctrinal glossolalia!—but were instead drawn from the already existing vocabulary of Greek philosophy. This means the theologian must familiarize themselves with the writings of the ancient philosophers if they are to decipher the way the technical concepts functioned in the early debates. With conceptual trails running in every direction, the theologian soon faces up to the enormity of their task.

However, the theologian cannot stop there. They must journey beyond Nicaea and Constantinople, examining the works of Augustine, Cyril, and

Maximus, for example, before following a path through the writings of Aquinas and the schoolmen, on into the Reformers, before taking a look at how the concepts were used—or not used!—in the post-Enlightenment period. Eventually they will run up against Barth and his *Dogmatics*, and then those theologians who write after him: Pannenberg, T. F. Torrance, Moltmann, Jüngel, Coakley, Rowan Williams, and Sonderegger, and the list could go on. Contemporary publications abound.

With countless books, articles, and essays piling up on their shelves, the theologian quickly realizes they do not have enough time to read everything on this subject. Life is too short.[1] That's why our teachers are so important, functioning as navigational aids who effectively map the terrain for us, a point to which I'll return. But with so many writings already in print, we should first ask whether we need yet another collection of essays on the Trinity. Some no doubt will say that we don't. But I'm convinced that we do. That's because changes are afoot.

The doctrine of the Trinity enjoyed something of a recovery during the latter part of the 20th century, or so it is often said. The doctrine began to play a prominent role in the work of a number of influential theologians, with the likes of Colin E. Gunton, Robert W. Jenson, and John Zizioulas writing extensively on the subject.[2] Of course, their constructive proposals varied enormously, but these theologians—and others like them—attempted to foreground the way in which the biblical God is eternally constituted through a dynamic event of perichoretic mutuality, in which the communion of Father, Son, and Holy Spirit makes God what it is to be God. In many respects, none of this was new, and rarely was it claimed to be.[3] Christian theologians have always grappled with the doctrine of the Trinity, as my opening paragraphs tried to indicate. But something seemed different with this current crop of theologians. They allowed their understanding of the Trinity to inform what they then said about everything else, with their accounts of creation, atonement, ecclesiology, and the like being shaped by their vision of the triune God. As a result, technical concepts like perichoresis and person began to get a mention in just about every theological exchange, with constructive proposals popping up left, right, and center.

---

1. "Some 130 million books have been published in history; a big reader will get through 6,000 in a lifetime. Choose carefully." Alain de Botton, Twitter, January 7, 2017.

2. Gunton, Jenson, and Zizioulas have written extensively on the subject. Amongst many others, see Gunton, *One, the Three, and the Many*; Zizioulas, *Being as Communion*; Jenson, *Systematic Theology*.

3. Robert W. Jenson, for example, clearly understands himself to be doing something unusual, though not without precedent in the tradition.

By the turn of the twenty-first century, a booming industry had been born. Any theologian worth their salt was talking about the Trinity.

As varied as their proposals were, the renaissance theologians—for want of a better adjective—often read the history of doctrine in a similar manner, a reading that was at once both positive and negative. Positively, the fourth century was said to mark a revolution in thought. The early church fathers had recruited concepts from the existing philosophical discourse and drafted them into their exegetical analysis of the God of Easter and Pentecost. In so doing, they had used the concepts to depict a God who is eternally to-ing and fro-ing in self-relation, with the tri-personal gospel event of dynamically mutual differentiation being posited as the unsurpassable life of God's substantial reality. This conclusion upset some deeply held assumptions, most notably the commonly held belief that "Being" is splendidly singular, unmoving, and unchanging, and pretty much un-anything at all. It meant that the inherited assumptions embedded *in* the concepts had to be redefined in real time *by* the novel use the of concepts that were being set. As a result, the technical words still looked the same, but their meaning was subtly changing as they were deployed in a nexus of statements about the peculiar God whose works are recounted in Scripture. In short, a new metaphysics was constructed as the Hellenic patterns of thought were evangelized. And this was obviously good news.[4] At least, that's what we were being told around the turn of the century.

But the silver lining had a cloud. According to the renaissance theologians the Hellenic concepts had been baptized, but not by full immersion. The church's best thinkers—both then and now—failed to grasp the revolutionary character of the new metaphysics, and were oblivious to the way the technical terms had been redefined through the course of the early exegetical labors. This meant the original philosophical meaning continued to determine the theological use of the concepts, which meant in turn that an alien metaphysics was shaping the church's speech about God. And this wasn't good. The doctrine of the Trinity had emerged from a penetrating analysis of the God of the gospel, but with the original philosophical definitions still entrenched within it, the doctrine somehow slipped its object and was set to serve a god undefined by Scripture. The doctrine of the Trinity thus became—and too often remains—an impenetrable puzzle, instead of a reasonable confession on the basis of theological exegesis, and this had happened because a category error had taken place: Christian theology was

---

4. The evangelization of our metaphysics is a key theme in the writings of Robert W. Jenson, who continues to use variations of the phrase in many of his works as he seeks to offer a "revisionary metaphysics." See for example, Jenson, *Systematic Theology*, 90, and his "Reply" and "Response."

being done on terms set by a rival religion. In short, the concepts had become a Trojan horse.

Substance, simplicity, omni-this, that, and the other were usually the villains in this tale, and were thought to owe more to Plato than to the teaching of the apostles. Blame was often laid at the feet of Augustine, who had failed to grasp the scale of the Cappadocian achievement, thereby erasing eventful differentiation from his account of God's being, and promoting instead his vision of a simplified deity possessed of a bland singular nature.[5] As a result, urgent remedial work was needing to be done, and the renaissance theologians were on hand to do it—or so it was claimed at the turn of the century.

But fast forward to today. The renaissance project is now under attack and beats a retreat on a number of fronts. Patristic scholars like Lewis Ayres have debunked the historical narrative, with Augustine long since sprung from the dock.[6] The concept of simplicity has returned from its exile, and is again doing the work perichoresis had done in the renaissance accounts.[7] The concept of oneness is once more prioritized, with theologians like Sonderegger distancing themselves from attempts to foreground the Three.[8] We even hear how the concept of person—so pivotal to the renaissance project—should be stripped of all content, effectively parked in eternity and utterly detached from any anthropological sense of the word.[9] As a result, leading theologians such as Stephen R. Holmes and Fred Sanders are repenting of their former ways, and now align their thinking to the classical tradition as they dismiss the renaissance as a mistaken dead-end.[10] Aquinas is the new Cappadocian, again all the rage, and as for using the doctrine of the Trinity to shed light on created reality, well don't. That would make you a "social Trinitarian," a term that is fast becoming derogatory in certain circles.

---

5. For example, see Gunton, "Augustine, the Trinity." For a summary of various critiques of Augustine, by Gunton and others, see the first chapter of Green's *Gunton and the Failure of Augustine*.

6. See, for example, Ayres, *Augustine and the Trinity*; and Ayres, *Nicaea and Its Legacy*. See also Barnes, "Augustine in Contemporary Theology."

7. See, for example, Dolezal, *God without Parts*; and Duby, *Divine Simplicity*.

8. Sonderegger, *Systematic Theology*.

9. See, for example, Holmes, "Classical Trinity."

10. Karen Kilby describes the recent work of Stephen R. Holmes as an act of repentance, see Kilby, "Trinity, Tradition, and Politics," 76. For the key text, see Holmes, *Holy Trinity*. In a recent article, Fred Sanders notes "I confess" as he indicates a change in his ways of thinking. Sanders, "We Don't Actually Need a Trinitarian Revival."

Whether or not this is a fair summary of the current state of play is for others to decide, but one thing seems certain: times have changed. I may of course be in danger of reading too much into these developments, imagining there is more at stake than is really the case. It might be no more than a War of the Schools, as it were, a localized squabble that interests only a few.[11] But the localized nature of the debate is one of the reasons it feels so pressing, albeit secondary to more urgent issues to do with the church's faithful witness. At the risk of sounding like a disgruntled groupie, it feels somewhat personal. Let me explain.

Like many other students, I did my postgraduate work at King's College, London, where Colin E. Gunton had attracted a large number of fledgling theologians. We all benefitted from the excellent faculty assembled at King's, as well as the weekly *Research Institute in Systematic Theology*. This public forum allowed us to engage with the world's leading theologians, and we regularly got to learn from Zizioulas, Jenson, and many more besides. There was a genuine sense of excitement in the air at King's, as students saw how the doctrine of the Trinity might unlock the issues that lay at the center of our own projects. Times were good, and Colin remains of blessed memory—which is one of the reasons why the recent backlash against the renaissance project is so troubling. As mentioned earlier, all of us are indebted to our teachers, trusting that they have grasped the issues with better minds than our own, with doctrine inevitably introduced to us in person, by persons. That's why it's difficult to be as objective as we should when our teachers come under attack. It's hard to accept that our own studies may have been fundamentally misguided, and as a result begin to unlearn the patterns of thought we've been taught to think. A lot feels at stake.

Of course, re-thinking issues isn't a bad thing, and personal contingencies—like those outlined above—cannot carry much weight. Our teachers are only human, and history is littered with influential thinkers who have turned against their teachers.[12] Besides, theological study follows baptism, and so it is invariably caught up in that ongoing conversion from one way of life to another. Just like the rest of our lives, any break between the old and the new is never as clean as we'd like, and so we must continually revisit previous judgements and decisions, ensuring that they were not built on sand,

---

11. I am indebted to Douglas Farrow for this way of putting it.

12. To keep things at arm's length, we need only consider famous cases in philosophy such as Nietzsche and Wagner, Wittgenstein and Russell, Heidegger and Husserl. Steve Holmes's comment, in his introduction to Gunton's work on Barth—which he thinks he may have heard from Gunton himself—is apt here: "The British academic career consists of spending three years learning how to think like your PhD supervisor, and thirty years of learning how not to." Holmes, "Introduction," 7.

and be ever alert to the fact that no one is infallible. Nonetheless, the recent backlash against the renaissance theologians has gained such momentum that their entire project is in danger of becoming a footnote, bracketed in time and no longer worthy of investment. And that doesn't seem right to me—at least not yet.

For a start, a lot of the recent criticism misses the mark. Quasi *ad hominem* attacks, for example, rarely prove fatal. Any deficiency in patristic studies doesn't mean someone's systematic proposal can be so easily dismissed. Misreading the tradition—notably Augustine and the Cappadocians—is a serious matter, and, given the terms of reference, especially troubling for Eastern theologians like Zizioulas. But historical footnotes only ever support constructive proposals, they don't constitute them in themselves. The true test is whether a proposal is biblical and in accordance with the creeds, and the renaissance theologians certainly listened carefully to Scripture and sought to allow it to determine their definition of who God eternally is. As a result, their status cannot be decided by quasi *ad hominem* attacks alone, and it certainly hasn't been yet.[13]

In addition, the problem the renaissance theologians were tackling hasn't disappeared, even if their explanation of its genesis is proved to be faulty. The doctrine of the Trinity remains peripheral to much of the church's thinking, with many of our clergy going about their business with no reference to the way in which God is eternally God. I think Rahner's diagnosis still holds true, with the content of too many sermons, for example, remaining unaffected if the doctrine of the Trinity was ever proved to be false.[14] That surely is a problem that still needs to be tackled, and God is much more beautiful—and exciting—than the bland singularity so often buried in the deadpan term "God." That's one of the reasons why I'm not yet ready to jettison my teachers. Their work serves the church well in this regard, and helps our clergy see that the Trinity is good news. The ecstatic nature of Personhood, mutually bestowing and receiving identity in subsisting

---

13. This points draws on the language I used in my appraisal of McNall's *A Free Corrector*, see Harvey, "Review." Besides, historians have made us all aware that Nestorius probably wasn't Nestorian and that Arius probably wasn't the Arian we think, and that their names now essentially function as short hand for the (unfairly) associated positions. If so, why not Augustine in this case, even if he wasn't the "Augustinian" that renaissance theologians made him out to be? For a list of texts that rehabilitate Nestorius, see Riches, *Ecce Homo*, 10. See also, Wiles, "In Defence of Arius."

14. It is still hard to argue with Rahner's opening diagnosis: "despite their orthodox confession of the Trinity, Christians are, in their practical life, almost mere 'monotheists.' We must be willing to admit that, should the doctrine of the Trinity have to be dropped as false, the major part of religious literature could well remain virtually unchanged." Rahner, *Trinity*, 10–11.

relation—the pure mutual act that is God—startles so many people, and allows us to see that the technical concepts are not abstract and arid, but instead trace the Gospel story of the *life* of this Son with his Father, in the Spirit they share. And that's important. Any of us who teach in the seminary context still encounter candidates who've been taught by their clergy that the doctrine of the Trinity is unrelated to a faithful life of worship, prayer, and the study of Scripture, and next to no use in the urgent missionary work of the church. Of course, the teacher's task is to help them overcome this prejudice, showing them how the philosophical concepts—which they too readily disparage—have been reworked in light of the gospel. We need to show how the church's vision is defined by the reality of our prayer and our Bible study, and that the doctrine of the Trinity possesses an intellectual beauty that puts the world to shame. And here's the point: I still find the God described by the renaissance theologians does just that. The doctrine comes alive for the student, with the technical interrelation of person and nature, perichoresis and communion, offering such a wonderful vision of God that they sometimes hope it's right even if it's proved to be wrong. The relational ontology that characterizes the work of Zizioulas, for instance, proves utterly compelling to so many future clergy, and invigorates their preaching and teaching in turn—and for the good in my opinion.[15] Students see how the renaissance accounts of God's eternal communion allow us to celebrate the irreducibly personal nature of God's existence, allowing them to invest meaning into their heartfelt belief that God *is* love. Suddenly what he does is identical with who he is, and their trust in him will often rocket, with the work of the renaissance theologians helping them imagine the eternal ground of God's self-giving grace—and again that is surely a good thing, the value of which cannot be dismissed. Academic theology must serve catechesis, faithful proclamation, and the right ordering of our worship, and if anyone's theology leaves God's people unmoved, something can't be right. And that's why the current shifts in theology are much more than personal. A great deal is at stake, regardless of who taught who.

  Of course, none of this means the renaissance project is the answer. We all know heresies prove popular, scratching the contemporary intellect exactly where it itches. But the pedagogical impact of the renaissance should earn it some slack, encouraging us to be patient, testing and probing its constructive proposals, grappling with the deployment of the technical concepts, and continuing the gospel-driven interrogation of the metaphysical assumptions that determine our own confession as we seek to worship the triune God. Hence this book.

---

15. See Zizioulas, *Being as Communion*.

This volume offers the reader a collection of contemporary essays on the Trinity. The essays have been drawn from various sub-disciplines, with some chapters written by biblical scholars, others by analytic theologians, and still more by systematicians—a varied bunch indeed. But I must add an important disclaimer: *this introduction is not a manifesto, and I'm certainly not speaking on behalf of any of the contributors.* This introduction only sketches the terrain as I see it, albeit with a polemical slant, and in no way attempts to position the essays themselves. In fact, none of the authors speak directly to the issues I've raised. Instead, the book gathers together some current work on the doctrine of God in the hope that it can contribute to the ongoing task of grappling with the doctrine of the Trinity. In short, this book is not a renaissance apology or defense.

However, in the first chapter, Robert W. Jenson does up the ante. With characteristic insight, Jenson sets a decision before us, asking whether we are prepared to take the biblical narrative seriously or instead duck the metaphysical revision it demands. Mapping the options before us—and the way they play out in contemporary theology—Jenson ventures into territory his regular readers will expect, exploring the way the persistence of an enfleshed Word in theological statements about the Trinity runs contrary to what we assume to be true when we stop to think. As Jenson sees it, the persistent incursion of the name of the resolutely incarnate Word—where we should expect the *Logos asarkos* to appear in the literature—results from our theological conversation being nudged along by God's own conversation, in which our identification of what makes God to be God intersects with God's own internal deliberation on the very same matter, a deliberation in which Jesus *is* the eternally spoken event of God's self-determination. As always, Jenson dares us to place Jesus front and center, and shape our metaphysics around him thereafter.

In the second chapter, Jeremy Begbie takes up a different issue. Aware of the dominant trends in contemporary theology, Begbie examines various conceptions of "space," arguing that auditory space—as opposed to visual space—provides an interpretative tool that can unlock some of the zero-sum games that define so much of our discourse. As Begbie understands it, musical space provides a way to conceptualize "interpenetration," and incorporate both unity and distinction, otherness and relation within it, and—with suitable analogical qualification—helps us imagine the life of God *ad intra* without confusing the life of the Three with our own. Begbie's attempt to redefine the terms of reference poses a question to renaissance Trinitarians and to those who oppose them. We all need to rethink how best to conceptualize "space."

In the third chapter, the New Testament scholar Chris Tilling ventures a bold thesis: the Apostle Paul was a Trinitarian. To substantiate his claim, Tilling examines Paul's thought, attempting to understand it on its own terms. Tilling refuses to draw lines between Paul and subsequent dogma, nor look for embryonic instances of later Trinitarian thought, but instead allows Paul's thinking to bear its own load. In so doing, Tilling identifies a series of patterns in Paul's theology by which Paul establishes what Tilling refers to as the *Godness* of God. Tilling is thus able to demonstrate that for Paul the transcendent uniqueness of God centers on a tri-unity of active agents who together share, and therein constitute, the God-relation that identifies which God is the true God. Tilling's work rewards careful reading. In any debate, Scripture is the trump card.

In chapter four, Lucy Peppiatt explores the relation between the participatory nature of our salvation and the way in which we conceive of the Trinity. Peppiatt critiques two popular moves in contemporary theology: an overemphasis on the apophatic nature of our knowledge of God, and a truncated—and therein misused—conception of inseparable works *ad extra*. Drawing from a range of ancient and modern sources, Peppiatt shows how the relation between a participatory ontology of salvation and a theological epistemology enables us to conceptualize the dynamic nature of the triune *taxis*, thereby finding a place for the monarchy of the Father and a christological anthropology in which we are free to speak of God's being *ad intra*. Peppiatt's work is an important corrective to our tendency to divorce the doctrine of God from the reality of salvation, and draws the doctrine back into a life of prayer.

In the fifth chapter, we turn to the work of an analytic theologian. William Hasker examines the claim that there is only one concrete divine nature that is simultaneously the nature of each of the three Persons. Hasker first outlines why we can't reject the concept of a single concrete nature, before pinpointing problems associated with a strong doctrine of divine simplicity. Highlighting the way identity and relation are incompatible in the strong accounts of simplicity, Hasker draws on a number of analogies to argue that the metaphysical idea of "constitution" is the best way to conceptualize the relation between the one concrete nature and the three Persons of the Trinity. With characteristic rigor, Hasker makes a very strong case indeed.

The sixth chapter is written by Claire Wright. Her contribution is in some respects the most unusual, though—like all the essays!—a must-read. Following on from Hasker, Wright again confronts us with the difficulty of conceptualizing the utterly singular nature of God. To this end, she examines the sermons of Gregory Nazianzus to explore the extent to which the being of God is in any way knowable through the reality of human language.

However, Wright shows how Gregory allows the doctrine of the Trinity to transcend the limited space within any analogy, thereby undermining our overconfidence *and* pointing the way ahead as he links (re)semblance to (con)substance within his analysis of encountering the Trinity. Wright's work is rich in textual insights, not only with regard to the nature of Gregory's unconfounded Three in self-same substance, but also to the need for a disciplined playfulness in our own theological labor. I'm confident that every theologian will benefit from reading this chapter, and likely take up a new skill as they continue their own writing projects.

In chapter seven, Chris Green draws from his own experience in the Pentecostal church, and turns his mind to the question of the relation between God's being-in-act and God's ongoing work in our lives. Green immediately recognizes the difficulty of reconciling the pure immutability of God's being-in-act with God's ongoing involvement in historical events, but Green offers a way to conceptualize how God is drawing creation toward its telic end in correlation with his eternal life. To do this, Green lays out the Trinitarian processions on the economic missions *in*, *outside*, and *upon* time, thereby ensuring that his account of the inseparable work *ad extra* is both constant and variegated, and thus offering a vision of faithful discipleship in which the reality of our lives—in their joys and sorrow, blessings and curse—bear witness to the nexus of threefold mutual action that opens creation up to its transfigured end in Christ. In short, the *lively* immutability of the pure act that God *is* constitutes the "texture" in which our lives happen. This essay will help all of us think carefully about the way the Father, Son, and Spirit are at work in our day-to-day lives.

In the eighth chapter, Stephen Wright also examines the relation between God's being and our history, but from a very different angle. Focussing directly on the work of Robert W. Jenson, Wright examines the commonplace critique that Jenson's theology is Hegelian, in that Jenson's construal of God's time historicizes God's being and thereby erases the difference between God and the creature in some kind of pantheistic theogony. Wright effectively turns the tables on many of Jenson's critics, showing that Jenson's opponents are often at best dealing in caricatures, essentially missing the truly dialectical nature of both Hegel's and Jenson's work. In contrast to these misreadings, Wright draws out the way both Hegel and Jenson agitate any premature settlement, disrupting the static polarities of dependence or independence through a "Chalcedonian logic" in which sublation situates difference in lively relation. Wright's work shows that Hegel and Jenson deserve a fairer hearing, while pinpointing the way Jenson differs from the great German thinker.

In chapter nine, Gijsbert van den Brink explores the extent to which the doctrine of the Trinity can function as a heuristic device within the natural sciences. To this end, van den Brink traces the thoughts of T. F. Torrance, John Polkinghorne, and Alister McGrath, bringing the issue into focus by setting out the promise and problems associated with a Trinitarian theology of nature. By clarifying the convergences and differences between these three thinkers, van den Brink demonstrates how epistemology and ontology coincide, thereby encouraging us to allow our knowledge of the created order to be shaped by the one who called it into being. Though van den Brink recognizes the perils associated with this approach, he rejects the widespread opposition to theologically-shaped science, and instead concludes that who God is *in himself* can function as a heuristic key in our scientific endeavors. Van den Brink's work indicates how our thinking about the Trinity makes a difference to how we understand the world.

In chapter ten, Julie Canlis turns our attention back to prayer, effectively showing how the ancient adage of *lex orandi, lex credendi* cuts both ways. First instilling an attitude of wonder in her reader's mind, Canlis draws on her own experience to explain how the stories we tell about God determine the way in which we pray to God. To chart the power of stories to shape our imagination and inform relationships, Canlis sketches the different narratives she imagines being told by Pharaoh, Moses, and Jesus, calling on her readers to accept their identity as children of God by entering further into the marvel of prayer *in* God and celebrating our freedom in the Spirit to speak to our Father with the Son. In so doing, Canlis shows how Christian prayer is personal participation in a God who *is* eternally love, and does so in a disarming way that resonates with our status as God's children.

In chapter eleven, Douglas Campbell takes us back to the writings of St Paul. Campbell shows how Paul's ethic is determined by his understanding of the triune nature of God, with the Apostle's desire to incorporate diverse peoples and cultures into the infant Christian community being fuelled by his knowledge that the Christian life is most basically a participation in the dynamic God who *is* love. Of course, this means Paul's understanding of how we should live depends on him making a conceptual move from confessional knowledge about the relational nature of God to the structuring of the created reality we inhabit, effectively allowing the first to determine his understanding of the second, and thereby refusing to uncouple the doctrine of the Trinity from creaturely life. In short, doctrine—as Barth put it—is ethics. If Campbell is right, then it seems Paul's thinking is travelling in precisely the opposite direction to those who claim that the doctrine of the Trinity has no place in any consideration of how we are to live together. Instead, our confession of the Trinity determines our ethic.

In the final chapter, Christoph Schwöbel exegetes the primary Christian act of worship, the Eucharist. Schwöbel illustrates the way in which the concept of orthodoxy posits the inherent connection between right worship and right thinking. In so doing, he explores the Trinitarian presuppositions that constitute the underlying logic of a eucharistic liturgy, and then allows the triune shape of the liturgical act to generate the key questions that must be answered in any attempt to articulate the doctrine of the Trinity. Schwöbel thus demonstrates how our theological proposals need to emerge from, and align with, the way in which we worship the triune God. In effect, constructive theology is provoked by what we do in church and needs to be measured by the difference it would make to the way Christians worship. Theological concepts therefore serve the primary task of adoring the Father, Son, and Holy Spirit, and so any technical ideas developed in the academy should be traceable to a liturgical setting. In short, Schwöbel shows how the two domains should never be separated, even if they remain fundamentally distinct.

As these brief summaries show, what we have here is a diverse range of essays whose unifying theme is the doctrine of God and his relation to us, rather than a polemical agenda or common cause. The topics covered are vast in scope, and the approaches taken markedly different. However, I'm confident that each essay will offer its reader a rich resource that will help them in the ongoing task of thinking faithfully about the Father, Son, and Holy Spirit. I hope this book is of service to the church and of benefit to theologians, clergy, and students alike. It is offered to the glory of God, Father, Son, and Holy Spirit.[16]

Bibliography

Ayres, Lewis. *Augustine and the Trinity*. Cambridge: Cambridge University Press, 2010.
———. *Nicaea and Its Legacy: An Approach to Fourth-Century Trinitarian Theology*. Oxford: Oxford University Press, 2009.
Barnes, Michel Rene. "Augustine in Contemporary Theology." *Augustinian Studies* 56 (1995) 237–50.
Dolezal, James E. *God without Parts: Divine Simplicity and the Metaphysics of God's Absoluteness*. Eugene, OR: Pickwick, 2011.
Duby, Steven J. *Divine Simplicity: A Dogmatic Account*. London: Bloomsbury, T. & T. Clark, 2016.
Green, Bradley. *Colin Gunton and the Failure of Augustine*. Eugene, OR: Pickwick, 2011.

---

16. I'm grateful to John Colwell, Paul Cumin, and my colleagues, Mark Knight, Donna Lazenby, and Michael Leyden, for critical comments on a draft of this chapter. As always, any faults remain my own. I am also very grateful to Chris Tilling for the original idea of putting together this collection of essays.

Gunton, Colin E. "Augustine, the Trinity and the Theological Crisis of the West." *Scottish Journal of Theology* 43 (1990) 33–58.

———. *The One, the Three and the Many: God, Creation and the Culture of Modernity.* Cambridge: Cambridge University Press, 1993.

Harvey, Lincoln. "Review of 'A Free Corrector: Colin Gunton and the Legacy of Augustine' by Joshua McNall." *Augustinian Studies* 47 (2016) 102–4.

Holmes, Stephen R. "Classical Trinity: Evangelical Perspective." In *Two Views on the Doctrine of the Trinity*, edited by Jason S. Sexton and Stanley N. Gundry, 25–48. Grand Rapids: Zondervan, 2014.

———. *The Holy Trinity: Understanding God's Life.* Milton Keynes, UK: Paternoster, 2012.

———. "Introduction." In *The Barth Lectures*, by Colin Gunton, transcribed and edited by Paul Brazier, 1–8. London: T. & T. Clark, 2007.

Jenson, Robert W. *Systematic Theology.* Vol. 1, *The Triune God.* New York: Oxford University Press, 1997.

———. "A Reply." *Scottish Journal of Theology* 52 (1999) 132.

——— "Response to Watson and Hunsinger." *Scottish Journal of Theology* 55 (2002) 225–32.

Kilby, Karen. "Trinity, Tradition, and Politics." In *Recent Developments in Trinitarian Theology: An International Symposium*, edited by Christophe Chalamet and Marc Vial, 73–86. Minneapolis: Augsburg Fortress, 2014.

Rahner, Karl. *The Trinity.* London: Continuum, 2001.

Riches, Aaron. *Ecce Homo: On the Divine Unity of Christ.* Grand Rapids: Eerdmans, 2016.

Sanders, Fred. "We Actually Don't Need a Trinitarian Revival." *Christianity Today*, May 23, 2017. http://www.christianitytoday.com/ct/2017/may-web-only/we-dont-need-trinity-revival-fred-sanders.html.

Sonderegger, Katherine. *Systematic Theology.* Vol. 1, *The Doctrine of God.* Minneapolis: Fortress, 2015.

Wiles, Maurice. "In Defence of Arius." *The Journal of Theological Studies* 13 (1962) 339–47.

Zizioulas, John D. *Being as Communion: Studies in Person and the Church.* London: Darton, Longman and Todd, 1985.

CHAPTER 1

Choose Ye This Day Whom Ye Will Serve . . .

ROBERT W. JENSON

I

At various times in the history of Christian theology, one might have stepped to the side, viewed the theological scene, and pronounced, "We are now urgently faced with an historically decisive choice, between theological proposals that do [A] and those that do [not-A]." And on very few occasions the claim would even have been true. I am about to make just such a risky move.

I urge: it is time to deliberately choose between (A) attributing decisive ontological weight to the overall narrative character of the Bible and to the plot of the story that it does seem to tell, and (not-A) holding that one or both of these cannot or should not bear such a burden. (My own conviction will not long remain secret.)

Perhaps there is general assent to the observation that the Bible on its face tells a history running from its first verses to its last, from Creation to creation's End—to be sure, with detours, subplots, and incorporated stories; memoirs of the prophetic word by which in Israel's understanding God drives history; and pauses for prayer and for lament or celebration of major turnings. Perhaps there is even widespread agreement that this observation is in some way theologically important. But in *what* way important? That is the question, I now propose, starkly before us. Let me begin with some possible not-As to my A.

II

Of course, if one is antecedently determined enough, one can use historical-critical regents to resolve the Bible's prima facie over-all narrative into a heap of detached bits and pieces, some of which are narratives and very many of which are not. Then you have departed from that "general assent," and can have the fun of putting the bits together in whatever fashion pleases you—or indeed leaving them in postmodern chaos. I mention this only because there are still a few such vandals out there, despite Irenaeus and the church's general rejection of gnostic-style exegesis.

Moving on to more respectable possibilities: one can plausibly treat many of the stories incorporated in the Bible, such as Jesus's parables, as intended to evoke a reality that is not itself narratable, that is not itself shaped by any before-and-after—as Jesus's parables are indeed often interpreted. Then we may, once launched on such reading, come to suppose that also the over-all story that the Bible tells must point to a reality that is itself not finally narratable. After all, the Bible reveals God; and God in and for himself, it will be said—often with outrage at the very thought—surely knows no before-and-after. Our knowledge of this atemporal sort of divinity must then derive from some available and prior metaphysics; and several have been on offer, one or two claiming biblical origin or sanction.

Or we may have encountered the power of narrative in another context, perhaps as a general theory of language, and applied it to theological discourse. At least some of what used to be called "narrative theology" seems to me to have proceeded in this fashion. It may be that the general theory was itself inspired by observations about Scripture and its exegetical tradition, but that is beside the present point.

It may even be that the doctrine of the Trinity—to which I am coming on A's behalf—is invoked and so shaped as to provide or suggest a metaphysics of divine timelessness. Father, Son, and Spirit must be somehow distinguished from one another. One not-A way in which this might be done is by distributing pieces of usual Trinitarian discourse. "The Son became incarnate" is indeed a narrative sentence, and thus can provide a parking place for any theologically weighty narratives found incorporated in the Bible. The Spirit is "breathed" by the Father with this Son. Thus, Son and Spirit, and their relation, are "of" the Father, who just so is himself prior to their doings. He is neither incarnate nor breathed; and he is the *fons trinitatis*, who defines what it means to be God.

There are many ways of using the mass of inherited language about the Trinity to construct a not-A doctrine. I have invented the above only as a sample.

Doubtless, the simplest way to assert not-A is just to denounce the proposal of A as by some criterion—however obtained—outside the bounds of legitimate theological development. This simplicity does, however, demand a further current choice, between two ways to read the theological tradition, to which we now turn.

III

The choice within which our A vs. not-A resides is between two ways of reading the long, intense, and richly profitable history between the gospel and pagan Greek religious reflection—effectively Aristotle and the Platonists. Von Harnack set the usual terms of discussion by describing that history as a progressive hellenization of the gospel. He regarded this as a bad thing, an alienation of the church from an original simple faith. But one can affirm the "hellenization thesis" itself and instead judge this history good. The gospel message—it is said—needs a presupposed "theism," which Platonism and/or Aristotle can provide. This claim, I suggest, is at least implicitly made in current versions of not-A known to me.

On the other hand, those like me who affirm A read the tradition just the other way around, either explicitly or in effect: what the Fathers were, in fact, up to was the gospelizing of Hellenism. The hellenization thesis, whether used negatively or affirmatively, got it exactly backwards.

On this latter view of the history, revisionary interpretation of Greece's religious metaphysics by the biblical gospel-narrative may be seen as a continuing task of Western theology. Thus Aquinas, to instance one—often very daring—reviser, regularly made "the philosopher" say the exact contrary of anything the historical Aristotle could have dreamed. The observation which occasions this essay is that work on this long project is under renewed dispute within Western theology. There are influential authors who vehemently deplore taking this aspect of theological history so seriously, and in fact hold to the hellenization theory in its above noted positive use.

IV

A chief locus of the history between Greece and the gospel is the teaching of God's Trinity, comprising dogmatic decisions, unchallenged tradition, and continuing work on questions which the at any time established orthodoxy leaves open for further thought and decision. And present necessities of Trinitarian reflection are a stated theme of this volume, so Trinity is the final—in both senses—matter of this essay.

Close to the heart of classical Greece's religious thinking was the apprehension of divinity as a predicate capable of degrees: deities could posses more or less of what makes them be deities. The second-century Christian "philosophers"—their word—whom we usually call "the Apologists," exploited this feature to interpret the Son's ability to mediate between God's presumed timeless and impervious eternity and creatures' needy temporality, conceiving this ability as constituted by the Son's being not *quite* as divine as the Father. Surely a clear case of von Harnack's hellenization! But consider what followed.

We often label this device of locating the Son's—and then the Spirit's—divinity down a tiny step from that of the Father "subordinationism." Under the spell of its use by the great Origen it was for a century a standard reliance in the theologically dominant East. But Origen also called for conceptually self-disciplined biblical exegesis, and if you heed this call you will sooner or later notice that in Scripture the line between Creator and creature admits of no such blurring, of no almost-gods or almost-creatures: everything is either the one or the other. At this point one strand of Origen's multifarious work undercut another strand. (Which often happens with the legacy of powerful thinkers.)

So—on which side of the line is the Son? The question could no longer be finessed after Arius stated the subordinationist principle altogether too bluntly: according to Arius the Son is indeed a *very, very* special creature, but if you insist on a straight answer, he is a creature. Compelled by Constantine's political needs to rule on the disputes that Arius had stirred up, the bishops at Nicaea finally blurted, "Ok already! So Arius and his closer followers must be wrong about that." Therewith they—many of them unwittingly—rejected that central feature of Greek religious wisdom on which they had been relying at a key juncture of their own thinking. It took some time and much further controversy before the church could settle down to this ruling.

Of course, Nicene thinkers could not just stop discoursing about deity with Plato and Aristotle, and in the process picking up much of their language. But now we were using—and if need be distorting—this language for our own purposes, step by step working toward speech about deity shaped to biblical commitments.

So that is one side of the matter. The other is a need for some ventures in Trinitarian thought itself. I will take up just one, that has recently been a center of controversy.

V

As we have noted, one dominant form of current not-A polemics posits the necessity of a "theism" not shaped by Christology and presupposed by Christology. This teaching has an inner-Trinitarian correlate, the posit of a *Logos asarkos*, an existence of the Logos "before" it is incarnate as Jesus of Nazareth.

To assert A we must challenge this language—among more obvious reasons, reliably to negate the heresy that "there was when the Son was not." I have been working on that project, and hope to have contributed a few bits. The following may perhaps add another.

For who exactly is this Son? Surely not an entity fully characterized *only* by *not* being incarnate, for such a negative entity could have no soteriological role and the concept "*asarkos*" could then have no place in theology. The notion thus undoes itself in use; or if it does not must evoke a vacancy "before" the birth of the Son, and so indeed dream a sort of "time" when the Son was not.

And indeed Christian discourse about the *Logos* has never gotten well along without somehow identifying the preexisting *Logos* soteriologically. To instance a surely orthodox author, Athanasius in the first volume of his work on the incarnation exhibits a language-habit that is often remarked—and regularly quietly dismissed. But there the passages sit on the page: precisely the *preexistent Logos* is identified as "our Lord and Savior Jesus Christ." Nothing compels us to take this as thoughtless or enthusiastic. We are free to note its possible kinship to certain other—to be sure, startling—phenomena, in which in various ways the Trinity's constitutive inner discourse seems to *intersect* with ours. Despite our initial recoil, the phenomena are many and unavoidable.

Prominent among such is prayer of petition, which must either be absurd, or be nothing less than our permitted mixing into the triune deliberation we call providence. As the Father and the Son deliberate in the Spirit, we as members of the "whole Christ" are invited to contribute our opinions. Then there are the places in John's gospel where the mutual verbal glorification of the Father and the Son opens to the disciples, to encompass *their* glorification and indeed that of those whom their addresses will bring into the same fellowship. Or what is going on in the Psalter's "hymns," where the assembly praises God not by saying "You are great, O God," but by exhorting unidentified others to do so? "Praise God from whom all blessings flow." Why this twist? Or what makes an absolution spoken by one of us reliable? Or. . .

Our present concern is places in churchly discourse that identify the eternal *Logos* on the pattern "Lord and Savior Jesus Christ." I propose: the persistent and logically various occurrence in the church's discourse of soteriological identifications of the eternal Son are nudges inflicted by intersections of our speech with the mutually identifying addresses of the Father and the Son themselves.

According to widely accepted teaching, in God persons are relations subsisting of themselves, without needing an x that *has* the relation. So far so good. But since in the church's faith the Son is equivalently the Word, these relations must be words, addresses between Father and Son in the Spirit: "Thou. . ." I propose that the aforementioned nudges cue our hearing of these God-constitutive addresses: "Thou Son, Lord and Savior Jesus Christ. Thou Father of the Lord and Savior Jesus Christ. Thou Spirit of the Lord and Savior Jesus Christ." Behind this converse of mutual identification there cannot be even nothing.

Those who like me take the A-road have many tasks ahead. Perhaps the way stretches to the end of Western theology itself.

CHAPTER 2

"A Semblance More Lucid"?
An Exploration of Trinitarian Space[1]

JEREMY BEGBIE

One of the most spectacular artifacts of the fifteenth century, the Van Eyck Altarpiece in Ghent, "The Adoration of the Sacred Lamb," introduces us to a richly Trinitarian world.[2] In the central lower panel an austere Father presides, and a diminutive dove, the Spirit, hovers over the enthroned Lamb. But rather more subtle Trinitarian elements are also present. A panel on the upper right shows an angel at a keyboard,[3] delighting her colleagues. She plays three keys (C, E, and G). If we were to gather those keys within the span of an octave, they would form what today we would call a major triad.

This painting dates from 1432, and this triad had not yet become the basic building block of Western music. But by the late sixteenth century it is being talked about as a kind of ideal: the celebrated Italian theorist Gioseffo Zarlino calls it the "perfect harmony" (*harmonia perfetta*).[4] Ignatius of

---

1. This essay was originally published in Westhaver, *Transforming Vision*.

2. An image of the Van Eyck Altarpiece can be viewed here: https://d32dm-orphc51dk.cloudfront.net/OwlWfVVnhTVhSdrgeBv7dw/larger.jpg.

3. An image of the angel on the keyboard can be viewed here: https://i.pinimg.com/originals/7a/b3/8f/7ab38ff4113b23701c855a2a38f16f88.jpg.

4. Zarlino, *Le Istitutioni Harmoniche*.

Loyola was profoundly impressed by its Trinitarian suggestiveness,[5] and in the early seventeenth century the German theorist Johannes Lippius writes:

> The triad is the image of that great mystery, the divine and solely adorable Unitrinity (I cannot think of a semblance more lucid). All the more, therefore, should theologians and philosophers direct their attention to it, since at present they know fundamentally little, and in the past they knew practically nothing about it.[6]

Lippius was by no means the last to exploit the triad in this way. For J. S. Bach it was almost second nature to use three consonant tones in Trinitarian settings, and we could name many others since Bach who have employed the chord in this way.[7] The question I want to press in this chapter is: to what extent is there something especially appropriate about what was hinted at in Van Eyck's musical panel and has been developed by countless musicians and music theorists since? Is there something unusually "lucid" about the "semblance" between three consonant musical tones and the Trinity?

I want to contend that there is, and that allowing music its voice in Trinitarian theology will do very much more than provide useful illustrations for anxious clergy on Trinity Sunday. Indeed, there is much to suggest that at least some of the West's protracted struggles with Trinitarian doctrine have been severely hampered by what might be called unmusical habits—patterns of thought and speech that muffle and distort the testimony of Scripture and the church's confessions, but that could have readily been avoided if more attention had been paid to something as unassuming as a three-note chord. I hope to show that music can yield remarkable resources not only for exposing some of theology's most intractable aporias but also for circumventing them, allowing the Trinitarian pressure of the New Testament to be conceived and articulated more fully and faithfully. Moreover, far from defusing the mysteriousness of the triunity of God, its ungraspable, uncapturable character will be made all the more evident. I aim to show this with respect to a theme in Trinitarian theology that has become the focus of intense discussion in recent years: divine space.

---

5. Ignatius, *Autobiography of St. Ignatius Loyola*, 37–38.

6. Lippius, *Synopsis of New Music*, 41.

7. For an illuminating and detailed discussion, see Bertoglio, "Perfect Chord," 485–501.

The Space of Visual Perception

To open up the distinctiveness of what music has to offer here, I begin by making some very basic observations about the contrast between aural and visual perception.[8] To take the visual first: objects in our visual field typically occupy bounded locations such that they cannot overlap without losing their integrity. We are unable see a patch of blue and a patch of yellow in the same space *as* blue and yellow. The colors either hide each other, or, if the colors are allowed to merge, they become green. The spatiality perceptible here is one of juxtaposition and mutual exclusion: things can be next to each other but cannot be in the same place at the same time. Things take up circumscribed places—so space becomes, in effect, the aggregate of places. This is a space that encourages zero-sum games: the more of one thing, the less of another. Discrete objects are related to each other against the background of a spatial whole. We distinguish "somewhere" from "elsewhere." We can measure intervals between things, and things have different magnitudes—objects can be larger than or smaller than others. And, we might add, this is the space afforded not only by the eye, but also by our sense of touch.[9]

At the risk of over-generalizing, conceiving space in this way is habitual for most of us, so much so we probably never stop to think that other options might be available. However, a moment's thought shows that in the world of theology, if left unchecked it can spawn considerable difficulties. Take, for example, the way in which God's relation to the world is imagined. As long as we remain wedded to visualizable pictures of distinct quasi-physical objects in bounded domains, it requires a constant struggle *not* to suggest that the more active God is in the world, the less the world can be itself. "Transcendence" will tend to be opposed to "immanence." It is hard to sidestep some form of univocity: where God and the created world are regarded as two objects belonging to the same *genus* or type of thing, each contending for the same space. Likewise, divine and human agency will tend to be imagined as ontologically comparable categories striving for the same territory. Contractual models of salvation will find a ready home in this kind of scheme: God occupies one share of the salvific space, and humans the other, making some kind of agreement necessary about how the available terrain is to be distributed. And, needless to say, human freedom

---

8. For a much fuller treatment of what I adumbrate here, see Begbie, *Music, Modernity, and God*, ch. 6.

9. Here I am drawing especially on Zuckerkandl, *Sound and Symbol*, esp. 82–85, 93–94, 275–76.

will tend to be envisaged primarily as freedom *from* the other (whether divine or human).

All this reaches acute form in Christology—when the deity and humanity of Christ are seen as properties on essentially the same plane, jostling for the same ground. Commonly, the two natures are nervously sustained in static equilibrium—like a tightrope walker with a double-weighted bar, poised far above heresy. Or else a compromise is negotiated by attenuating one of the natures—so, for example, the eternal Son is said to engage in some form of pulling back, non-exercise, or even abandonment of divine powers or attributes; or Jesus's humanity becomes a truncated version of the real thing, in order to cope with a potentially overpowering divine presence.[10]

Our main concern here is with Trinitarian theology, and it is readily apparent that similar struggles and dangers apply here also. If our theological imagination is (over-)determined by visualization, it becomes challenging, to say the least, to comprehend how there can be irreducible threeness and oneness. Again, some type of precarious equilibrium is commonly suggested: the divine *hypostases* are strongly affirmed as distinct and inseparable but left in a lifeless tension that seems to have little to do with, for example, the energetic Trinitarian testimony of John's gospel. Or failing that, some kind of compromise is advanced—swerving dangerously toward an association of individuals on the one hand (tritheism), or a collapse of distinctiveness (modalism) on the other.

Musical Space

Things are strikingly different if we turn to the space perceptible through our ears. If I press a key on a piano, the tone I then hear fills the whole of my aural field, my heard space. It does not occupy a bounded location. It is not "here" as opposed to "there." It is "everywhere" in my aural space; there is no spatial zone where the sound is not present. If I play another note along with the first, that second tone fills the entirety of the *same* (heard) space; yet I hear it as distinct. In this aural environment, two distinct entities, it would seem, can occupy the same space at the same time and yet be perceived as irreducibly distinct.

In modern times no one has done more to expound this sonic spatiality, especially in relation to music, than the twentieth-century Austrian

---

10. Significantly, the New Testament passage from which such Christologies take their cue—Phil 2:5–11—does not seem to carry any of these connotations, even if it is maintained that Paul is here holding to the "pre-existence" of Christ. See e.g. Fee, "New Testament and Kenosis Christology."

musicologist Victor Zuckerkandl.[11] He points to several features of musical space-as-heard that are relevant here. Perhaps most striking is the phenomenon of "interpenetration." As we have just noted, when one tone is heard along with another of a different pitch, the second does not drive the first away, nor is it in a different place, nor does it merge with the first. We are not dealing with the space of juxtaposition and mutual exclusion, or an aggregate of places, nor with a magnitude of parts—one tone does not take up more space than the other. Zero-sum games are gone; there is no question of "the more of one the less of the other." We do not set notes in relation to each other against the backdrop of a spatial whole. Both tones make up the one heard space. They sound "through" one another. They can be *in* one another while being heard *as* two full and distinct tones.

No less significant, Zuckerkandl writes of musical space as "coming from" / "coming toward."[12] This sounds somewhat mysterious at first, but only because of our tendency to over-rely on visualization. Zuckerkandl's point is that when we perceive a sound we are not perceiving the object that produces it, and therefore we are not perceiving an object at a distance, in a particular place. Philosophers have long reflected on the way in which perceiving sounds need not involve perceiving the objects that produce them.[13] Roger Scruton describes sounds as "pure events," by which he means that although they are happenings, they do not happen *to* the entities that caused them. They are not qualities of objects.[14] *Contra* John Locke, who spoke of sounds as "secondary qualities" of objects, when we call a sound rough we are ascribing a quality to the sound, not to the object that produced it, nor to any physical alteration in the object. Yet it is an event, something happens. I perceive a depth of sorts, but not the depth that enables me to distinguish some entity as "near" or "far." A sound has the depth of "coming from," "coming toward." What we hear is not *at* a distance, it comes *from* a distance. In this way, we hear space not as an inert vessel or container through which things can move but space as an intrinsic dimension of a living sound; a living space, we might say.

11. Zuckerkandl, *Sound and Symbol*, esp. chs. 14, 15, and 16.

12. Zuckerkandl, *Sound and Symbol*, ch. 16.

13. This is one of the differences between music and what we call "noise." When we hear a noise, we typically follow the sound through to its source. We hear a noise in the children's bedroom upstairs, so we take action with respect to the presumed cause of the noise. In the case of musical sounds, no such action is required. Music is not interesting to us because of what it tells us about the physical objects that cause it. We can enjoy the interplay of sounds without following them through to the objects that gave rise to them. Indeed, recognizing music as such seems to *depend* on our ability to do this.

14. Scruton, *Aesthetics of Music*, 6–13; "Sounds as Secondary Objects," 50–68.

Zuckerkandl also highlights a phenomenon he calls "the order of auditory space."[15] Depending on its frequency, a vibrating string can provoke another to vibrate—a phenomenon known as sympathetic resonance. This is because a single string vibrates in multiple ways, creating a series of tones (overtones) along with its basic tone. If I play middle C and open up the string an octave above by silently depressing the appropriate key, the upper C string will vibrate even though it has not been struck. And the more the lower string sounds, the more the upper string sounds in its distinctiveness. The strings are not in competition, nor do they simply allow each other room to vibrate. The lower string enhances the upper string, brings it to life, frees it to be itself, compromising neither the integrity of the upper string nor its own. We hear the resonant order of musical space.

By this time, the phrase "merely metaphorical" may well be coming to mind. It will be objected that this heard sonic space is not "real space" at all, despite the inescapable investment in spatial metaphors when describing it. Music is essentially non-spatial, or a-spatial. This was the position taken in a celebrated article by philosopher P. F. Strawson,[16] and it has been picked up and developed by a number of authors since, including Roger Scruton: "The essential feature of a spatial dimension," he writes, "is that it contains places, which can be *occupied* by things, and between which things can move."[17] In other words, authentic space is found not in the eyes-shut world of hearing music but the eyes-open world of visual and tangible perception.

But are things quite so simple? Obviously, musical space does not correspond in all respects to the spatial order of three-dimensional objects. And metaphor is certainly unavoidable in this context. But need we assume that all our spatial language is to be evaluated according to the degree to which it measures up to what we have determined in advance is "essential" or "real" space? More pointedly: need we suppose that the only possible existent spatial order is that which can be straightforwardly visualized? I hardly need point out that this is a latently theological question, or at least one that pushes us in that direction, provoking us to wonder: might there be a type of spatial order that underwrites and perhaps enfolds the space we like to call "real" space, and might our aural experience of music be gesturing toward it, perhaps even to some degree embodying it?

The relevance of all this to Trinitarian reflection will be fast becoming clear. The very term interpenetration may well call to mind the ancient concept of *perichoresis*. The theological associations of Zuckerkandl's "coming

---

15. Scruton, *Aesthetics of Music*, ch. 17.
16. Strawson, *Individuals*, 59–86.
17. Scruton, *Understanding Music*, 14. Italics original.

towards" are also surely potent, as is the phenomenon of resonance. On a wider front, we can begin to see how some of the West's most arduous theological struggles might be re-cast, and in some cases exposed as misdirected and unnecessary. I am thinking, for example, of the way in which the church has conceived of God's transcendence, two-natures Christology, divine and human agency, and interpersonal freedom. Not least, the vexed notion of our "participation" in God (or Christ) no longer needs to be hampered by zero-sum schemes that try to coordinate divine and human agency in somewhat lifeless balances (the more of God, the less of us). Through sonic or musical space, fresh languages and thought-patterns are released that are arguably far more appropriate to Scripture and the church's conciliar confessions than many of the default options on which we habitually rely.[18]

In this essay we have a particular focus in mind: God's triune life, with particular attention to that life *ad intra*. Before we delve into this, however, two caveats need to be borne in mind. First, and most obviously, to show that the kind of spatiality opening up here is at least conceivable does not of itself say anything about the truth or falsity of this or that formulation of God's triunity. Such issues cannot be resolved without reference to other more ultimate criteria. Second, we should be distinctly cautious about extending this spatial model without qualification to the relation between God and the created world. In the case of two strings vibrating, we are hearing two sounds that belong to the same ontological class, and when both are activated they are mutually constitutive. The Creator-creature relation is—most would argue—not amenable to any such pattern. To expand the point: we need to be wary of sliding into an indiscriminate reduction of all relations to a single type.[19] The intra-Trinitarian relations, the relation of Creator and creature, divine and human in the hypostatic union, Christ and church, and the relations between persons in the church—all these need to be assiduously differentiated. Unqualified appeals to "relationality" are to be treated with suspicion.[20]

Bearing these caveats in mind, however, and with what I hope is a due apophatic reserve, I propose to explore a question very much alive and a matter of pointed controversy in contemporary Trinitarian theology: in what sense, if any, is it appropriate to speak of God as possessing space?

18. Begbie, *Music, Modernity, and God*, ch. 6, *passim*.

19. For discussion of these matters, see Polkinghorne, *Trinity and an Entangled World*.

20. For strong exhortations to caution regarding *perichoresis*, for example, see Crisp, "Problems with Perichoresis," 119–40. Otto, "Use and Abuse of Perichoresis," 366–84. On the hazards of applying Trinitarian relations to the church, see Husbands, "Trinity Is Not Our Social Program," 120–41.

God's Space?[21]

For good reasons a large part of the Christian tradition has found itself resisting any notion of space as applied to God. It is said that space is a dimension belonging to the created, contingent world, not to God. Creation is composite; God is without parts. Further, there can be no space antecedent to God, "in" which God could reside. As with time, God creates all things *with* space, not *in* space. Granted, we can and must affirm God's direct engagement with the space of this world, climaxing in the incarnation: the Son comes amongst us as a spatially located, embodied human. And spatial metaphors are probably impossible to avoid when articulating the God-world relation, as Scripture makes clear: God is "close" at hand, "far off," "high above all," and so forth. But none of this warrants predicating space of God's own self in anything other than an extremely stretched, metaphorical sense. Moreover, much vigilance is needed not to allow our spatial metaphors to trick us into imagining that God and world share some common type of being. The doctrine of God's immensity—or non-spatiality—underlines the absolute qualitative distinction between divine and created reality and protects us from the huge risk of projecting what is proper to the creature onto the Creator.

Understandable as all this is, in its more extreme forms this kind of position is in considerable danger of succumbing to the very positions being opposed. If we construe God's non-spatiality purely or primarily in terms of the negation of this world's space—as if this divine non-space could be thought of as created space without bounds (our space, but infinitely extended), then whatever our good intentions we are open to the charge of imposing creaturely categories onto the Creator. And arguably, these difficulties are exacerbated by visual-spatial conceptuality (models of space dependent upon our visual perception) in which God and world are plotted as if against the background of a "hyper-space" that embraces both.

At the other end of the spectrum we find schemes that liberally employ spatial language of the Trinity and of God's relation to the world, but in ways that also quickly invite the charge of projection. Some of the highly "socialized" doctrines of the Trinity emerging in the late twentieth century are a case in point, where Father, Son, and Spirit can come close to being imagined as discrete individual quasi-personalities, engaged in a sort of triadic drama.[22] Other examples can be found in varieties of panentheism, in which

---

21. In this section I gratefully acknowledge my considerable debt to a highly lucid and perceptive article by Murray Rae: Rae, "Spatiality of God," 70–86.

22. To be fair, however, most of these theologies resist the idea that behind the three persons lies a more ultimate space, in the form of an undifferentiated substrate

the world is said to be "in" God, but where God and world are in danger of being imagined against the backdrop of a prior "super-space."[23] Again we should note that whatever the investment in metaphysical technicalities, it is hard to avoid the impression that fuelling many such proposals are visual-spatial habits of mind, where God and creation are being mapped onto a larger, pre-conceived spatial whole.

Webster and Barth

It is to the great credit of the much-lamented John Webster that he recognized the dangers of both extremes. His long-time allergy to even a whiff of social Trinitarianism (let alone panentheism) was legendary. But he was equally resistant to expounding God's non-spatiality simply by maximizing creaturely notions of spatiality. In a penetrating article on our theme he insists that we conceive God's immensity strictly through attention to the self-enactment of God as Father, Son, and Spirit: "To offer a dogmatic presentation of the attributes of God is, therefore, to indicate *this one* in the supreme radiance and completeness of his triune being and act in which he freely turns to his creatures, claiming them and directing them to himself."[24] God's infinity with regard to space cannot be expressed by magnifying creaturely properties and thus making it an "inverted image of the finite";[25] rather we are speaking of the immensity of God's goodness, the "boundless plenitude of his being, in which he is unhindered by any spatial constraint, and so is sovereignly free for creative and saving presence to all limited creaturely reality."[26] In this way immensity and omnipresence can be seen as twin doctrines: God's immeasurability enables God to be redeemingly present to all places.[27] Immensity is to be understood, therefore, not by positing an abstract contrast between created and uncreated being, for then we are thrown back on ourselves to construe it in creaturely terms, and certainly not as a property of the one God anterior to God's triune life, but only out of the fullness of the eternal Trinitarian relations.

---

or essence.

23. The classic instance is Jürgen Moltmann, who memorably portrays God's creative act in terms of self-retraction, God vacating a space for what is not God. Moltmann, *God in Creation*, 86–93.

24. Webster, "Immensity and Ubiquity of God," 87–108 (88). Italics original.

25. Webster, "Immensity and Ubiquity of God," 92.

26. Webster, "Immensity and Ubiquity of God," 92.

27. Webster, "Immensity and Ubiquity of God," 93.

However, despite a repeated and robust adherence to God's irreducible triunity, Webster does not appear to go as far as ascribing spatiality to God. This is perhaps not surprising given a particularly fervent commitment in his later work to an especially uncompromising doctrine of the simplicity of God (broadly, the belief that God is not a composite being, constituted of parts).[28] In fact, recent years have seen a significant stream of writing that has sought to recover and re-invigorate an affirmation of divine simplicity.[29] And in this environment one can meet a sharp suspicion of the notion that, for example, Father and Son are substantively present to each other in a relation of love, or that at Gethsemane the eternal *Son* prays (as man) to the Father. Social Trinitarianism of almost any shade is shunned. Stephen Holmes, for example, insists that the three divine *hypostases* are to be distinguished by relations of origin (unbegotten, begotten, and proceeds) and in no other way, and that this articulates by far the most pervasive tradition in the history of Trinitarian doctrine.[30] Clearly, this makes the language of spatiality as applied to God especially problematic.

On these matters Karl Barth is a good deal bolder. Although acutely alert to the hazards of projecting individualistic notions of human personhood onto the members of the Trinity, he nonetheless wants to insist that in the light of God's activity *ad extra*, we can and should affirm that God possesses his own space *ad intra*, by virtue of his differentiation as Father, Son, and Spirit. Space is a condition by which Father, Son, and Spirit are distinguished from one another. There is "proximity" and "distance" within God, and the latter is the source of the ontological distinction between God and world.[31] "The space everything [other than God] possesses is the space which is given it out of the fullness of God. The fact is that first of all *God has space for Himself* and . . . subsequently, because he is God and able to create, *He has [space] for everything else as well.*"[32] In other words, the differentiation-in-love of God's own being is the antecedent condition of the otherness to each other of God and world. Barth even goes so far as to say that the non-spatiality of God is a "more than dangerous idea," for space is the *a priori* of otherness.[33] To insist on God's non-spatiality (i) threatens

28. "The creator is radically incomposite. As the cause of finite being, God is not one term or agent in a set of interactions, not a 'co-eval, co-finite being', but unqualifiedly simple and in himself replete." David Braine quoted in Webster, *God without Measure*, 107, see also, ch. 6, esp. 86–89.

29. See, for example, Dolezal, *God without Parts*; Duby, *Divine Simplicity*.

30. Holmes, *Holy Trinity*, 200; Holmes, "Classical Trinity," esp. 43.

31. Barth, *Church Dogmatics*, 461–64.

32. Barth, *Church Dogmatics*, 474. My italics.

33. Barth, *Church Dogmatics*, 468.

the qualitative distinction between Creator and creature (God without "distance" implies God's identity with the world); and (ii) threatens to dissolve the differentiation of Father, Son, and Spirit (without "distance," the three collapse into absolute identity). Thus, Barth can daringly claim that omnipresence belongs first of all to God *in se*: Father, Son, and Spirit are present to and for one another in the eternity of divine love. To use more technical language, omnipresence does not merely belong to the "relative" attributes of God (those exercised by God with regard to the created world) but in the first instance characterizes God's own being.[34]

On these matters my sympathies are decidedly with Barth over against Webster, and over against the more fervent advocates of divine simplicity. This is principally for biblical-exegetical reasons. On Scriptural grounds it is difficult to sustain the view, for example, that the only distinctions that can be made between the Persons are those between relations of origin. Many texts of the Apostle Paul are exceedingly hard to square with this outlook, not to mention Gethsemane or Golgotha, or indeed large portions of the Gospel of John—a text conspicuous by its absence in current discussions of divine simplicity.[35] Indeed, the witness of the Fourth Gospel to the mutual love of Father and Son would seem to be drastically distorted if it is held that the Father's love is directed only to the humanity assumed by the Son and not to the eternal Son from all eternity—a position that entails something close to Nestorianism.[36] Speaking of John 17:3 ("Now this is eternal life: that they know you, the only true God, and Jesus Christ, whom you have sent"), Andrew Lincoln writes, "For the evangelist, Jesus in his relationship as Son to the Father is intrinsic to this one God's identity. As the second petition will make clear [i.e. as in vs. 5] Jesus was always included in the identity and glory of the one God, even before the foundation of the world."[37] More pointedly, commenting on John 17:26, C. K. Barrett writes, "The love which inspires and rules the church, and is its life, is the essential inward love of the Godhead, the love with which the Father eternally loves the Son (the love which God *is*, 1 John 4:8, 16)."[38]

---

34. Barth, *Church Dogmatics*, 461–78.

35. Tilling, "Paul, the Trinity," esp. 36–42; Hill, *Paul and the Trinity*.

36. In other words, splitting up the divine and human in Christ. For the Trinity in John's gospel, see Bird, *Evangelical Theology*, 98–113. Lincoln, *Gospel According to Saint John*, 435.

37. Lincoln, *Gospel According to Saint John*, 435.

38. Barrett, *Gospel According to St. John*, 515. Italics original. For an exceptionally clear exposition of John 17 in relation to these issues, carrying the argument that we have in Jesus's so-called "high-priestly" prayer a manifestation of "an intersubjective relationship of love between the Father and the Son in eternity," see Bauckham, "Trinity

If this Jesus, the one into whose filial relation of love and knowledge of the Father we are granted access by the Spirit, is authentically *God from God*, the eternal Son enfleshed as one of us, then it is hard to see how we can *not* speak of a relation or exchange of loving and knowing belonging to God's own being, and thus of a divine spatiality *in this sense*.[39] Whatever post-biblical metaphysical apparatus we employ, we can hardly forget that the theological stakes are extraordinarily high here: in what sense does love belong to who God actually *is*?

Having said all this, if Barth's account of divine space is taken out of its distinctive theological matrix in the *Dogmatics*, his audacious prose is liable to significant misunderstanding (and misuse), especially if approached through a visual-spatial mind-set of the kind I have been questioning from the start of this chapter. Can we find a way forward here?

Rehearing Trinitarian Space

Assuming, then, that there are grounds for speaking of divine spatiality along the lines suggested by Barth, but at the same time bearing in mind the pitfalls of such language that we have been highlighting, we can ask: what would a biblically responsible account of divine spatiality require, and how might "musical space" speak to those requirements? Here I think we can identify one general *desideratum*, and three more particular *desiderata*.

To begin with, the general one. Clearly we are going to need habits of thought and speech that avoid construing space as an inert receptacle, a mere frame into which things and events are installed. As we saw earlier, this has often caused many a theological shipwreck. In debates about divine spatiality all parties in one way or another are struggling to extricate themselves from just this—the notion that there is a logically prior "meta-space" encompassing both God and world, or a logically prior (perhaps even ontologically prior) divine space into which the Trinitarian Persons fit. Here the aural perception of musical tones would seem to have much to offer, for it entails a kind of space not bound to these schemes: space not as a container

---

and the Gospel of John," 92–93. (I am not convinced that "intersubjective relationship" is the best phrase in this context, given the connotations of enclosed mutuality that it is almost bound to evoke in late modernity, but the thrust of his exegesis here is surely very much to the point.)

39. Christoph Schwöbel writes, "If the *homoousios* ['of one substance'] is simply taken to mean that Father, Son, and Spirit instantiate the same divine essence three times over, without rooting how God is in relation to the world in how God is in God's own being, one has effectively made the doctrine of the Trinity meaningless for understanding the divine economy." Schwöbel, "Where Do We Stand?," 9–72 (23).

through which sounds travel but space as an intrinsic dimension of sounds-in-motion. Music can serve to remind us that space is always the space *of* this, the space *of* that, and that theologically, we should be careful not to operate with a concept of space in general but only with the distinctive space manifest in the self-presentation of the triune God.[40]

Now for three more particular *desiderata*: and here we can return to the features of musical spatiality outlined by Zuckerkandl highlighted above, and draw on some major currents in John's gospel.

First, we recall that Zuckerkandl wrote of the "interpenetration" of sounds in our aural perception. This speaks to the need to do justice to the "in-one-anotherness" of the divine Persons, a term coined by Richard Bauckham to speak of the mutual indwelling of Father and Son in the Gospel of John.[41] The interpenetration of heard musical tones offers a remarkably apt way of allowing this extraordinary language of the Fourth Gospel to be heard more fully and profoundly, releasing us from some of the more damaging snares associated with visual-spatial discourse. We avoid any suggestion of God possessing "parts" (the three heard notes are not parts of a whole, they *are* the whole) and we avoid the pitfalls of terms like "proximity," "remoteness," and "distance" that opponents of divine spatiality rightly warn us about.

Second, Zuckerkandl spoke of sounds "coming from" / "coming toward." This speaks to the need to do justice to what we can call the "*for-one-anotherness*" of the Persons. So, for example, if we are to describe the Father's love for the Son and the Son's love for the Father as a dynamic of self-giving or self-dispossession that reaches its epitome at the cross, this language must not be allowed to push us into imagining some kind of shift of content from one location to another, or a self-evacuation of one for the sake of the other. In John's gospel, the Father gives life to the Son such that the Son "has life in himself" *as he, the Father, has life in himself* (John 5:26)—in other words there is no diminishment of the Father's divinity in the process; quite the opposite—for this is who God *is*. And there is no hint of a diminishment of the Son's deity as the Son in turn gives life to, and for, others in the world. In hearing a musical tone, we do not perceive anything moving within a pre-existing space, still less do we perceive anything diminished; the life of the sound *is* the life of coming-from/coming-toward (going to/going toward). Again, this evades the cruder visual-spatial assumptions that those who oppose divine spatiality quite properly oppose.

---

40. The work of T. F. Torrance is especially relevant here; see for example, Torrance, *Space, Time and Incarnation*; and *Space, Time, and Resurrection*.

41. Bauckham, *Gospel of Glory*, 9–13.

Third, Zuckerkandl identified a resonant "order of auditory space" arising from the sympathetic resonance of strings. This addresses a double-need: to do justice to (i) the *mutual enlivening* of the Trinitarian Persons, and (ii) the *uncontainability* of this mutuality. By mutual enlivening, I have in mind the reciprocal activation of the sort we hear between two resonant tones. There is arguably something of this in the concept of "glorification" in the Fourth Gospel; the mutual glorification of Son and Father, climaxing at the crucifixion (e.g. John 12:23, 28; 13:31–32; 17:1). And, as with love, we are told this has characterized the life of Son and Father from before the foundation of the world (John 17:4–5). Glory carries with it a sense of honor as well as splendor; to glorify is to honor and magnify the other *as other*.[42] If all this feels too dangerously "social" or plural, undercutting divine unity, we need to recall what we have just said about in-one-anotherness. To repeat, this is not a space with different objects inside it; it is a space *constituted by* the differentiated life of the three. The three tones I hear do not each *have* a space (akin to *having* an essence); they *are* that space in action.

With mutual enlivening goes uncontainability. Resonance is abundant (another key concept in John's gospel). In hearing two resonant strings we are being introduced to a space of liveliness that by its very nature far exceeds the giving and receiving between these two. Here it is difficult not to invoke a lively tradition that speaks of the Holy Spirit as the excess of the mutual love of Father and Son, the pressure toward outgoingness within God's life, the divine capaciousness that saves the Father and Son becoming, as it were, a private duet.[43]

Of course, in this chapter I have been able to do no more than sketch possibilities, but they are ones that I believe have considerable bearing on contemporary debates in Trinitarian theology. I have not even begun to discuss melody, dissonance, and numerous other musical phenomena. But I hope I have done enough to show that the phenomenology of the perception of musical sound yields conceptual tools that can clarify, expose and even correct some of theology's worst habits, and thus enable the theologian to discover in fresh ways something of the New Testament's Trinitarian pressure and shape. Theologically, music helps us realize there is far more in what the church says than we think, and far more in what we think than we can ever say.

---

42. Bauckham, *Gospel of Glory*, ch. 3.

43. See Williams, "Deflections of Desire." "God is no lonely monad or self-absorbed tyrant, but one whose orientation to the other is intrinsic to his eternal being as God. . . .The Spirit, we might say, is the motor of that divine movement outwards." Gunton, *Father, Son, and Holy Spirit*, 86.

Bibliography

Barrett, C. K. *The Gospel According to St. John : An Introduction with Commentary and Notes on the Greek Text*. 2nd ed. Philadelphia: Westminster, 1978.

Barth, Karl. *Church Dogmatics*. Translated by Geoffrey W. Bromiley and Thomas F. Torrance, vol. II/1. Edinburgh: T. & T. Clark, 1957.

Bauckham, Richard. *Gospel of Glory: Major Themes in Johannine Theology*. Grand Rapids: Baker Academic, 2015.

———. "The Trinity and the Gospel of John." In *The Essential Trinity: New Testament Foundations and Practical Relevance*, edited by Brandon Crowe and Carl R. Trueman, 91–117. London: Apollos, 2016.

Begbie, Jeremy. *Music, Modernity, and God: Essays in Listening*. Oxford: Oxford University Press, 2013.

Bertoglio, Chiara. "A Perfect Chord: Trinity in Music, Music in the Trinity." *Religions* 4 (2013) 485–501.

Bird, Michael F. *Evangelical Theology: A Biblical and Systematic Introduction*. Grand Rapids: Zondervan, 2013.

Crisp, Oliver. "Problems with Perichoresis." *Tyndale Bulletin* 56 (2005) 119–40.

Dolezal, James E. *God without Parts: Divine Simplicity and the Metaphysics of God's Absoluteness*. Eugene, OR: Pickwick, 2011.

Duby, Steven J. *Divine Simplicity: A Dogmatic Account*. London: Bloomsbury, T. & T. Clark, 2016.

Fee, Gordon D. "The New Testament and Kenosis Christology: The Self-Emptying of God." In *Exploring Kenotic Christology*, edited by C. Stephen Evans, 25–44. Oxford: Oxford University Press, 2006.

Gunton, Colin E. *Father, Son, and Holy Spirit: Essays Toward a Fully Trinitarian Theology*. London: T. & T. Clark, 2003.

Hill, Wesley. *Paul and the Trinity: Persons, Relations, and the Pauline Letters*. Grand Rapids: Eerdmans, 2015.

Holmes, Stephen R. "Classical Trinity: Evangelical Perspective." In *Two Views on the Doctrine of the Trinity*, edited by Jason S. Sexton, 69–95. Grand Rapids: Zondervan, 2014.

———. *The Holy Trinity: Understanding God's Life*. Milton Keynes, UK: Paternoster, 2012.

Husbands, Mark. "The Trinity Is Not Our Social Program: Volf, Gregory and Barth." In *Trinitarian Theology for the Church: Scripture, Community, Worship*, edited by Daniel J. Treier and David Lauber, 120–41. Downers Grove, IL: InterVarsity, 2009.

Ignatius. *The Autobiography of St. Ignatius Loyola, with Related Documents*. Edited by John C. Olin, translated by Joseph F. O'Callaghan. New York: Harper & Row, 1974.

Lincoln, Andrew T. *The Gospel According to Saint John*. Peabody; London: Continuum, 2005.

Lippius, Johann. *Synopsis of New Music = Synopsis Musicae Novae*. Translations— Colorado College Music Press 8. Colorado Springs: Colorado College Music Press, 1977.

Moltmann, Jürgen. *God in Creation: An Ecological Doctrine of Creation*. London: SCM, 1985.

Otto, Randall E. "The Use and Abuse of Perichoresis in Recent Theology." *Scottish Journal of Theology* 54 (2001) 366–84.

Polkinghorne, John C., ed. *The Trinity and an Entangled World: Relationality in Physical Science and Theology*. Grand Rapids: Eerdmans, 2010.

Rae, Murray. "The Spatiality of God." In *Trinitarian Theology After Barth*, edited by Myk Habets and Phillip Tolliday, 70–86. Eugene, OR: Wipf & Stock, 2011.

Schwöbel, Christoph. "Where Do We Stand in Trinitarian Theology? Resources, Revisions, and Reappraisals." In *Recent Developments in Trinitarian Theology: An International Symposium*, edited by Christophe Chalamet and Marc Vial, 9–72. Minneapolis: Augsburg Fortress, 2014.

Scruton, Roger. *The Aesthetics of Music*. Oxford: Clarendon, 1997.

———. "Sounds as Secondary Objects and Pure Events." In *Sounds and Perception: New Philosophical Essays*, edited by Matthew Nudds and Casey O'Callaghan, 50–68. Oxford: Oxford University Press, 2009.

———. *Understanding Music: Philosophy and Interpretation*. London: Continuum, 2009.

Strawson, P. F. *Individuals: An Essay in Descriptive Metaphysics*. London: Methuen, 1959.

Tilling, Chris. "Paul, the Trinity, and Contemporary Trinitarian Debates." *The Pacific Journal of Baptist Research* 11 (2016) 19–43.

Torrance, Thomas F. *Space, Time and Incarnation*. London: Oxford University Press, 1969.

———. *Space, Time and Resurrection*. Grand Rapids: Eerdmans, 1976.

Webster, John. *God without Measure: Working Papers in Christian Theology*. Vol. 1, *God and the Works of God*. London: Bloomsbury T. & T. Clark, 2016.

———. "The Immensity and Ubiquity of God." In *Confessing God: Essays in Christian Dogmatics II*, 87–108. London: T. & T. Clark, 2005.

Westhaver, George, ed. *A Transforming Vision: Knowing and Loving the Triune God*. London: SCM, 2018.

Williams, Rowan. "The Deflections of Desire: Negative Theology in Trinitarian Disclosure." In *Silence and the Word: Negative Theology and Incarnation*, edited by Oliver Davies and Denys Turner, 115–35. Cambridge: Cambridge University Press, 2002.

Zarlino, Gioseffo. *Le Istitutioni Harmoniche*. Venice, 1558.

Zuckerkandl, Victor. *Sound and Symbol: Music and the External World*. Translated by Willard R. Trask. London: Routledge & Kegan Paul, 1956.

CHAPTER 3

Paul the Trinitarian

Chris Tilling

The Apostle Paul was a Trinitarian. That at least is the controversial thesis I will defend in this essay.[1] To that end, I will first outline the three main ways Pauline theology has been articulated in relation to the Trinity. Following this, I will present a rather different way of understanding the issues, thereby defending my claim that Paul was a Trinitarian, one explicable in terms of the epistemological and theological resources within Paul's letters as instances of Second Temple Judaism.

Of course, I realize how this might sound. The mere suggestion that Paul be understood as a Trinitarian will likely strike one as problematic for a host of reasons. Yet others, too, have been known to speak about Paul's theology in Trinitarian terms. Kavin Rowe, for example, argues that although Paul is not explicitly articulating Trinitarian theology, it is still to be understood as the "deeper presupposition" that (retrospectively) makes specific Pauline arguments intelligible.[2] That being said, Rowe hesitates to speak of *Paul* as a Trinitarian due to the issue of anachronism, and for this same reason some of the most conservative scholars will avoid speaking of Paul's own theology directly in these terms. Even Benjamin Warfield of inerrancy

---

1. The argument here anticipates, in summary form, a more complete treatment to be pursued in a forthcoming monograph entitled *Paul the Trinitarian*. This essay is based upon a paper I delivered at Duke University, November 2016.

2. Rowe, "Trinity in the Letters," 50.

fame wrote that "[w]e cannot speak of the doctrine of the Trinity as revealed in the New Testament."[3]

So what am I doing in this essay, trying to argue that Paul was a Trinitarian? Well, that will become apparent. To begin, I will first present a threefold taxonomy of contemporary views on Paul's thinking in relation to the doctrine of the Trinity.[4] This road map will facilitate locating my own constructive proposal in relation to recent scholarship, after which I will argue that the various approaches fail sufficiently to take Paul on his own terms. And that, for me, is the key. When Paul's letters drive the interpretative agenda more concretely, we will see that his thinking is rightly described as Trinitarian.

From Paul to the Trinity and Back Again

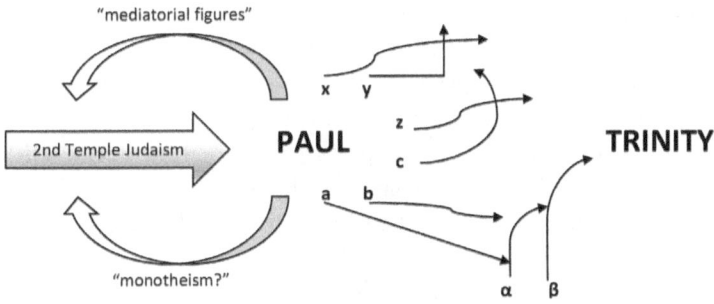

Model A

Model A suggests that there is a long and complex relationship between Paul's theology and later Trinitarianism. If different aspects of Paul's own theological rhetoric, here represented by the letters "a, b, c, x, y, z," are taken up into the tradition in different ways, it is to be noted that not all (if any) of them point to the Trinity. Examples include Paul's language about Christ being appointed (ὁρισθέντος) Son of God in Rom 1:4, the manner in which Paul can speak of the Father as Christ's *God* (e.g., 2 Cor. 1:3), and so on.[5]

---

3. As cited in Yarnell, *God the Trinity*, Kindle Loc 389.

4. Of course, as with all taxonomies, this is an imperfect scheme, suggesting isolated hermeneutical spaces when reality is indeed messier and overlapping. But the distinctions still make some heuristic sense for my purposes in this essay.

5. Such verses naturally, though not exclusively, become the focus of those wishing

Hence, the legitimacy of any straight path between Paul and later creedal Trinitarianism is called into question. This case can be underscored by tying "high christological" statements in Paul to exalted Jewish mediatorial and messianic figures, by emphasizing so-called subordinationist language in Paul (e.g., 1 Cor 15:24–28), and by distancing Jewish God-talk from "exclusive monotheism."[6]

There is thus no logical (and certainly no necessary) path from Pauline theology to later dogmatic articulations of the Trinity. Perhaps some of it will get close (as Jimmy Dunn would argue),[7] but the only way Paul's language ultimately lands on the shores of later Trinitarian dogma is by joining hands, or rather by being appropriated, by very different ontological and epistemological concerns, associated with such terms as *hypostasis* and *ousia* (here marked by α and β). Without these alien (usually called "Hellenistic") elements, Trinitarian dogma would have been unthinkable. So, famously, Harnack, or more recently Maurice Casey.[8]

Clearly there is much to commend in model A. For starters, it takes the historical task seriously. If the job of New Testament scholarship is to foreground the historical particularity of New Testament language, and to understand that language as an instance of Second Temple Judaism in the Hellenistic world, not something apart from it, then the dual emphases on the Jewish God and mediatorial language has sought to honor this task.

This model is thus correct to insist on care in the use of the word "monotheism." Scholarly calls for the retirement of the word (Paula Fredriksen),[9] or redefinition (William Horbury),[10] or merely its re-envisioning (Nathan MacDonald),[11] are important,[12] if extremely uneven, contributions. Any engagement with Paul's theology certainly needs to be alert to these debates (as we shall see). A further strength is its concern to note the complex *Wirkungsgeschichte* of Paul's letters. To assert only a *single* straight line between Paul and creedal Trinitarianism seems like an apologetic move. Finally, later Trinitarian dogma indisputably deployed its rhetoric in philosophical categories and language borrowed from the Hel-

---

to distance Paul from later Trinitarian dogma.

6. On the distinction between mediatorial and Messiah figures, see Waddell, *Messiah*, 183.

7. Dunn, *Theology of Paul*, 258.

8. Harnack, *Lehrbuch der Dogmengeschichte*; Casey, *From Jewish Prophet*, e.g., 175.

9. Fredriksen, "Mandatory Retirement," 25–38.

10. Horbury, "Jewish and Christian Monotheism," 16–44.

11. See, e.g., MacDonald, *Deuteronomy*.

12. Horbury, "Jewish and Christian Monotheism."

lenistic world, particularly the middle Platonism that became dominant in the Cappadocian Fathers.

The problems with this model are, however, equally apparent. Perhaps most importantly, the proposals of scholars within its orbit have not paid sufficient attention to the patterns and interconnections within Paul's own language. The upshot is that inadequate, unhelpful, or misleading parallels are drawn to explain Paul's Christ-rhetoric, simply because Paul's letters have been sidelined in explaining Pauline theology.[13]

Finally, very occasionally I read offhand comments which suggest that to speak of Paul in terms of Trinitarian theology would be to commit an *ideological* sin. Paula Fredriksen, for example, when critiquing the use of the word "monotheism" in terms of these very debates, speaks of "tortured Chalcedonianism" and "austere and exclusive monotheism."[14] These claims reveal an ideological pressure that require a little more self-reflection if accompanied by knee-jerk rejection of association between Paul and the Trinity.

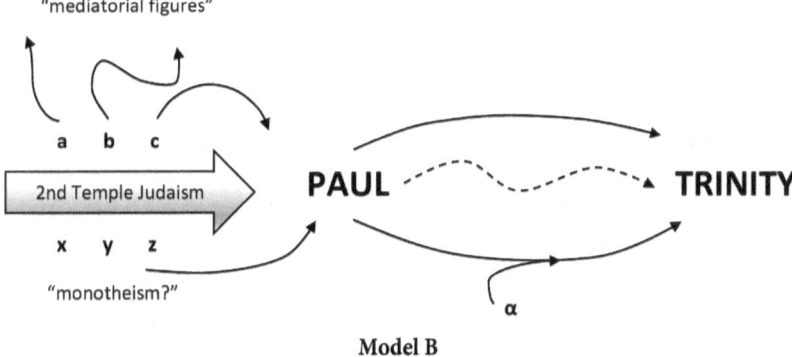

Model B

The second model tends to affirm a greater continuity between Paul's own theology and later Trinitarian dogma (here indicated by the arrow

---

13. For example, and as I have argued in previous publications, I instance the scholarship of William Horbury, valuable as it is. He explains Paul's high christological language via recourse to the praise of Jewish kings, and so Paul's Christ-devotion is explained without need to paint it in terms of the worship of the One God. But this overlooks the fact that Paul does not speak of Christ as the object of worship in direct terms, and ignores the texture and depth of Paul's own Christ-devotion language (Tilling, *Paul's Divine Christology*, 230–32). In this, Horbury reflects a wider trend, against the evidence in Paul's letters, to understand the relationship between God and the risen Lord in terms of mediatorial or messianic figures. Simply put, representatives of this model have overestimated the explanatory power of their proposed historical precedents. They are looking at the wrong ones, I have argued.

14. Fredriksen, "Mandatory Retirement," 35, 37.

connecting "Paul" and "Trinity"). While particular accounts of "Jewish monotheism" are presented with some care and sophistication, in such a way that feeds into presentations of Paul's so-called "christological monotheism," links with mediatorial or messianic language, insofar as it purports to explain the relationship between Father and Son, tend to be down-played. This trend is exemplified by Bauckham's divine identity approach, but it is by no means a rule for those in this broad camp. For example, Dunn and Hurtado indeed make extensive use of such mediatorial language.[15]

Scholars broadly representing this model draw connections between Paul and the Trinity in hard and soft forms, hence the variety of depicted arrows, some wavy, others dotted and so on.

First, the harder version, which is exemplified by Neil Richardson in his *Paul's Language About God*. He concludes his study with the claim that "the later doctrines of the incarnation and Trinity were the *logical consequences* of [Paul's] theological grammar."[16] Another similar voice, important in these debates, is that of Gordon Fee, who deserves a closer look for reasons that will become clear later on. In *God's Empowering Presence* he spoke of Paul's Trinitarian theology,[17] but he has since adjusted these views. So he states:

> In light of some (legitimate) objections to my use of "trinitarian" in [*God's Empowering Presence*] as proper nomenclature for Pauline theology—mostly because the word carries too much baggage from later discussions that are concerned with how the three divine "persons" cohere in unity of being—I have chosen to use "proto-trinitarian" for those moments in Paul.[18]

The dogma of the Trinity is what later church traditions articulated with the language of ousia, hypostasis, etc. Hence, even though what Paul writes in some ways corresponds with this dogmatic language, it needs nevertheless formally to be distanced from it. The prefix "proto" performs this crucial function.

What Fee objects to is his earlier claims from the mid-90s, where he opines that Paul's letters contain "explicitly trinitarian texts," namely 2 Cor 13:14; 1 Cor 12:4–6; Eph 4:4–6.[19] Such language, Fee later maintains, overestimates what can be found in Paul. At most one can speak of Paul's

---

15. See, importantly, Dunn, *Christology in the Making*; Hurtado, *One God*.
16. Richardson, *Paul's Language*, 315, italics mine.
17. See, e.g., Fee, *God's Empowering Presence*, 834.
18. Fee, *First and Second Letters*, 300n96.
19. Fee, *Paul, the Spirit*, 39.

"trinitarian assumptions,"[20] "presuppositions,"[21] and "implications."[22] The reason for this is explained by the following passage that Fee penned in the '90s:

> One may grant that Paul's trinitarian assumptions and descriptions, which form the basis of the later [creedal] formulas, never move toward calling the Spirit "God" and never wrestle with the philosophical and theological implications of those assumptions and descriptions.[23]

Later dogma had the theological and philosophical resources for parsing a doctrine of the Trinity, but this was not available to Paul and so should not be called "explicitly Trinitarian." Ignore this point and one will commit the sin of importing anachronistic, creedal dogma into descriptions of Pauline theology. Hence Fee's self-correction.

In clarifying himself, Fee was attempting to respond to criticisms, such as that proffered by Dunn, who reproached the early Fee with the assertion that such Trinitarian language, when used in relation to Paul, imports "analytic categories which took several centuries of sophisticated debate even to formulate."[24] This is why the arrow connecting Paul and the Trinity is so important in this model. Although it stresses continuity between Pauline theology and the Trinity, the distinction between the two means that one should not speak simply of Paul as Trinitarian.

Similar rhetorical tensions, if that is what they indeed are, can be witnessed in the scholarship of Douglas Campbell. He writes:

> We should note first that Paul's thinking about God's activity in Christ is trinitarian. Obviously he lacks the specialized terminology for the Trinity that was developed in the church by the fifth century after much reflection and discussion. But three persons are distinguishable in Romans 5 and 8, acting not only in concert but in an overlapping fashion.[25]

So far so clear: Paul's thinking is Trinitarian. But Campbell then goes on to qualify this by stating that "Paul operated with 'an inchoate trinitarian grammar' [here referring to Christoph Schwöbel]. This means in turn that

---

20. Fee, *Paul, the Spirit*, 45.
21. Fee, "Christology and Pneumatology," 330–31.
22. Fee, *Paul, the Spirit*, 41.
23. Fee, *Paul, the Spirit*, 45.
24. Dunn, *Theology of Paul*, 263n157.
25. Campbell, "Christ and the Church," 119.

Paul's writings witness to the Trinity."[26] As Luke Timothy Johnson writes in response to this set of claims: "Well, no, an inchoate logic does not constitute a witness to the Trinity, especially not with a capital T."[27] Is Paul's theological vision inchoate, not fully formed, one that is rudimentary? Or is Paul's theology actually Trinitarian? Which is it?

Softer versions suspect a theological heavy-handedness in any use of the word "Trinity" in terms of Paul, even if qualified by "proto-" or "inchoate." Most in this camp will deploy production or agricultural metaphors ("build," "seeds," and so on). It would require later theologians to piece things together, to form what became the *concept* of the Trinity. Hence, the link between Paul and the Trinity is an evolutionary one.

Representatives of this approach include Hurtado, Wright,[28] Schreiner,[29] Schnelle,[30] and so on. It is certainly a popular option, and it is instructive to see repeated the concern about anachronism. So Hurtado opines, "To be sure, it would be anachronistic to read back into [the New Testament] the developed theological categories of the doctrine of the Trinity, which required a few centuries of debate and intellectual exploration." What we have in the New Testament are the "seeds of an impetus for" later Trinitarian dogmatic reflection.[31] Jimmy Dunn likewise resists speaking of Paul as a Trinitarian, implying the claim does not respect the "time-conditioned and relatively inchoate character" of Paul's theology.[32] He is very happy to claim that aspects of Pauline theology were a vital impulse toward later Trinitarian thinking,[33] but that is a long way from claiming that Paul himself was a Trinitarian, especially as—according to Dunn—Paul's Christology isn't quite as "high" as others have reckoned.

In other words, in both hard and soft versions, Paul's relationship to the Trinity is plotted according to a developmental schema, in which the Apostle laid the grounds for later Trinitarian theology, *without conceptualizing it himself*. For Paul, it is at most only an inchoate grammar, a presupposition, or even just a seed.

---

26. Campbell, "Christ and the Church," 121.

27. Johnson, "Response to Douglas A. Campbell," 151. However, I am not sure why Johnson places so much ideological weight on the presence or absence of a capital letter.

28. E.g., Wright, *Paul and the Faithfulness*, 721.

29. "Paul did not believe that worshiping Jesus Christ as Lord compromised monotheism. We have here the raw materials from which the theology of the Trinity developed" (Schreiner, "Paul," 23).

30. Schnelle, *Apostle Paul*, 492.

31. Hurtado, *God in New Testament Theology*, 114–15.

32. Dunn, *Theology of Paul*, 440n37.

33. Dunn, *Theology of Paul*, 264.

The strengths of this model overlap with those of the previous to a certain extent, especially the concern to honor the historical particularity of the Pauline rhetoric. It also, by and large, manages better than the previous model to take more seriously language, in Paul, which bespeaks a divine Christology, a conclusion that Crispin Fletcher-Louis has rightly described as an "emerging consensus" in Pauline scholarship.[34]

But weaknesses are also apparent. Many scholars representing this model tend to neglect broad thematic, overlapping concerns in Paul, and overly atomize their exegetical endeavors, particularly when speaking about the Trinity. Even the harder versions underestimate Paul's theological coherence—and by "theological," I mean something specific, as I shall explain soon.[35]

One also wonders whether a *single* straight line between Paul and the kind of dogmas articulated hundreds of years later can really take the complexities of the journey seriously, whether, in other words, it acknowledges the variety of Christian theologies in the early church.

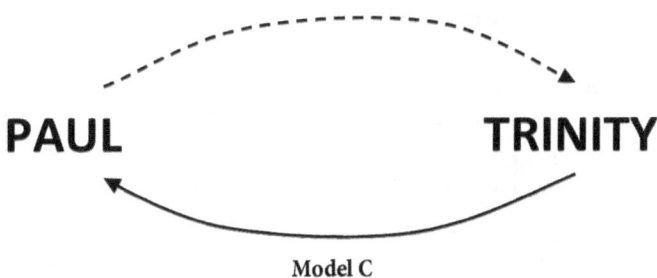

Model C

The final model is best portrayed as a hermeneutical approach, which aims to show how the later dogmatic categories of the Trinity illuminate a reading of Paul's language understood—to a certain extent—in terms of the results of usual critical exegesis. In order to elucidate this position, I will interact with the recent work of its main representative, Wesley Hill, in order to show its strengths and weaknesses. This will then lead to my own constructive proposals.

---

34. Fletcher-Louis, *Jesus Monotheism*, 3–59.

35. There is also, apart from a few notable exceptions, not enough accounting for Paul's pneumatological language in terms of these debates, leading some to speak of "binitarian theology" (as in Fletcher-Louis, *Jesus Monotheism*, 81). The lens adopted by Hurtado, which emphasizes "binitarian devotion," can be plausibly adduced as a cause for these problems.

In *Paul and the Trinity*,[36] Hill argues that modern Pauline scholarship creates interpretative problems when it seeks to understand Paul's christological language in terms of whether it is merely "high" or "low" (thereby deploying a new term, "monotheism," against which Paul's christological rhetoric is to be measured). But such vertical metaphors do not help the interpreter understand the nature of Paul's language, which very much concerns the relationship between specific actors, namely the Father, the Son, and the Spirit. What Hill seeks to achieve is a reading that takes seriously the mutually interpreting nature of these actors, and to do this he will deploy a reading that draws on later Trinitarian categories. This is not to say that Hill seeks to find the Trinity in Paul, as he is quick to point out. This would mistake Paul's theology for a static "given," something requiring "no constructive effort on the part of . . . interpreters."[37] In dialectical fashion, rather, "trinitarian theologies will be employed as *hermeneutical resources*" that "enable a genuinely historical exegesis." In this way, Hill seeks to present "self-consciously *historical* readings" of Paul.[38]

Having outlined classical and twentieth century accounts of Trinitarian discourse, Hill alights upon two verses in Romans that involve, he asserts, "identity descriptions" of God in relation to Jesus.[39] In chapters 3 and 4 of his book, Hill examines certain texts that portray some asymmetry in the relationship between God and Jesus (Phil 2:6–11; 1 Cor 8:6 and 15:24–28). The element of subordination within these texts, often seen as problematic for those who merely endorse a Pauline "high Christology," are read in terms of the Trinitarian strategy of "redoublement" (translatable as repetition or reduplication).[40] In chapter 5, and on the basis of exegetical work relating to 1 Cor 12:3 and Gal 4:4–6, Hill understands Paul to say that the Spirit mediates the presence of the risen Lord, and claims that in this way the Spirit is identified. Turning to Rom 1:3–4 and 8:9–11, Hill further claims that the sonship of Jesus and the fatherhood of God are indeed "constituted in and through the Spirit's role in raising Jesus."[41]

Again, there is much to commend in this.[42] But in this essay I focus on two problems, the elucidation of which will serve as an appropriate

36. Hill, *Paul and the Trinity*.
37. Hill, *Paul and the Trinity*, 45–46.
38. Hill, *Paul and the Trinity*, 45.
39. Hill, *Paul and the Trinity*, 53. Why these are "identity descriptors" over against other passages that might speak of the "God and Father of our Lord Jesus Christ" (e.g., 2 Cor 1:3), is not explained.
40. Hill, *Paul and the Trinity*, 99.
41. Hill, *Paul and the Trinity*, 138.
42. See my longer discussion, Tilling, "Paul, the Trinity," 19–43, from which I lift

launch-pad to present my own proposals. First, Hill claims that his Trinitarian assertions do not "'trump' what Paul's texts may be plausibly shown to have communicated within his own context."[43] But one may suspect that some theological trumping has indeed taken place. For example, in addition to Hill's reasonably sparse engagement with the variety of relevant and important Second Temple Jewish literature throughout his argument, his lack of engagement with the category of Second Temple Jewish agency figures (so prominent in models A and B) is to be noted. In many relevant Second Temple texts an exalted intermediary agent of some sort reigns alongside God, receives worship, and so on (so *1 En.*). Jesus Christ is in many ways much like one of these agents alongside God, so a legitimate historical question remains: why would a Trinitarian conceptuality be preferred over this Jewish language of (broadly speaking) "divine agency"? Hill does not answer this. So when Hill describes his task as "self-consciously *historical*," he may be claiming too much.

My second point of criticism relates to the way Hill interprets the claim that "Paul's theology does not exist in a static form to which its interpreters are then beholden as passive receivers."[44] The problem, I suggest, is that in denying Pauline theology its own givenness and structure, he oversimplifies the hermeneutical task in favor of one side of the helpful dialectical conversation between historical exegesis and creedal Trinitarian grammar. In Hill's argumentation the volume of the symphony of Paul's voice is turned down, and only certain Pauline sound-bites, deemed worthy of entering into this conversation with creedal formulations, are heard. Hill's concrete argumentative practice, therefore, exhibits a philosophical constructivism,[45] a hermeneutical posture that should not be confused with more helpful christological, and non-foundationalist accounts of the knowledge of God.[46] Hill's atomistic engagement with Paul is the result. Of course, Hill needed to decide on a particular focus, draw lines around his research to stop it becoming unwieldy. But I submit that his hermeneutical practice, and consequent focus on just the relations between the divine actors, obscures matters, as we shall see.[47]

---

some of this analysis.

43. Hill, *Paul and the Trinity*, 45.

44. Hill, *Paul and the Trinity*, 46.

45. I do not think it an accident that the word "construct" and its cognates are multiplied in these pages (45–46).

46. Harvey, "Theological Promise," 62.

47. In reading Paul, Hill states that "each [divine] person is only identifiable by means of reference to the others" (Hill, *Paul and the Trinity*, 44). But had Paul's language been taken more seriously, it becomes clear that each "divine person" is identifiable,

What This Teaches Us

So what lessons do we learn from this overview of these three models? Common to all of them is a recognition of the conceptual distance between Paul and later Trinitarian dogmas. Any articulation of Paul and creedal faith needs to acknowledge this, and claims of a *single* straight line between Paul and Nicene Trinitarianism looks like an apologetic move.

And yet this valuable insight contains an unexplored and problematic flip side. Namely, the implication that Paul did not have the epistemological or ontological resources to articulate the Trinity on his own terms. *Of course* reading Paul in terms of the philosophical and ontological categories worked out in creedal Christianity is an anachronism (even if it remains heuristically useful). But, and this is crucial, it is equally an anachronism to judge the presence of a Trinity in Pauline theology on those same terms. Anachronism cuts both ways![48] We can't expect Paul to evidence Nicene Trinitarianism. But that should not cause us to say "move on, nothing but seeds or, at best, an inchoate grammar to see here!"

But I argue that this is precisely what has happened. The nature and depth of Paul's own rhetoric is consistently underestimated in these models. It is evident in model A's atomistic exegesis, as well as in model B in both hard and soft varieties. Likewise, model C tends to ignore the theological coherence already present within Paul, treating Pauline theology as soundbites. Our constructive proposal will refocus attention on those wider patterns and themes across Paul's letters, precisely as it involves the question of the Trinity.

Finally, and as models A and B consistently remind us, foregrounding the historical particularity of the Pauline texts is not to be neglected. It should remain incumbent on us to read Paul's texts as far as possible within their own contextual idiom, cultural encyclopaedia, symbolic universe—insert your preferred phrase. That there is a concerted effort in the first two models to take the exigencies of Second Temple Judaism seriously, and to understand the Pauline letters as an instance of Second Temple Judaism, and not something apart from it, is something to be applauded. But that so much of the discussion relating to Paul *and the Trinity* has ignored this point in practice is something my own constructive proposals will now seek to rectify.

---

known, spoken about, and confessed, in terms of that Spirit animated and graced *human relationship* with God and Christ. Exegetical issues will otherwise be overlooked, and this is a matter of no small significance.

48. See the suggestive but brief comments by Blackwell, "Biblical Trinitarianism."

Paul's Trinitarianism

My argument consists of four consecutive theses.

> Thesis 1:
>
> Paul's Jewish God-relation pattern of language is the articulation of the transcendent uniqueness of God, Paul's exclusive monotheism, and as such creates the space for speaking, in Paul's idiom, about that which is God over against that which is not God.

This can be unpacked in three steps.

a) A relational epistemology lies at the heart of Paul's Jewish-style God-rhetoric. By "relational" I do not necessarily mean more than "[t]he way in which one person or thing is related to another"[49] and intend the meaning of the word to gain purchase from its particular use in concrete contexts. This is to say, here, that God was not simply an object of neutral discourse, but rather one to whom the faithful were (or at least were meant to be) completely devoted.[50]

For example, in 1 Cor 8 Paul responds to the knowledge of the Corinthian "knowledgeable," and does so on these relational epistemological grounds. They say "all of us possess knowledge" (8:1), so Paul responds by counterclaiming "knowledge puffs up, but love builds up." That Paul is not against knowledge, just a certain understanding of it is obvious from the way Paul immediately goes on to speak of a "necessary knowledge" (NRSV—δεῖ γνῶναι, 8:2), knowing as one "ought to know" (NIV, ESV). In 8:3 this knowing is further parsed in terms of loving God and being "known by him,"[51] which echoes scriptural language about God's special relationship with his chosen people (see Amos 3:2, for example). So Eric Waaler concludes his study of 8:3 by maintaining that "to love God and to be known by God (1Cor 8:3) describes the personal relationship between the believer and God,"[52] themes clearly echoed, of course, also in 8:6 where Paul draws

---

49. Pearsall and Trumble, *Oxford English Reference Dictionary*, 1216.

50. May I suggest that those who argue the word "relational" should not be used, because it is a slippery term, underestimate the slipperiness of all such load-bearing words. Indeed, "relational" attempts to articulate something important, and so should not be retired, just defined sufficiently by its use.

51. This formulation ("to know" as a passive perfect with God as subject) is likely best understood in terms of the word ידע. Schnabel explains: "ידע with God as subject means 'to attend to a person' and describes the special relationship between Jahwe and Israel or individual Israelites." Schnabel, *Der erste Brief des Paulus an die Korinther*, 442–43, translation mine.

52. Waaler, *Shema*, 351.

on the language of the *Shema* to pursue his argument.⁵³ Waaler's study of the reuse of the *Shema* and the First Commandment in first century culture maintains that "to know that 'God is the only God' or that 'he is one' implies that one *relates* to one God only."⁵⁴ MacDonald's important study of the *Shema* argues that its confession is not about the nonexistence of other gods. Rather, it emphasizes the *personal and relational* in terms of the confession that YHWH is one. Monotheism, for MacDonald, is not simply "a truth to be comprehended." In Deuteronomy, it is "a relationship in which to be committed."⁵⁵ So it makes sense for Paul to draw on this in 1 Cor 8:6, given his relational concerns.

It is no surprise, then, to find Paul repeating this relationally accented knowledge of God in various other texts.⁵⁶ Hence, Dunn correctly argues that to

> know God is to worship him.... To know God is to be known by him, a two-way relationship of acknowledgment and obligation.... As in the (Jewish) scriptures, the "knowledge of God" includes experience of God's dealings, the two-way knowing of personal relationship.⁵⁷

Importantly, specialized studies relating to Paul's epistemology affirm this basic point.⁵⁸ So as Mary Healy has argued, for Paul, knowledge is expressed as relationship.⁵⁹

---

53. Which I take to mean at least Deut 6:4–9.

54. Waaler, *Shema*, 202, italics mine.

55. MacDonald, *Deuteronomy*, 97.

56. Tilling, *Paul's Divine Christology*, 70. One could also refer to 2 Cor 6:16; Gal 4:8–9; 1 Thess 1:9; and so on.

57. Dunn, *Theology*, 47, italics mine.

58. I refer to the work of Ian Scott, as well as the collection of essays in the Healy and Parry edited volume (Scott, *Implicit Epistemology*). Scott submits that knowledge of God, for Paul, involves "a harmonious *relationship* with the Creator" (Scott, *Implicit Epistemology*, 150, italics mine). Murray Rae, summarizing the findings of this collection of essays, argues that knowing is relational, involving participation and requires indwelling (This follows the summary of Rae and the following two scholars in Johnson, *Biblical Knowing*, 190–93).

59. Cf. the section title in Healy, "Knowledge of the Mystery," 142, as well as 145–56. Likewise, Dru Johnson's recent study, *Biblical Knowing*, confirms the importance of knowing-in-relationship in scriptural texts. He surveys a number of very recent works, all of which make recourse to relational metaphors when articulating the epistemology of a variety of texts. He maintains that the "epistemic objectives found in Scripture are generally ascribed to knowing-in-relationship" (Johnson, *Biblical Knowing*, xviii). Douglas Yoder's analysis of epistemology in the Tanakh speaks of knowing as "relational" (as one of the three main emphases, along with the rational and phenomenological).

b) It follows that to map Paul's God-discourse, one should pay attention to relational themes in the identification of this God, otherwise how would Paul have understood it as God-knowledge? When this is done—when we attend to Paul's own theological idiom—we see *Paul's God-language expressed in terms of a broadly consistent and identifiable pattern.* This list is not exhaustive, but appropriately representative.[60]

- *Communication.* We read that God speaks (2 Cor 4:6; 6:1), and humans pray to God (Rom 1:9–10; 10:1; 15:30; 2 Cor 11:13; 13:7; Phil 1:3–4; 1 Thess 3:10–13).

- *Presence and activity.* God is active (Rom 4:17; 8:9; 9:16; 11:23; 13:1–2; 1 Cor 1:29; 2:12) in Paul's mission (Rom 14:20; 1 Cor 2:4; 3:6; 2 Cor 2:17; 3:4–6; 4:7; 6:7; 12:19; 13:4; 1 Thess 3:11–13), in the church (1 Cor 3:16; 7:24; 12:18, 24, 28; 14:25; 2 Cor 6:16; 9:8, 14; Gal 3:5; Phil 1:6; 2:13; 4:19), in the church's worldly situations (1 Cor 10:13), and in individuals (Rom 9:16–18; 2 Cor 8:16).

- *Spirit.* This presence and activity is spoken of also in terms of the Spirit (Rom 5:5; 8:9; Gal 3:5).

- *Absence.* There is, however, a sense in which God is not fully present in the way he will be in the *eschaton* (1 Cor 13:12; 15:28; 2 Cor 4:18).

- *Character.* God is characterized in typical ways, as faithful (2 Cor 1:18), loving (Rom 5:5), wrathful (Rom 5:9), gracious (Rom 5:15), wise (Rom 16:27), acting with forbearance and patience (Rom 2:4), and so on.

- *Devotion.* It is expected that people serve, are slaves of, and belong to God (Rom 1:9; 6:22; 1 Cor 3:9). They boast in God (Rom 2:17; 5:11; 1 Thess 1:9), know God (Rom 1:19, 28; 1 Cor 15:34; 2 Cor 2:14; 10:6), love God (Rom 8:28; 1 Cor 8:2), fear God (Rom 3:18; 2 Cor 7:1), hope in God (Rom 4:18; 8:20), believe in God (Rom 4:17, 20–22, 24; Gal 3:6; 1 Thess 1:8), believers have turned to God (1 Thess 1:9); are "alive to" God (Rom 6:11; Gal 2:19), live to please God (Rom 8:8; Phil 4:18; 1 Thess 2:4, 15; 4:1), present themselves to God (Rom 6:13, 16; 12:1), praise God (Rom 14:11), and are eschatologically accountable before

---

Ryan O'Dowd's analysis of epistemology in Deuteronomy and the Wisdom Literature again emphasizes the relational aspect of knowing. Across the literature analyzed by Johnson, he notes a number of recurring themes, one of the most dominant of which is "personal knowledge" (Johnson, *Biblical Knowing*, 193).

60. More exhaustive references can be found in Tilling, *Paul's Divine Christology*, 236–39. I have also lifted, and lightly adjusted, some of the following from those pages.

God (Rom 14:12), etc. Naturally, God is strongly associated with Paul's ultimate goals, motivations, and aims: (Rom 11:36; 2 Cor 1:20; 5:13; Phil 1:11; 2:11; 4:20). God-devotion language is contrasted in typical ways. The wicked do not know God (Rom 1:21, 28), do not please God (Rom 8:8), nor fear God (Rom 3:18). They practice idolatry instead of turning to God (Rom 1:25), and so on. This God-devotion language is, of course, expressed in a way that shows it was an energetic and lively devotion. So Paul speaks of serving God in his spirit (Rom 1:9), that tongues, which is a language spoken to God (1 Cor 14:2, 28), is something Paul practices "more than all of" the Corinthians (1 Cor 14:18). Likewise, Paul regularly speaks of his constant praying to God (Phil 1:4; 1 Thess 1:2-3; 2:13; 3:10-13).

c) As I have begun to argue elsewhere, it is to be noted that this God-relation pattern involves one, and only one, actor across Second Temple Jewish texts, the one God. This is so whether one negotiates the Pentateuch or the Prophets, the Psalms or the Histories, or those texts often cited as problematic for so-called "exclusive Jewish monotheism," such as the *Similitudes*, Daniel, and so on. Even in those texts one finds God described in precisely the relational terms I have outlined, deploying this relational pattern of overlapping themes.[61] Embedded in various narratives, this unique-to-God pattern of data corresponds to the highlighted relational epistemological tendencies.

Bauckham uses the language of God's "transcendent uniqueness,"[62] which indicates that the texts consistently present the one God as "in a class of his own."[63] This results from his examination of the multiplication of "Most High" language,[64] and his isolation of divine identity categories. But not only have the hermeneutical appropriateness of his categories been challenged, but the phrase "transcendent uniqueness" is an etic descriptor,

---

61. I indeed base my defense of the phrase precisely on the texts Bauckham deems problematic, namely the *Similitudes*, in order to show the robustness of the case. The transcendent uniqueness of God is seen in the God-relation language, which is only ever used with reference to the one God and not, in any Second Temple texts, in terms of any intermediary figures, however exalted. See Tilling, *Paul's Divine Christology*, 196-233, for a substantiation of this claim in relation to three texts that supposedly problematize the transcendent uniqueness of the one God.

62. Bauckham, "Biblical Theology," 210-11.

63. I am (usually) sympathetic to concerns relating to the use of gender specific language when speaking of God, but I will adopt the male pronoun in the following. On this, see now Hinlicky, *Beloved Community*, 84-93.

64. This realization dovetails with the multiplication of "Most High" language, as analyzed in Bauckham, *Jesus and the God*, 107-26.

and as such potentially suspicious.⁶⁵ But our more inductive focus on the unique-to-God-relation-pattern, itself prompted by Paul's relational epistemology, suggests that Bauckham's language expresses something accurate in useful shorthand.⁶⁶

So the God-relation pattern expresses God's transcendent uniqueness. And it does so in Paul's relational idiom, such that we speak not merely about God's unique metaphysical status, but of this expressed in terms of a lived, exclusive, covenantal relationship with God over against capitulation to idolatry. I speak, then, of "Jewish monotheism" in this highly particularized manner, to articulate a lived, concrete, and exclusive commitment to God over against capitulation to idols. In this way I can affirm God's "transcendent uniqueness" or "exclusive monotheism," and doing it in this way avoids some major problems with the terminology of "monotheism" highlighted by Fredriksen, Horbury, and others.⁶⁷ What is more, it accounts for the uniqueness of this relational pattern, ignored by other approaches.⁶⁸

The upshot of all of this is highly significant. The unique-to-God-relational-pattern expresses Paul's exclusive monotheism, God's "transcendent uniqueness," and therefore creates the space for speaking, in Paul's idiom, about that which is God over against that which is not God. Otherwise put, this relationally formulated account of God's transcendent uniqueness speaks of *God's Godness*, a phrase I will use as shorthand for these realizations in what follows.⁶⁹

---

65. Certain strands of social anthropology describe fieldwork in two ways, as either emic or etic. The former attempts description of a subject from within a social group, i.e., within the epistemological framework of a given subject. The latter pursues description of a subject in terms of the outsider, the observer.

66. In conversation, Fred Sanders has counselled me to use the language of "transcategorial" (following John Hick) to speak of God as outside or beyond the range of our categories.

67. Fredriksen, "Mandataory Retirement"; Horbury, "Jewish and Christian Monotheism."

68. Arguably second best is Horbury's "inclusive monotheism," recently given popular voice in Ehrman's treatment (Ehrman, *How Jesus Became God*). But their case problematically gains its cogency by deploying charges against "exclusive monotheism" that themselves involve unreasonable and anachronistic metaphysical expectations. So, the existence of heavenly beings is problematically understood to challenge exclusive monotheism.

69. I need to note that I make these claims primarily *in view of Paul's own language*. I need to offer some accounting for Second Temple God-language, but given my focus, I do not intend this to be understood as a totalizing claim about the nature of all Jewish God-language in every Second Temple text, even if I do think the basic argument holds across the board. My point is that I am not defending the wider thesis in this essay.

Thesis 2:

The Christ-relation pattern of language is Paul's divine Christology articulated in terms of the transcendent uniqueness of God (which, remember, is Paul's way of speaking about that which is God over against that which is not God), *so it follows that God's Godness is expressed in terms of both the Father and the risen Lord.*

Here are the key steps in my reasoning, a–g, which, I emphasize, build on our first thesis.

a) In the epistemological argument in 1 Cor 8 noted earlier, Paul continues to speak not about relation to God over against capitulation to idols, but of relation to the risen Lord (see 1 Cor 8:6, 12: 10:1–22), and Paul makes this case about the Christ-relation by deploying the range of language and interrelated themes used across Second Temple texts to speak of Israel's relationship with the one God. Hence, it makes sense to examine the contours of the Pauline Christ-relation, which I here present in summary form with a few verses referenced as examples:

- *Communication.* Christ is prayed to and Christ speaks back (Rom 10:9–13; 1 Cor 16:22; 2 Cor 10:18; 12:8–9; 13:3; 1 Thess 3:11–13).
- *Presence and activity.* Christ is present and active in various ways (Rom 1:7; 8:9–10; 14:4; 15:18–19, 29; 16:20; 1 Cor 1:3; 3:5; 4:19; 7:17, 25; 16:17, 23; 2 Cor 1:2; 2:10, 12; 3:3; 12:7–10; 13:3–5, 13; Gal 2:20; 4:6; 6:18; Phil 1:2, 19; 3:21; 1 Thess 3:11–13; 5:28; Phlm 3, 25).
- *Absence.* Christ is at the same time also strangely "absent" (1 Cor 11:26; 15:23; 2 Cor 5:6–8; Phil 1:20–24; 1 Thess 2:19; 3:13; 4:17; 5:10, 23).
- *Spirit.* So Christ is present and active by the Spirit (Rom 8:9–10; 15:18–19; Gal 4:6; Phil 1:19).
- *Character.* Christ is characterized in ways that overlap considerably with his own, and other, Jewish God-talk (Rom 8:35; 10:12; 14:4, 9; 11:27–30; 15:45; 2 Cor 4:13; 5:14; 10:1; 13:5; Gal 1:1, 11–12; 2:20; Phil 1:8; 3:21; 1 Thess 4:6).
- *Devotion.* Paul expresses devotion to Christ—which includes so-called "cultic worship," but also goes beyond it—in striking, lively, and consistent ways. Just as in Jewish God-language, this devotion is contrasted with certain themes such as sin, idolatry, and the like (Rom 1:5; 12:11; 14:6–9; 16:5; 1 Cor 1:7 [cf. also Phil 3:20]; 1:31; 2:2; 6:13, 16–17; 7:25–38; 8:12; 10:9, 20–22; 11:23–26, 30–32; 12:3; 15:19, 58; 16:18, 22; 2 Cor 3:16–18; 4:4–5; 5:9–10, 15; 8:5, 19; 10:7; 10:17; 11:2–3; 12:7–10;

Gal 1:10; 2:20; 3:29; Phil 1:20, 23; 2:6–11, 21; 3:1, 8; 1 Thess 1:2–3; 3:8; 4:17; 5:10; Phil 6).[70]

b) What is immediately apparent is that this overlaps, both in terms of structure and detail, with the God-relation pattern, and explicitly so. The whole discussion relating to food offered to idols in 1 Cor 8–10 attests to this, as do the majority of examples noted above relating to the Christ-relation pattern. In other words, dozens of texts across the Pauline corpus attest to Paul's articulation of the Christ-relation in terms of the transcendent uniqueness of God, or the Godness of God.

c) This is not merely to list random passages, driven by apologetic intent. This Christ-relation data is, I contend, a pattern that Paul would have recognized as such (namely, as a pattern) as it constitutes, to a rather greater than lesser extent, an existential reality in Paul's life. These themes are not merely a collection of loose, unrelated ideas. They are also regularly found together in single arguments in Paul's letters, and conceptually overlap. So, for example, Paul's intense devotion to Christ in his longing for the presence of Christ, bespeaks the absence of Christ, as well as the character of the risen Lord, and so on.

d) As we have concluded that, for Paul, knowledge is expressed as relationship (to cite Healy), it follows that the Christ-relation pattern *is* Paul's Christology (at least insofar as it pertains to our theme in this essay). Paul's Christ-relation is a form of knowing and so the Christ-relation is *Christology* in Paul's very particular Jewish idiom.

e) This Christ-relation, as a pattern, is analogous *only* with Paul's Jewish God-relation language, which itself expresses the transcendent uniqueness of God. Against those who argue that divine agency figures are the key for understanding Christ in Paul's letters, I argue that when Paul's Christ-relation language as a whole is kept in mind, it becomes obvious that agency figures are less helpful for understanding the breadth of Paul's divine Christology. None of these intermediary figures, however exalted, are described in comparable fashion. None can be mapped on to the God-relation pattern. Indeed, even in those texts that say the grandest things about intermediary figures, it is the way God is spoken of *even in those texts* that corresponds best with Paul's Christ-relation.

f) This means that the Christ-relation, and only the Christ-relation, has the same shape, major themes, and basic content as Jewish God-language, Paul's included, and as such articulates Paul's divine Christology.

---

70. As before, this summarizes findings presented earlier in Tilling, *Paul's Divine Christology*. The results of that previous study also inform the following paragraphs of this second thesis.

Paul's Christ-relation is Paul's divine Christology understood in precisely the way the "transcendent uniqueness" of the one God was expressed. It is his divine Christology, articulated in relational terms.

g) Hence, and finally, the unique-to-God-relational-pattern which expresses God's transcendent uniqueness, or God's Godness, involves, for Paul, both the Christ- and God-relations. God's unique Godness is expressed in both the God and Christ relations.

Thesis 3:

The Spirit mediates and actualizes both the God and Christ relations, hence the Spirit's activity is that relationality which articulates Paul's way of speaking about the Godness of God.

I will now focus on just two steps in this argument.

a) Mehrdad Fatehi made a strong case, now almost seventeen years ago, that "all Spirit-language in Second Temple Judaism (and in Paul) . . . speaks of 'God's activity *as he relates himself* to his world, his creation, [and] his people.'"[71] Certainly the Pauline data consistently presents God as relating to the world, or as present and active in it, by the Spirit. Hence, "*God's love has been poured into our hearts through the Holy Spirit*" (Rom 5:5), Paul's proclamation to the Corinthians came with "*a demonstration of the Spirit and of power, so that your faith might rest not on human wisdom but on the power of God*" (1 Cor 2:4–5), God supplies the Galatians with his Spirit, and so he works miracles among them (Gal 3:5), and so on.[72] The Spirit, then, is God relating to his people, the activity of the Spirit *is* the "transcendent uniqueness" of the one God, and so expresses the Godness of God.

b) The second point has indeed already been noted in the second thesis, but I will elaborate a little more on its content here. It presents Christ as both present and active in the communities of the faithful and in "the world." A small sampling of data suffices to demonstrate this. So, the risen Lord is able to make believers stand (Rom 14:4), is active in Paul's mission (1 Cor 15:18–19, 29), in appointing leaders (1 Cor 3:5), within Paul himself, is active in assigning the social and communal situatedness of all people (1 Cor 7:17), and so on. Paul's prayers to the risen Lord likewise show his expectation that Christ is *able*, sufficiently present, and active to answer his prayers, whether it be for the removal of the "thorn," or that the

---

71. Fatehi, *Spirit's Relation*, 303, italics mine.

72. God reveals through the Spirit (1 Cor 2:10, 12–14), puts his seal on the faithful by giving the Spirit (2 Cor 1:22), enables the same to cry "Abba! Father!" again by sending the Spirit (Gal 4:6) etc. See also Rom 8:27; 15:13, 16; 1 Thess 4:8; Eph 3:14–16.

Thessalonians would "increase and abound in love for one another," having their hearts strengthened in holiness (1 Thess 3:12–13).

But the noteworthy point to insist on is that this Christ is at the same time, for Paul, *absent*. Hence he celebrates the Lord's Supper *until* he comes (1 Cor 11:26). Christ cannot yet be seen face to face (1 Cor 13:12) because he is not yet present (παρουσία, 1 Cor 15:23; 1 Thess 2:19; 3:13) but absent (ἀπουσία, see Phil 2:12). This absence explains Paul's longing for the presence of the Lord, during the time, as Paul puts it in 2 Cor 5:6–8, that "we are at home in the body" and thus "*away* from the Lord."[73]

Paul, therefore, speaks of this absent Christ as *present by the Spirit*. This relation between the risen Lord and the Christ-communities, which *is* Paul's divine Christology, is actualized or realized by the activity of the Spirit, and so the Spirit's mediation constitutes Paul's divine Christology. Hence, for example, Paul does not venture to speak of anything to the Romans, "except what *Christ has accomplished through me* to win obedience from the Gentiles." And this agency of Christ is actualized, Paul goes on to explain, "by the power of the Spirit of God" (Rom 15:18–19). Likewise, Paul explains in 2 Corinthians 3 that they "are a letter of Christ," a genitive construction which most likely should be understood to denote a letter written *by* Christ. And how does Christ write this letter? It is one "written not with ink but *by the Spirit of the living God*" (2 Cor. 3:3). This same Spirit exclusively enables the confession "Jesus is Lord" (1 Cor. 12:3) and so on.[74]

Hill at least accounts for this kind of language, even if his approach did not allow for a sufficiently Pauline character. Our purpose has been to explore what that character looks like, and to suggest that, within Paul's idiom, one may speak of the God and Christ relations as articulating the Godness of God, or the "transcendent uniqueness" of God, both in terms of the risen Lord and God the Father. The activity of the Spirit, then, uniquely actualizes or realizes both the God and Christ relations, which means that both the God- and the Christ-relations are made relational, hence expresses the Godness of God, by the activity of the Spirit.

These first three theses present us with Paul's theological idiom in terms of God, the Lord Jesus, and the Spirit, and it is with these realizations that we turn to the fourth thesis.

> *Thesis 4:*
>
> The fourth thesis is two-part. *Presentations of Pauline theology in terms of the trinity, as represented in all three models of my taxonomy above, are superficial precisely as exegetical engagements*

---

73. See also Phil 1:20–24; 1 Thess 4:17–18; 5:10–11.
74. See also Rom 8:2, 9–10; 1 Cor 15:45.

with Paul. But, and this is the second part, *when Paul's texts are read in terms of the Apostle's own theological idiom, they achieve new levels of salience, leading to the affirmation of Paul the Trinitarian.*

a) The first step in this case is to note those typical texts. (There are also a sweep of related methods, but for reasons of space we will only focus on the texts in this essay. They would include interaction with the so-called "economic Trinity" method, analysis of the ascent and descent motifs in Paul's christological rhetoric,[75] and enumerate the prosopological exegetical method outlined in Matthew Bates's important contributions.[76]) They are taken to be relevant because they involve the explicit naming of God (or the Father), the Lord Jesus (or Christ) and the Spirit *in close proximity*. Important are the following:

- Romans 15:30: "I appeal to you, brothers and sisters, by our *Lord Jesus Christ* and by the love of the *Spirit*, to join me in earnest prayer to *God* on my behalf."
- 1 Corinthians 12:3–6: "Therefore I want you to understand that no one speaking by the *Spirit of God* ever says 'Let *Jesus* be cursed!' and no one can say '*Jesus is Lord*' except by the *Holy Spirit*. Now there are varieties of gifts, but the same *Spirit*; and there are varieties of services, but the same *Lord*; and there are varieties of activities, but it is the same *God*."
- 2 Corinthians 13:13: "The grace of the *Lord Jesus Christ*, the love of *God*, and the communion of the *Holy Spirit* be with all of you."
- 1 Thessalonians 1:2–6: "We always give thanks to *God* for all of you and mention you in our prayers, constantly remembering before our *God and Father* your work of faith and labor of love and steadfastness of hope in our *Lord Jesus Christ*. For we know, brothers and sisters beloved by *God*, that he has chosen you, because our message of the gospel came to you not in word only, but also in power and in the *Holy Spirit* and with full conviction; just as you know what kind of persons we proved to be among you for your sake. And you became imitators of us and of the *Lord*, for in spite of persecution you received the word with joy inspired by the *Holy Spirit*."[77]

---

75. See, e.g., Yarnell, *God the Trinity*.

76. Bates, *Hermeneutics*. For interaction with these themes, please see my forthcoming, *Paul the Trinitarian*.

77. Reference may also be made to 1 Cor 6:11; Gal 4:4–9; and Rom 8:9.

Immediately, one may understand why the three models enumerated above have developed as they have done. At best these passages, when read in isolation from Paul's theological idiom, look like seeds of later Trinitarian thought. One may thus prefer to deploy hermeneutical solutions, and suggest that these texts are *best understood* in light of later Trinitarian dogma. Others want to say more than this by arguing that there is still a Trinitarian grammar in Paul himself, albeit an inchoate or unreflected one. Or again, others argue that any logical connection between these passages and Nicene theology is merely apologetic, especially when Second Temple divine agents are factored in.

b) On the contrary, I argue that all of these positions have underestimated the theological richness and coherence of Paul's own letters, and thus offer atomistic or superficial accounts of these texts precisely as *Pauline*. Positively put, when one reads these texts in light of the wider relational pattern expressing the Godness of God in terms of the Father, the Lord Jesus, and these relations actualized by the Spirit (theses 1–3 above), they express, in a nutshell, what we have uncovered by focusing on Paul's *own* theological grammar.

And lest there be doubt that these texts belong within this proposed grammar, please note that they are all bound up in the communal and relational realities we have emphasized, and as such constitute a Pauline mode of theological articulation. This is either explicit in these verses, which speak in relational terms about God, whether by emphasizing prayer, confession, liturgical presence, and so on, or evident in the immediate textual frame.

Hence, the Pauline articulation of the "transcendent uniqueness" of God, or Paul's "exclusive monotheism," which involves the God and Christ relations as actualized by the Spirit, must impinge upon and guide our analysis of these passages which name Christ, God, and the Spirit in close proximity. Otherwise we risk anachronism, at the very least.

To cash this claim out in practice, let us briefly focus on one example from that list, namely 1 Corinthians 12:4. There, Paul contrasts the varieties of gifts, services, and activities with the "same" Spirit, Lord, and God. While this can be spoken of in terms of later creedal Trinitarianism, it is also entirely logical to read this within Paul's theological idiom, for the unique-to-God-relation, which expresses the transcendent uniqueness of God, is consistently parsed, by Paul, in terms of the Father and the risen Lord, both of which are relations realized by the Spirit. It states, in a nutshell, what our wider overview of Pauline rhetoric has already demonstrated, that Paul's articulation of the unique Godness of God exhibits a threefoldness. This is why it is entirely pertinent to speak of the unity of this threefold transcendent uniqueness, and hence to deploy it as exemplifying unity in diversity in 1 Corinthians 12. The logic which makes Paul's argument work, in 1 Corinthians 12, is that there is a "tri" in the "unity" of his articulation of the Godness of God. *Hence, we can speak of Paul's tri-une faith, and thus of Paul the Trinitarian.*

These texts are thus instances of that wider Pauline theological grammar. They express moments of *Paul's* Trinitarian rhetoric, and do so in the Apostle's own relational idiom. This is indeed why a Trinitarian hermeneutic is a resource rather than a liability,[78] and why analysis of so-called "economic" Trinitarian dynamics are helpful: because such readings alight on aspects of Paul's relationally articulated theological idiom. This is why prosopological exegesis plumbs the depths and digs up *what is there*, and does not simply provide raw data useful for later Nicene Trinitarian speculation. All of these various ways for speaking about the Trinity in terms of Paul find exegetical legitimation *as readings of Paul* in view of Paul's own robust and relational theology. To speak of Paul the Trinitarian in this way is, I suggest, not arbitrarily to impose later dogmatic categories, but indeed to read Paul in terms of his own historical particularity, as an instance and variation within wider themes and patterns across Second Temple Judaism.

Conclusion

By way of conclusion, I have argued that the transcendent uniqueness of God, for Paul, is expressed as the unique-to-God-relation-pattern, one suggested by realization of Paul's relational theological epistemology. God's Godness, or that which indicates that which is God as opposed to not God, is then expressed, by Paul, in terms of both the God and Christ relations, meaning that both God and Christ are spoken of in terms of that unique Godness of God. We then maintained that these relations are actualized as theologically significant relations *due to the agency of the Spirit*. As such, Paul can make recourse to this threefold articulation of God's "transcendent uniqueness" precisely to exemplify unity in diversity. One can therefore rightly speak of Paul's tri-une theology, and hence of Paul the Trinitarian.

It should be evident that I am not, therefore, positioning my own approach as an alternative to any of the three models outlined at the start. Rather, my goal is to insist that Paul remain our focus when speaking of Paul's theology. When this is done, we can meaningfully speak of Paul the Trinitarian as *articulated on his own terms*. For each model has underestimated what can be said about Paul, a factor that has allowed the hermeneutical balance to shift our gaze away from the Apostle, in so far as it pertains

---

78. Cf. Hill, *Paul and the Trinity*, 31.

to the Trinity. Paul's theology is then judged on anachronistic terms, which has led to each of the models summarized in our threefold taxonomy.

And there was truth in each of them. In terms of Paul's *Wirkungsgeschichte*, of course there is not only one line to draw from Paul to the Trinity, but multiple, with all kinds of results, ranging from anti-Trinitarian adoptionism to Marcionism. Of course, Paul may be read in such a way that suggests that the seeds of later Trinitarian theology are present in Paul, and now we have further shown why Trinitarian hermeneutical methods indeed shed light on Paul, rather than distort. And of course there is conceptual distance between Paul and Nicaea, both of which use different terms to articulate particular *theologoumena*. Paul and Nicaea are not saying *exactly* the same thing, for any re-articulation of a complex set of theological proposals in two disparate if overlapping philosophical idioms necessarily means that there is some degree of difference.[79] It is appropriate, therefore, to speak of the *translation*—as opposed to transposition—of Paul's theological and Trinitarian idiom into an alternative but related conceptual framework. And translations can be more or less faithful.

I am not thereby suggesting that later Trinitarian dogma is something radically different from what we find in Paul. Nicene Trinitarian theology, I think it is fair to say, represents a *faithful translation* of what is already present in Paul, but I have not attempted to defend this thesis today. All I can do is suggest that the relationship between the two, based on my proposals in this essay, is a logical one, and that this is precisely why a Trinitarian hermeneutic sheds meaningful light on Paul's own argumentation, as Hill ably demonstrates.

But this is not to say that Nicene dogma is a *necessary* development from Paul, at least if necessity is understood in prospective terms. Indeed, it seems to me far more pertinent to speak of the necessary accounting for Paul's historical particularity as an instance of Second Temple Judaism, which I have sought to do here. But as Hegel taught us, necessity need not be so understood. One may rightly speak of Nicaea as the necessary outcome of Paul's Trinity when necessity is comprehended in *retrospective* terms.[80]

---

79. This is because it is by means of words that we articulate those proposals. If the words change, so does the nature of the articulation.

80. Throughout the debates relating to Trinitarian theology in the early church, a lot of contingent issues played a part, and something else might have happened. But given that Nicene theology eventually became creedal, a retrospective account will insist that it becomes necessary. As Fritzman writes, "One of Hegel's deepest lessons [is] that what was contingent can become necessary" (Fritzman, *Hegel*, 8). I flew to Durham, North Carolina, in November 2016 to present an earlier version of this essay in a colloquium at Duke. The only way I could get to Duke from London on time was to catch my flight. Of course, I might have missed my flight, due, perhaps, to one of those typical British

So understood, Nicene dogma is both a logical and a necessary translation of Paul.

Of course, one might object that this kind of reasoning is simply the result of a Christian reading of Paul's language, one already committed to the Trinity. I'd be happy to capitulate to this point, although I would take issue with the word "simply" in that charge. Gadamer was right that our "understanding of texts is not in spite of a historical situation, but rather by means of it,"[81] so I do not claim to stand outside of my own tradition, as if I have somehow attained objectivity in my description of Paul's own theological idiom.

But that said, nor should my own Christian commitments suggest that all of my exegetical endeavours, in this essay, are thereby automatically suspicious. Gadamer's observation cuts both ways. In acknowledging that I am a Trinitarian interpreter of Paul, I hope that my preceding arguments will not be dismissed simply because of the suspicion that theology is trumping historical exegesis, or simply because it is asserted that my own agenda is pulling Pauline rhetoric out of shape. Rather, it is the arguments themselves that need to be assessed. And when that is done, it is my contention that we should indeed speak of Paul the Trinitarian.[82]

Bibliography

Bates, Matthew W. *The Birth of the Trinity: Jesus, God, and Spirit in New Testament and Early Christian Interpretations of the Old Testament*. Oxford: Oxford University Press, 2015.

———. *The Hermeneutics of the Apostolic Proclamation: The Center of Paul's Method of Scriptural Interpretation*. Waco, TX: Baylor University Press, 2012.

Bauckham, Richard J. "Biblical Theology and the Problems of Monotheism." In *Out of Egypt: Biblical Theology and Biblical Interpretation*, edited by Craig Bartholomew, Mary Healy, Karl Möller, and Robin Parry, 187–232. Milton Keynes, UK: Paternoster, 2004.

---

traffic-jams on the M25. If that had happened, I would have missed my flight and would not have been able to deliver the paper at Duke. But given that I did present the paper, it was necessary that I successfully caught my flight (A similar example is proffered in Fritzman, *Hegel*, 8, which inspired this one). So the creedal doctrine of the Trinity is necessary, and all the more so if one considers theological ontology, but that would take me beyond my argument in this essay.

81. I lift this useful summary of the import of Gadamer's language on reading New Testament texts from Blackwell, *Christosis*, 16. For a more complete overview of this aspect of his work, I refer to Gadamer, *Truth and Method*.

82. My thanks to members of the New Testament faculty at Duke Divinity School and the Duke Department of Religious Studies for critical feedback on an earlier draft of this essay.

———. *Jesus and the God of Israel*. Milton Keynes, UK: Paternoster, 2008.
Blackwell, Ben C. "Biblical Trinitarianism and Anachronism: Historical Criticism." https://dunelm.wordpress.com/2016/10/17/biblical-trinitarianism-and-anachronism-historical-criticism/.
———. *Christosis: Engaging Paul's Soteriology with His Patristic Interpreters*. Grand Rapids: Eerdmans, 2016.
Campbell, Douglas A. "Christ and the Church in Paul: A 'Post-New Perspective' Account." In *Four Views on the Apostle Paul*, edited by Michael F. Bird, 113–43. Grand Rapids: Zondervan, 2013.
Casey, Maurice. *From Jewish Prophet to Gentile God: The Origins and Development of New Testament Christology*. Cambridge: James Clarke, 1991.
Dunn, James D. G. *Christology in the Making: A New Testament Inquiry Into the Origins of the Doctrine of the Incarnation*. London: SCM, 1989.
———. *The Theology of Paul the Apostle*. Grand Rapids: Eerdmans, 1998.
Ehrman, Bart D. *How Jesus Became God: The Exaltation of a Jewish Preacher from Galilee*. New York: HarperCollins, 2014.
Fatehi, Mehrdad. *The Spirit's Relation to the Risen Lord in Paul: An Examination of Its Christological Implications*. Tübingen: Mohr Siebeck, 2000.
Fee, Gordon D. "Christology and Pneumatology in Romans 8:9–11—and Elsewhere: Some Reflections on Paul as a Trinitarian." In *Jesus of Nazareth: Lord and Christ. Essays on the Historical Jesus and New Testament Christology*, edited by Joel B. Green and Max Turner, 312–31. Carlisle, UK: Paternoster, 1994.
———. *The First and Second Letters to the Thessalonians*. Grand Rapids: Eerdmans, 2009.
———. *God's Empowering Presence: The Holy Spirit in the Letters of Paul*. Peabody, MA: Hendrickson, 1994.
———. *Paul, the Spirit, and the People of God*. Peabody, MA: Hendrickson, 1996.
Fletcher-Louis, Crispin. *Jesus Monotheism*. Vol. 1, *Christological Origins: The Emerging Consensus and Beyond*. Eugene, OR: Cascade, 2015.
Fredriksen, Paula. "Mandatory Retirement: Ideas in the Study of Christian Origins Whose Time Has Come to Go." In *Israel's God and Rebecca's Children: Essays in Honor of Larry W. Hurtado and Alan F. Segal*, edited by David B. Capes, April D. DeConick, Helen K. Bond, and Troy A. Miller, 25–38. Waco, TX: Baylor University Press, 2007.
Fritzman, J. M. *Hegel*. Polity Classic Thinkers. Cambridge: Polity, 2014.
Gadamer, Hans-Georg. *Truth and Method*. Translated by Garret Barden and John Cumming. New York: Seabury, Continuum, 1975.
Harnack, Adolf. *Lehrbuch der Dogmengeschichte*. 1909. Tübingen: Mohr, 1990.
Harvey, Lincoln. "The Theological Promise of Michael Polanyi's Project: An Examination Within the Contemporary Context of Atheism and the Constructivist Critique of the Natural Sciences." In *Critical Conversations: Michael Polanyi and Christian Theology*, edited by Murray A. Rae, 56–73. Eugene, OR: Pickwick, 2012.
Healy, Mary. "Knowledge of the Mystery: A Study of Pauline Epistemology." In *The Bible and Epistemology*, edited by Mary Healy and Robin Parry, 134–57. Milton Keynes: Paternoster, 2007.
Hill, Wesley. *Paul and the Trinity: Persons, Relations, and the Pauline Letters*. Grand Rapids: Eerdmans, 2015.

Hinlicky, Paul R. *Beloved Community: Critical Dogmatics After Christendom*. Grand Rapids: Eerdmans, 2015.

Horbury, William. "Jewish and Christian Monotheism in the Herodian Age." In *Early Jewish and Christian Monotheism*, edited by Loren T. Stuckenbruck and Wendy E. S. North, 16–44. London: T. & T. Clark, 2004.

Hurtado, Larry W. *God in New Testament Theology*. Nashville: Abingdon, 2010.

———. *One God, One Lord*. 1988. London: Bloomsbury T. & T. Clark, 2015.

Johnson, Dru. *Biblical Knowing: A Scriptural Epistemology of Error*. Eugene, OR: Cascade, 2013.

Johnson, Luke Timothy. "Response to Douglas A. Campbell." In *Four Views on the Apostle Paul*, edited by Michael F. Bird, 149–52. Grand Rapids: Zondervan, 2013.

MacDonald, Nathan. *Deuteronomy and the Meaning of "Monotheism."* Tübingen: Mohr Siebeck, 2003.

Parry, Robin, and Mary Healy, eds. *The Bible and Epistemology: Biblical Soundings on the Knowledge of God*. Milton Keynes, UK: Paternoster, 2007.

Pearsall, Judy, and William R. Trumble, eds. *The Oxford English Reference Dictionary*. Oxford: Oxford University Press, 1995.

Richardson, Neil. *Paul's Language About God*. Sheffield, UK: Sheffield Academic, 1994.

Rowe, C. Kavin. "The Trinity in the Letters of St Paul and Hebrews." In *The Oxford Handbook of the Trinity*, edited by Gilles Emery and Matthew Levering, 41–54. Oxford: Oxford University Press, 2011.

Schnabel, Eckhard J. *Der erste Brief des Paulus an die Korinther*. Wuppertal, DE: R. Brockhaus Verlag, 2006.

Schnelle, Udo. *Apostle Paul: His Life and Theology*. Translated by M. Eugene Boring. Grand Rapids: Baker Academic, 2005.

Schreiner, Thomas R. "Paul: A Reformed Reading." In *Four Views on the Apostle Paul*, edited by Michael F. Bird, 19–47. Grand Rapids: Zondervan, 2012.

Scott, Ian W. *Implicit Epistemology in the Letters of Paul: Story, Experience and the Spirit*. Tübingen: Mohr Siebeck, 2006.

Tilling, Chris. "Paul, the Trinity and Contemporary Trinitarian Debates." *Pacific Journal of Baptist Research* 11 (May 2016) 19–43.

———. *Paul's Divine Christology*. Grand Rapids, MI: Eerdmans, 2015.

Waaler, Erik. *The Shema and the First Commandment in First Corinthians: An Intertextual Approach to Paul's Re-Reading of Deuteronomy*. Tübingen: Mohr Siebeck, 2008.

Waddell, James A. *The Messiah: A Comparative Study of the Enochic Son of Man and the Pauline Kyrios*. London: Bloomsbury, 2011.

Wright, N. T. *Paul and the Faithfulness of God*. Minneapolis: Fortress, 2013.

Yarnell, Malcolm B., III. *God the Trinity: Biblical Portraits*. Nashville: B & H Academic, 2016. Kindle edition.

CHAPTER 4

That We May Know Him . . .

Lucy Peppiatt

And this is eternal life, that they may know you, the only true God, and Jesus Christ, whom you have sent. (John 17:3)

For the Apostle says . . . *But we have not received the spirit of this world, but the Spirit which is of God, that we may know the things that are given unto us by God.* We receive Him, then, that we may know. (Hilary of Poitiers, *On the Trinity*, II.35)

Introduction: Salvation as Participation

In our thinking on the Trinity, two extremes must be avoided: tritheism on the one hand and modalism on the other. Avoiding them, however, is not easy. With an emphasis (or over-emphasis) on the three, God is three "persons" who all relate to one another in loving relationship sometimes described as if they were three distinct centers of consciousness. In extreme versions of this, it is both the mutual love and, rather confusingly, either the hierarchical structuring *or* the mutual submission of the three persons in relation that seem to define and inform much of what we might want to say about God.[1] The emphasis is on the unity of the Godhead constituted

---

1. Whenever there are sharper distinctions drawn between the persons of the Trinity as if each of the three persons operate from a distinct center of consciousness, what follows necessarily is speculation as to *how* those persons "relate." Where Moltmann

in the relationship of the three persons and in the way that they relate as persons, rather than in the oneness of God expressed in the three persons subsisting as one essence, as in what is now purported to be the more classical view. In my view, the latter is more doctrinally correct than the former, despite the former perspective gaining great popularity in recent years. The challenge, however, for those countering a strongly tri-personal account of the Trinity is to avoid eliding the distinctions between the persons in such a way that the three simply blend into a monolithic one, and we lose sight of the triunity of God all together. Despite my commitment to the classical approach, my concerns center on two dogmatic issues that I wish to address in this essay.

The first is to caution against placing too great an emphasis on apophaticism in relation to the concept of the knowability/unknowability of God. The second is to caution against emphasizing only the first half of the principle of inseparable operations (that the works of the Trinity *ad extra* are undivided) while ignoring the second qualifying clause in the original maxim.[2] Twenty years ago, Henri Blocher pointed out that the rule of inseparable external operations "too often goes in a truncated form" omitting the second part of the rule, *servato discrimine et ordine personarum* (the distinction and order of the Persons being preserved).[3] Unfortunately, this

---

and Boff, for example, argue for a non-hierarchical structure of the three persons of the Trinity who all relate to one another in mutual love, others such as Wayne Grudem argue that the Son and the Spirit have eternally subordinate roles to the Father. These views are two different sides of the same tri-personal coin. See Moltmann, *Trinity and the Kingdom*; Boff, *Trinity and Society*; Grudem, *Systematic Theology*.

2. I see hints of both these moves in those arguing against social Trinitarianism. In a more apophatic vein, Karen Kilby writes, "My own proposal, then, is not that one should move from the social back to, say, a psychological approach to the Trinity—this would simply be to look for a *different* insight—but rather that one should renounce the very idea that the point of the doctrine is to give insight into God." Kilby, "Perichoresis and Projection," 443. Kilby then develops this idea in more detail in "Is an Apophatic Trinitarianism Possible?" Sarah Coakley appeals specifically to the apophaticism of Gregory of Nyssa in relation to knowing and unknowing in order to respond to what she sees as the overstated claims of social trinitarians in the analytic philosophical tradition. I bring out one particular aspect of her use of Gregory below. See Coakley, "'Persons' in the 'Social' Doctrine." Steve Holmes's summary of Trinitarian doctrine up until the mid-eighth century illustrates this emphasis on the one divine essence and inseparable operations, "God is, and is ineffable. God is triune: Father, Son, and Holy Spirit. The church believes, adores, and worships the one simple divine essence, which exists three times over, as Father, Son, and Holy Spirit, inseparably united in life and action, one in everything save in their relations of origin." Holmes, *Holy Trinity*, 120.

3. Blocher, "Immanence and Transcendence," 120. Blocher here cites Emil Brunner, *Dogmatique I: la doctrine chrétienne de Dieu*, translated into French by Fréderic Jaccard (Geneva: Labor & Fides, 1964) 253. I am unclear as to the origins of this precise wording used by Blocher/Brunner. The principle of inseparable operations is normally

is still often the case, and it only serves to attenuate the singular significance of the missions of the Son and the Spirit to bring humanity to the Father. I propose that if the two theological commitments—apophaticism and the undivided act—converge, there is a danger of diminishing the soteriological significance of the doctrine of the Trinity, which itself was fundamental to the classical understanding of the doctrine as it is enumerated in early church writings. A properly classical view of the Trinity, therefore, needs to take this into account.

In the first place, then, we should be cautious of emphasizing the ineffability of the one essence of God to such an extent that we might wonder about the legitimacy of claims regarding the possibility of "knowing" God, a claim that is central both to the gospel and to the early accounts of God as triune.[4] In addition, leaning heavily on the inseparable operations should not come at the expense of an account of the missions of the Son and the Spirit, which in the biblical narrative and in early church thought were un-

---

associated with Augustine. In IV.5.30 of *On the Trinity*, Augustine claims that the Father, Son, and Holy Spirit "act inseparably," and goes on, "But they cannot be manifested inseparably by creatures which are so unlike them, especially material ones." He adds, the "trinity together produced both the Father's voice and the Son's flesh and the Holy Spirit's dove, though each of these single things has reference to a single person. Well, at least the example helps us to see how this three, inseparable in itself, is manifested separately through visible creatures." I am arguing that we should not downplay the significance of this separate manifestation.

4. Lewis Ayres discusses the complex relationship of knowing and unknowing in his chapter "On the Contours of Mystery" in *Nicaea and Its Legacy*. Space prohibits a discussion of the question of Trinitarian language as anagogic, and the epistemic implications of this which Ayres discusses in his work. Ayres's point in this chapter is that "Pro-Nicenes argue that we can have no knowledge of God in which we can rest as if we finally understood: all knowledge of God is useful within what we might term an anagogic context." (284). This is a point well made and should be taken into consideration in discussions regarding "knowing" God. Interestingly, despite an insistence by Ayres that inseparable operations and the simplicity of God led Pro-Nicenes to claim that there is an unknowable, ineffable essence of God, he also concludes, "The pro-Nicene life of the mind finds its core in attention, on the one hand, to the dynamics not simply of 'revelation', but of the divine economy that condescends to our categories but does so only to draw us slowly toward a contemplation of the divine realities of which they speak." (300). Ayres is another example of someone who brings out the prominence of the simplicity of God, the ineffable essence, and inseparable operations in classical thought. He includes in a footnote to this chapter, rather tantalizingly, that he could have chosen to go on to "investigate common themes among pro-Nicene presentations of the individual persons of Father, Son, and Spirit. That is a large task for which I intend only to lay the groundwork for future work here. It should be clear, however, that pursuing such an investigation would involve being attentive not only to how individual theologians and traditions present the three persons, but also to how they relate their presentations to their (perhaps implicit) understandings of appropriation and common operation." (300).

derstood as the very means by which humanity can, in fact, come to know God and to participate in his being.

Gijsbert van den Brink makes these very points in a recent article where he first draws the explicit link between "proto-trinitarian patterns and assertions" in the New Testament in the context of salvation history, claiming that they "occur in such a pervasive manner that they form a more or less consistent pattern throughout the New Testament, a kind of punch-line which, if properly understood, enables us to make sense of the overarching story of God's involvement in history for us and our salvation."[5] He describes salvation in terms of a "participatory ontology, according to which human beings are transformed in the Spirit through Jesus Christ into fellowship with the Father."[6] This "communion and participation in God . . . is realized in the double movement of incarnation and ascension of the Son, to whom believers are united by the Spirit."[7] Of course, these claims are hardly new. They have their roots in the New Testament and in patristic reflections where the doctrine of the Trinity is expressed in relation to salvation articulating "the fact that Christ died for us and lives in us, that the Spirit prays for us and in us, and that in such ways we are reunited with the Father."[8] But van den Brink's Trinitarian insights give us both a helpful backdrop and a framework for further discussion. With a view of salvation as participation, we can explore the question of knowing and unknowing and from there analyze the concept of inseparable operations.

Methodologies and Commitments

In response to the two commitments referenced above (a strong apophaticism in league with a strong account of inseparable operations) I will begin by touching on the complex topic of the idea of knowing God in patristic writings, thereby demonstrating that knowledge of God was viewed as a possibility, even a goal, with certain provisos in place. I hope to make the point that discussions about our knowledge of God, especially in relation to the Trinity, cannot appeal to apophaticism as some kind of epistemological cop-out as that defeats the point of the doctrine, which is at its heart, revelatory. I will then examine a few Trinitarian principles and concepts with a view to demonstrating that they are most useful in relation to an understanding that the Trinitarian God is the God who *saves* rather than understanding them

---

5. Van den Brink, "Social Trinitarianism," 345.
6. Van den Brink, "Social Trinitarianism," 349–50.
7. Van den Brink, "Social Trinitarianism," 350.
8. Van den Brink, "Social Trinitarianism," 350.

primarily as explanatory concepts in respect to God's inner being. For this I revisit the principle of inseparable operations, the missions of the Son and the Spirit, the notion of taxis, and the monarchy of the Father.[9] I propose that we return to one of the patristic threads that is woven throughout early discussions on the Trinity, and focus on the significance of the doctrine of the Trinity for our understanding of the God who saves humanity by first making himself known through the sending of the Son and the Spirit with a view to drawing humanity to himself to participate in his being by the same means. I will argue that Trinitarian nomenclature and categories were never intended to be abstracted from the story of salvation, and by extension to the human experience of God through his self-sending as the Trinitarian God, and make *most* sense not just as technical language pertaining to God's inner being, but as descriptive (albeit analogical) language pertaining to God's relation to humanity.

On the question of method, many recent discussions on the Trinity start from what we might posit to be true of the nature of God in himself as a triune being, and then move from there to posit what we believe to be true of the human condition. This is sometimes extrapolated in such a way that the proposals regarding the nature of God *in se* are then mapped onto structures in society, politics, relationships, marriages, church life, etc. Thus, Trinitarian categories and nomenclature such as processions, relations, monarchy, eternal begottenness, spiration, perichoresis, and taxis are employed in the service of describing the inner nature of God with a view to drawing anthropological analogies, with eclectic results. This methodology is used both by so-called "social Trinitarians" and "anti social Trinitarians" (as opposed to anti-social Trinitarians!). Ostensibly, the method as it stands is sound; we begin with the knowledge of God and proceed to the knowledge of humanity. However, as we well know, the process can quickly unravel. Given the proclivity of human beings to project our desires, fears, hopes, and agenda onto the being of God, and then to use that projection to justify said desires, fears etc., this method should be treated with caution. Although space limits an extended discussion, my final point, with reference to the work of Kathryn Tanner, is that in the light of the fact that the primary way of relating to God for humanity is in the Son through the Spirit, we should expect that the life, witness, and person of the Son

---

9. I have chosen to use the language of the "missions" of the Son and the Spirit rather than appealing to the doctrine of appropriation as a means of distinguishing the persons of the Trinity in what Augustine calls their "separate manifestation" as this expression retains the connotations of the dynamic of "sending" at the heart of the gospel narratives that is also later taken up by early church writers, especially Augustine.

communicated to us by the Spirit provides an all-sufficient foundation for Trinitarian-shaped anthropological and ethical claims.

The Unknown Made Known

It has never been deemed an easy task to describe the nature of God. In early Christian writings, we find an emphasis on the idea that language limits us, analogies fail us, and the human mind is a poor, fragile, and limited receptacle for the revelation of the Divine. All these conspire to mean that the theologian is faced with a challenging task when attempting to give expression to the ineffable. For this reason, when it comes to describing the nature of God, it is no wonder that early thinkers would appeal to a *via negativa* in order not to say more than we can or ought. So we read in Gregory of Nyssa,

> we find that all else which results from the significance involved in the names expressing the Divine attributes either forbids us to conceive what we ought not to conceive of the Divine nature, or teaches us that which we ought to conceive of it, but does not include an explanation of the nature itself.[10]

God is uncircumscribed and uncircumscribable; he is beyond our descriptive capabilities. For this reason, we exercise necessary caution and requisite humility in our claims regarding the Divine nature. This, too, is why some contemporary theologians discussing the Trinity might want to lean more heavily on the insights of the apophatic tradition, perhaps as some kind of safeguard for the transcendence of God on the one hand, and against human presumption on the other. Thus, it is salutary to recall, as the ancients taught, that not only is God's nature ineffable but full knowledge of this nature is beyond the frail capacities of the human mind. Moreover, humanity is blinded to God's revelation by the sinful nature and the passions and desires arising therefrom. We cannot *think* our way to the knowledge of God, neither are we capable in and of ourselves of understanding. In addition to this our language limits us.

But it is equally important to recall that this is only half the story. We must be careful not to blur the line between a claim about what humanity might know of God and how we might know this, and what we are claiming regarding the nature of God himself. One is an epistemological claim and the other doctrinal. As Ian McFarland writes, "God is certainly unknowable, in the sense of transcending all finite, creaturely capacity; but God is not for

---

10. Gregory of Nyssa, *Ad Ablabium*.

that reason unknown."[11] It is not wrong to stress the ineffability of God's essence, as long as we remember that this is as much, if not more, a claim in relation both to human intellectual frailty and human sin as it is to the nature or, more importantly, the intentions of God.

A statement about the ineffability of the essence of the Divine should not, therefore, be employed in a blunt fashion as a premise upon which to make a claim that God is simply unknowable. To make such a move would be to miss the point a) of the biblical testimony, and b) of how the concept of knowing God is developed by early Christian thinkers. What is of interest here is how these ideas are developed in relation to the doctrine of the Trinity. The doctrine of the Trinity as spelled out in early Christian writings is inextricably linked to the idea that the unknowable God has come to humanity precisely to make himself known, and through doing so has given us the means by which we may know him—the gifts of the Son and the Spirit—a movement (descent and ascent) that is elucidated as a pivotal aspect of salvation. Knowledge of God through Christ and in the Spirit is not only possible, but is a foundational soteriological concept.

In the history of God's people, I suggest that on balance there is a greater emphasis on the idea that God makes himself known in various ways and at various times, than that he is essentially unknowable. Craig Keener refers to precisely this in his book, *The Mind of the Spirit: Paul's Approach to Transformed Thinking*. Keener outlines both Greek and Jewish thought in relation to the knowledge of God in ancient Mediterranean thinking, beginning with the point that even Greek philosophers of different schools who held that knowledge of God was rare, believed it was something to aspire to.[12] "Philo insists on proper knowledge about God; he even replaces manna with heavenly knowledge and indicates that the Logos dwells in knowledge. Those with true knowledge of God are aptly entitled God's children."[13] He goes on, "Knowledge of God" in the Hebrew Bible usually indicates a right relationship with him, one predicated on proper knowledge about him and expressed in genuine piety. Knowing God also can express intimacy with God and can indicate the covenant relationship (cf. Hosea 2:20). In Scripture God often acts in a self-revealing way so that people "might know that I am YHWH."[14] (On this point see also Exod 24:11 and Num 12:8.) In addition to this it should be noted that knowledge of God often has an ethical as well as a cultic component (cf. Jer 22:16).

11. McFarland, *Divine Image*, 20.
12. Keener, *Mind of the Spirit*, 6.
13. Keener, *Mind of the Spirit*, 7.
14. Keener, *Mind of the Spirit*, 7.

In the New Testament witness, the self-revelation of God in order to make himself known reaches its apotheosis in the coming of Christ (Col 1:15; Heb 1:1–2; 1 John 1:1–4). McFarland, who himself strikes a balance between apophaticism and cataphaticism, notes, "God is beyond all speech and beyond all knowledge, but there is knowledge of God that makes 'meaningful talk about God possible.'"[15] In this brief statement he sums up the paradox of knowing. The slightly amusing irony in relation to claims regarding the unknowability of God is that they are almost invariably made by those engaged in wordy and detailed discussions of his nature! This was certainly true of early discussions on the nature of God as triune, which were conducted by men who were, in fact, sure of many aspects of their knowledge of God in Christ and the Spirit. Moreover, it was precisely this that they were attempting to convey in response to various critics and even enemies of the orthodox faith. It was important for them to "get it right," and getting it right required prayer, worship, and intellectual activity. But more than this, or rather, more importantly than this, through this exercise, they were defending the gospel as they understood it. For a good example of this very exercise see Gregory Nazianzen's *Theological Orations* 29.21, where he both acknowledges the limitations of language and the human mind in articulating truths and at the same time claims the need for, and indeed the possibility of, faith-directed and Spirit-filled responses in articulating the truth to those who would come against the gospel through false ideas.

The early writers on the Trinity believed that the doctrine of the Trinity, in fact, only makes sense to the human mind as a story of salvation. In their version of the story of salvation, God gives himself to humanity as three in one to be known, and the distinction of the persons of the Trinity in this process is a crucial aspect of God's dealing with humanity. It is a shame, therefore, that discussions of the Trinity can lose sight of the fact that early accounts of God as triune were focused as much on epistemology and soteriology as they were on ontology. That is not to say that technical terms, nuance, and precision were lacking—quite the opposite. It is simply to say that technical terms, nuance, and precision were employed in the service of articulating truths about the God who *saves* in Christ, and who brings us to *know* him by the work of his Spirit.[16] Theological reflection on the tri-unity of God, and the divinity of Christ, were reflections on how, in Christ and the Spirit, the unknowable had become knowable, or as Austin

---

15. McFarland, *Divine Image*, 3.

16. I am thinking here of both Hilary of Poitiers's and Augustine's writings on the Trinity, Gregory Nazianzen's *Theological Orations*, Gregory of Nyssa, *Ad Ablabium*, and Athanasius, *On the Incarnation of the Word*.

Farrer puts it, "The unbearable to mere humanity made both bearable and sweet in Christ, by his grace."[17]

To reiterate then, there are a number of caveats when speaking of the knowledge of God. First, we accept the limits of language and human comprehension. Second, we must acknowledge the scriptural teaching that this knowledge cannot be complete in this life—the unclouded knowledge of God awaits humanity in the eschaton with the beatific vision. We now only see as through a glass, darkly, and it is only in the life to come when we will see God face to face. Only then will we know as we are known, and we will see God as he is (1 Cor 13:12; 1 John 3:2). Nevertheless, despite the fact that God is not fully comprehensible, we are called to seek him continuously, with the promise that those who seek him not only will find him but also be found by him and, I would add, be found in him (Isa 55:6; Jer 29:13–14). This is a point we will come to shortly. In addition to this, it is important to recognize the knowledge of God referred to by the church fathers is a gift from God that transcends natural knowledge, belonging as it does to a different category of knowing.

A New Knowing

Early Christian writers on the Trinity understood that the human mind labored under limitations in relation to its comprehension of the Divine. We are not God, and therefore we do not have access via our intellect, language, and expression to the essence of God. This was expressed, however, in the context of their belief that the prayerful, faithful, worshipping theologian might receive revelation to her frail mind, which, through contemplation and sanctification, would be lifted toward God, and to knowledge of him. Patristic accounts of knowing God have an unapologetically devotional cast to them, i.e., the one who worships God will also know him. In addition to this, they have an ethical slant in that the expectation is that faith, prayer, worship, and loving God will lead to the selfless love of others.[18]

Thus, despite the belief that knowledge of God lies beyond the capacity of the natural mind, the corresponding belief was that God is capable of touching the mind and endowing a new, essentially spiritual capacity to apprehend himself, thus rendering himself knowable. Athanasius, for

---

17. Farrer, *Words For Life*, 74.

18. See for example Augustine, "If this is difficult to understand [the nature of God], then you must purify your mind with faith, by abstaining more and more from sin, and by doing good, and by praying with the sighs of holy desire that God will help you to make progress in understanding and loving." *On the Trinity*, IV.5.31.

example, in *On the Incarnation of the Word*, views the unknowability of God as a tragic result of the Fall, which has led to the dimming and distortion of humanity's reasonable capacity to apprehend the Divine. The Fall is a crisis of knowing leading to the destructiveness of idolatry: "They defiled their own soul so completely that they not only lost their apprehension of God, but invented for themselves other gods of various kinds." (III.3) Indeed, one of his main themes in his work is that God restores humanity by renewing "His Image in humankind" so that through this "men might once more come to know Him." (III.13) As Athanasius elucidates, God himself rids us of idolatry and false knowledge. (III.16) He cites Eph 3:17ff,

> And I pray that you, being rooted and established in love, may have power, together with all the Lord's holy people, to grasp how wide and long and high and deep is the love of Christ, and to know this love that surpasses knowledge—that you may be filled to the measure of all the fullness of God.

The invisible has become visible, revealing the truth about God through human acts in Christ, so that we may know the Father (III.16). The work of Christ and the Spirit brings creation to the knowledge of God (VII.45).

The theme running through patristic writings is that God himself gives humanity the means by which to know him, but that it is a new way of knowing. Hilary of Poitiers sees the remedy for our dulled faculties of reason and our clouded vision in the gifts of God, namely the Word/Logos and the Spirit, which engenders in us the gift of faith. Faith and the gift of the Spirit give us a different way of knowing, a more perfect knowledge.

> I must pray also for the gift of Your help and compassion, that the breath of Your Spirit may fill the sails of faith and confession which I have spread, and a favoring wind be sent to forward me on my voyage of instruction. We can trust the promise of Him Who said, Ask, and it shall be given you, seek, and you shall find, knock, and it shall be opened unto you (Luke 11:9); and we in our want shall pray for the things we need. We shall bring an untiring energy to the study of Your Prophets and Apostles, and we shall knock for entrance at every gate of hidden knowledge, but it is Yours to answer the prayer, to grant the thing we seek, to open the door on which we beat. Our minds are born with dull and clouded vision, our feeble intellect is penned within the barriers of an impassable ignorance concerning things Divine; but the study of Your revelation elevates our soul to the

comprehension of sacred truth, and submission to the faith is the path to a certainty beyond the reach of unassisted reason.[19]

We find the same themes in Augustine on the Trinity. The chief capacity of the human mind is that by which it knows God, and this is the image of God in humanity (XIV.3.11). Augustine calls this "contemplative wisdom," distinguished from "knowledge," but nevertheless a pursuit of the rational and intellectual mind (XIV.5.26). Humanity is the image of God in that we are capable of knowing God with minds that have been renewed and restored by him. The image is slowly restored and renewed in the Christian as she grows in the knowledge and vision of God (XIV.5). In both Athanasius and Augustine knowledge and vision converge. In addition to this, one of the key concepts for understanding this particular way of knowing is "participation." It is not just that we "see" God in Christ by the gift of the Spirit, it is that we are also given the means by those same gifts to participate in his being. There is no such thing really as objective knowledge of God; knowledge of the Divine can only be obtained by those who participate in the Divine life. It is an emic rather than an etic knowledge. That is, inside, rather than outside, the object of enquiry.

McFarland complexifies the topic somewhat in a discussion of Maximus's "logic of knowing and unknowing" in *Centuries of Love*, describing this variously as "hyperknowing," "unknowing," and "participatory knowledge" elucidating a nuanced version of this knowing.[20] Despite the references also to unknowing, I suggest that Maximus is still describing a concrete, if limited, form of knowing. He writes, "The perfect mind is the one that through genuine faith supremely knows in supreme ignorance the supremely unknowable, and in gazing on the universe of his handiwork has received from God comprehensive knowledge of his Providence and judgment in it, as far as allowable to men." (*Centuries of Love*, III.99) Participation in God's life is a key category for this form of knowing, re-forming the human intellect. McFarland comments that "Maximus teaches that participation in God comes through a divine penetration of the intellect that overcomes the opposition between subject and object characteristic of conceptual knowledge."[21] So Maximus, "God who is beyond fullness did not bring creatures into being out of any need of his, but that he might enjoy their proportionate participation in him and that he might delight in his

---

19. Hilary, *On the Trinity*, 1.37.

20. See McFarland, *Divine Image*, 36–37, who cites *Centuries of Love* III.99 and III.45.

21. McFarland, *Divine Image*, 37.

works seeing them delighted and ever insatiably satisfied with the one who is inexhaustible" (*Centuries of Love* III.46).

There are two aspects of Maximus's teaching on participation referenced in McFarland's work that I wish to highlight. The first is Maximus's understanding of *how* God penetrates the human mind to endow this new knowledge, and the second is the particularly christological and pneumatological cast to this movement. In respect of the first point, McFarland cites Maximus, "But this does not come to us through the loss of our own intellectual power; nor does it come to us as a supplementary part added to our intellect; nor does it pass essentially and hypostatically into our intellect. Rather, it illumines the power of our intellect with its own quality and conforms the activity of our intellect to its own. In my opinion the person who has Christ's intellect is he whose intellection accords with that of Christ and who apprehends Christ through all things."[22] Maximus states that Christ's intellect "illumines the power of our intellect with its own quality and conforms the activity of our intellect to its own." In terms of *how* we know, revelation of the Divine comes to humanity from outside of itself as illumination "comparable to the granting of sight to the blind." There is no natural pathway to the knowledge of the Logos, and it is the Logos himself who is the precondition for the knowledge of God.[23] Capturing the true essence of perichoresis, and with characteristic insight, Umberto Eco describes "Christ, insofar as He was the *Logos*" as "the knowledge that the Father had of Himself."[24] If we extend this principle to the Spirit (John 14:26; 16:13), we have a properly Trinitarian pattern for the manner in which the knowledge of God is imparted to humanity, retaining the principle of inseparable operations in its entirety, i.e., with both halves of the rule. We will develop this idea further below.

According to McFarland's reading of Maximus, this gift of the *Logos* to our intellect changes both how we see and what we see. Grace "enables the

---

22. Maximus, *Centuries on Theology*, II.83 cited in McFarland, *Divine Image*, 39.

23. McFarland, *Divine Image*, 38.

24. Eco, *Semiotics*, 148. Eco is here speaking of the interpretation of "the Holy Scriptures" as a semiosic web centered on the *logos* who is at once "the *verbum mentis* and *verbum vocis*, as well as the name and the nature of the second person of the Trinity." Christ is the interpreter of the ancient law and the one through whom all Scripture is interpreted. Eco's understanding of the relation of the Father and Son here is remarkably reminiscent of Maximus who writes, "Just as our human word which proceeds naturally from the mind is messenger of the secret movements of the mind, so does the Word of God, who knows the Father by essence as Word knows the Mind which has begotten it (since no created being can approach the Father without him), reveal the Father whom he knows. As the Word of God by nature he is spoken of as the 'messenger of the great counsel.'" (*Chapters on Knowledge*, II.22).

mind 'to see with knowledge what is [already] in front of it.'"[25] This is echoed centuries later by Aquinas. "Therefore the created intellect cannot see the essence of God, unless God by His grace unites Himself to the created intellect, as an object made intelligible to it." (ST 1, q.12 a.4) It is common to find this transforming work described by the term "grace," which McFarland himself does. However, when he cites Maximus on the transfiguration, we find Maximus attributes the disciples' new understanding to the work of the "Spirit."[26] I prefer Maximus's own terminology, articulating as it does a role for both the Logos/Christ and the Spirit, and with Eco's insight, a way of understanding how the Son and the Spirit endow the knowledge of the Father.

On the Usefulness of Trinitarian Concepts

Having established that participatory knowing is a way of understanding how we might know God, and that this is via the Son and the Spirit, I now turn to a few Trinitarian concepts to demonstrate that they are best understood when employed as explanatory tools for the portrayal of the God who saves, especially when we understand salvation in terms of a participatory ontology. Here I mention the four Trinitarian concepts that I see as most relevant to the discussion: inseparable operations, the missions of the Son and the Spirit, taxis, and the monarchy of the Father. Placing an emphasis on the inseparable and indivisible operations of the works of the Trinity *ad extra* (strictly the first half of the rule) is extremely useful for holding a number of Trinitarian stakes in the ground; for example, when used to illustrate the oneness of the essence and will of the three persons. In addition to this, it is excellent for combatting subordinationist tendencies in respect to the Son or the Spirit or both. It helps to eliminate overtones or undertones of a superior issuing orders to an inferior that are so often read into the language of "sending." Again, this is most useful. It becomes problematic, however, if we omit the second half of the maxim added in order to safeguard the Trinitarian theologian from forms of modalism. This is precisely the problem that Ralph Del Colle identifies when he asks: "If the persons of the trinity cannot be distinguished on the basis of the divine operation ad extra, where the *relationis oppositio* does not function since the work of God is common

---

25. McFarland, *Divine Image*, 39.

26. McFarland writes, "Instead, the disciples are enabled to see what was there all along by virtue of 'a change in the powers of sense that the Spirit worked in the[m], lifting the veils of the passions from the intellectual activity that was in them.'" Here he is citing Maximus, "Difficulty 10" from Louth, *Maximus the Confessor*, 109, in *Divine Image*, 40.

to all three persons, then how are the persons distinct in their respective missions, since they are an ad extra manifestation of the divine working?"[27]

Adonis Vidu recently addressed the question of marrying the doctrine of inseparable external operations with a strong theology of the missions, arguing that OAE (*opera ad extra*) as he calls it can be adhered to in concert with the idea that the incarnation is also exclusively a work of the Son, and the gift of grace a work of the Spirit. Employing scholastic nomenclature and categories, he achieves the balance of the inseparable operations maxim in its complete form emphasizing both the oneness of the work of God in this world and the distinctiveness of the missions of the Son and the Spirit. His argument *in nuce* is that the Father, Son, and Spirit "truly present the Son to us in his secondary (human) nature; they truly present the gift of the Spirit to us in (created) grace."[28] In addition to his dogmatic claims, he also describes the "descent" of "the Trinity in its missions" corresponding to an intellectual "ascent" of humanity through reflection on their created effects.[29] His work, therefore, is a good example of taking the rule of inseparable operations in its entirety (even though he does not actually cite the second half of the rule) while also locating the doctrine of the Trinity in the context of salvation history and human experience.

Similarly, Fred Sanders in his recent book, *The Triune God*, also emphasizes the distinction of persons on the basis of the revelatory and salvific missions of the Son and the Spirit, explicating the doctrine of the Trinity as uncompromisingly soteriological. The self-revelation of the Godhead in the missions of the Son and the Spirit reveals the triune nature of God. "The Father's sending of the Son and the Holy Spirit makes it possible and necessary to discern distinctions within the life of the one God. The distinctions drawn by Trinitarian doctrine are the ones that must be presupposed if it is true that the two missions are the ultimate self-revelation of God. There are, therefore, in the eternal essence of God three persons."[30] Or, as he states, "missions reveal processions."[31] Moreover, this revelation of the Godhead comes to us in salvific acts. With reference to the church fathers, he writes, "What becomes gradually clearer is that the missions and processions are what enable theology to distinguish between the persons of the Trinity *on the basis of the history of salvation.*"[32]

27. Del Colle, *Christ and the Spirit*, 102.
28. Vidu, "Trinitarian Inseparable Operations," 123.
29. Vidu, "Trinitarian Inseparable Operations," 123.
30. Sanders, *Triune God*, 121.
31. Sanders, *Triune God*, 121.
32. Sanders, *Triune God*, 121. My italics.

Applying the principle of inseparable operations in its entirety allows us to hold to the oneness of the Godhead while also acknowledging that the opposition of relations (paternity, filiation, spiration, and procession), tell us something significant about both distinctions in the Godhead, the missions of the Son and the Spirit, and the intentions of God toward humanity. These are not just academic terms. Ralph Del Colle, in his book *Christ and the Spirit*, argues that our Trinitarian theology should be articulated in such a way as to enable us to speak of the "hypostatic individuation" of the persons of the Trinity, with a strong emphasis on both inseparable operations *and* the missions.[33] Where Sanders emphasizes what feels like a type of chronological distinction, enumerating as he does the relation of the Old Testament revelation followed by the coming of Christ followed by Pentecost as distinct but related salvific events, Del Colle places greater emphasis on the Spirit in constant relation to Christ as attested to in the New Testament witness; hence his term the "coinherent missions" of the Son and the Spirit. In other words, in Del Colle's view there is a simultaneity about the sending of the Son and the Spirit in salvation events, which in my view not only corresponds more faithfully to the biblical witness but also accommodates inseparable operations more effectively. Here is an example of this from his work:

> [O]ur original Irenaean theme ("the two hands of God") is thoroughly played out in Orthodox christology and pneumatology. Neither hand is subordinate to the other and neither replaces the other. The Spirit was present in the Son's incarnation, baptism, ministry, death, and resurrection and because of this is now sent by the risen and exalted Christ. The pentecostal Spirit, however, is neither a substitute for Christ . . . nor merely the instrument of his presence. . . . Rather, the Holy Spirit is the person of the trinity who "forms Christ within us and renders Him present to us," and by preparing us for Christ "achieves in us the Parousia, the eternal coming and Presence of Jesus the Lord." Without the *Spiritus praesens* the reality of the *Christus praesens* would be an exercise in pious imagination instead of the communication of the divine being.[34]

David Coffey in his Trinitarian theology makes a similar claim regarding coinherence. Where Sanders stresses the incarnation and Pentecost as properly belonging to the Son and the Spirit respectively, Del Colle's and Coffey's projects are aimed at constructing a different role for the Spirit,

---

33. Del Colle, *Christ and the Spirit*, passim.
34. Del Colle, *Christ and the Spirit*, 27.

where the Spirit has a constitutive role in the person and work of Christ. In this sense, the Spirit is also one who sends and can be said, in some sense, to precede the Son.[35] So whereas Del Colle, Coffey, and Sanders are all in agreement that the divine self-communication is mediated through the two temporal missions of the Son and the Spirit which bear distinct manners of operation, they have different emphases on how those distinct manners of operation might be described.

Nevertheless, the foundational premise of the Trinity as a soteriological doctrine remains the same. Those who encounter the Holy Spirit are encountering the Spirit of Christ, through whom they are drawn, by grace, into union with Christ and thus into a filial relationship with the Father (Rom 8:14–17). This is the salvific process by which humanity is drawn into the life of God, by which we come to know him and thus are saved. Retaining the Trinitarian framework for salvation allows us to construct a theology of the knowledge of God and participation in his being while being able to hold together both halves of the inseparable operations principle, including the distinct missions of the Son and the Spirit. In addition to this I think it places the language of taxis and the monarchy of the Father in its proper context. It is to this that I now turn.

Taxis and Monarchy

The concept of taxis (the ordering of the divine life) and the monarchy of the Father have in recent years become controversial issues among Trinitarian theologians. Do these concepts in some way undermine the co-equality and co-divinity of the three persons? Do these concepts lend themselves, misleadingly, to the idea that there is some hierarchy within the Trinity? Does it sound as if there is both some sort of divine precedence and divine ultimacy in the Father alone? These conclusions would, of course, be wrong, hence the nervousness of modern Trinitarian theologians who began to

---

35. This is not a wholly new idea. See, for example, Gregory Nazianzen, *Theol. Or.* 31.29. "This, then, is what may be said by one who admits the silence of Scripture. But now the swarm of testimonies shall burst upon you from which the Deity of the Holy Ghost shall be shown to all who are not excessively stupid, or else altogether enemies to the Spirit, to be most clearly recognized in Scripture. Look at these facts: Christ is born; the Spirit is His Forerunner. He is baptized; the Spirit bears witness. He is tempted; the Spirit leads Him up. He works miracles; the Spirit accompanies them. He ascends; the Spirit takes His place. What great things are there in the idea of God which are not in His power? What titles which belong to God are not applied to Him, except only Unbegotten and Begotten? For it was needful that the distinctive properties of the Father and the Son should remain peculiar to Them, lest there should be confusion in the Godhead Which brings all things, even disorder itself, into due arrangement and good order."

question classical Western and Eastern categories and models.[36] If we locate these concepts within a soteriological framework, however, it is possible to see how they are still useful and to resist the charge that they somehow establish a hierarchy or order of precedence within the Trinity.

It is clear when reading some early reflections on the Trinity that while it was held that the works of God in the world were the works of the one God, it was also held that God was present as Father, Son, and Spirit ordered in relation to himself (the opposition of relations) and ordered in relation to humanity for a specific purpose. This is nicely illustrated in Gregory Nazianzen's *Theological Orations*, where taxis and monarchy come into their own in relation to the story of salvation. Here Gregory describes a journey of incremental apprehension of the Godhead enabled by progressive illumination through the Son and the Spirit, given in accordance with the capacity of humanity to receive the divine. This enables Gregory on the one hand to claim that monarchy is not, in fact, limited to one person of the Trinity as they all share in the same essence. The Father is eternally the Father as the Son is eternally the Son (29.2). There is, therefore, no progression in the Godhead and there is only one motion in which, as the other Gregory describes, "there is no delay, existent or conceived, in the motion of the Divine will from the Father, through the Son, to the Spirit."[37] It is more complex than this though, as there is a taxis, or order of communication, in relation to revelation and salvation that is both progressive and linked to the return of humanity to God the Father, the source.

Gregory of Nyssa speaks of the indivisible operations of the Father, Son, and Holy Spirit in the context of taxis and monarchy. First he states the indivisible operations, "But in the case of the Divine nature we do not similarly learn that the Father does anything by Himself in which the Son does not work conjointly, or again that the Son has any special operation apart from the Holy Spirit." He goes on, "but every operation which extends from God to the Creation and is named according to our variable conceptions of it, has its origins from the Father, and proceeds through the Son, and is perfected in the Holy Spirit."[38] The Father is the *fons divinitatis* and the work of God proceeds through the three persons, but always only as the one God. Monarchy, therefore, is both shared by all three persons of the Trinity but in relation to the taxis of Father, Son, and Holy Spirit, belongs to the Father alone.

36. See, for example, Weinandy, *Father's Spirit*, 54, in which he argues that we need to be careful not to see the doctrine of the monarchy of the Father as saying that the Godhead resides in the Father alone.

37. Gregory of Nyssa, *Ad Ablabium*.

38. Gregory of Nyssa, *Ad Ablabium*.

To return to my earlier point, there are distinct doctrinal issues at play here: one pertains to epistemology, one to soteriology, and one to ontology. One is a question of how we experience God and how we come to know him. The second to how he has chosen to save us. The third, what that tells us of the Divine being. Ephesians 2:18 states that "through Christ we have access in one Spirit to the Father." There is some kind of progression described where we have an entry point to the Father through Christ and in the Spirit. There is a unity of will, action, and motion, but at the same time there is a movement in the Trinitarian life toward humanity in order to draw humanity back to the source, the Father, and this is the point of the taxis.

Sarah Coakley comments on Gregory of Nyssa's *Ad Ablabium* that "the Spirit acts as the experiential point of entry into the divine flow from the 'spring' of the Father." She goes on, however, to say, "But since the operations of the three are by definition inseparable, even this apparent experiential distinctness has an illusory quality to it: 'there is *one* motion . . .'"[39] I appreciate the point made that "*there is no suggestion that three 'consciousnesses' are in play*,"[40] but I think to claim that experiential distinctness has an "illusory quality" is a misapplication of inseparable operations and loses the point of the taxis, which is founded on the relations of opposition. In defense of the distinction of the three persons of the Trinity, Coffey cites the following axiom "*In Deo omnia sunt unum ubi non obviat relationis oppositio* (In the Godhead all things are one except where the opposition of relationship rules this out)."[41] He writes, "This means, at least in part, that the ultimate ground of distinction between persons is the relationships between them, which make it impossible for them to be totally identical with each other."[42] Or as Gregory Nazianzen points out, Father is not a name of an essence or an action, "But it is the name of the relation in which the Father stands to the Son, and the Son to the Father." He goes on to make the point that these names make known a "genuine and intimate relation" on a human level, and at a Divine level denote an identity of nature between Him that is begotten and Him that begets" (*Theol. Or.* 29.27).

Whereas taxis is often traditionally understood as an order of Father, Son, Spirit, both Coffey and Del Colle argue that there are two taxeis including Father, Spirit, Son. As we saw in an earlier footnote, we find references to this in Gregory Nazianzen, "Look at these facts:—Christ is born; the Spirit is His Forerunner. He is baptized; the Spirit bears witness. He is tempted; the

---

39. Coakley, "'Persons' in the 'Social' Doctrine," 133.
40. Coakley, "'Persons' in the 'Social' Doctrine," 133.
41. Coffey, "Proper Mission," 229.
42. Coffey, "Proper Mission," 229.

Spirit leads Him up. He works miracles; the Spirit accompanies them. He ascends; the Spirit takes His place." Drawing attention to the two taxeis in the Trinity in many ways makes for an easier amalgamation of inseparable operations, the unity of the persons, and the missions. As Coffey claims, "it is the co-presence of the persons in the working of the economic Trinity that reflects their circumincession in the immanent Trinity."[43]

I propose, therefore, that inseparable operations should not be applied without reference to other Trinitarian rules and maxims, most specifically, the missions of the Son and the Spirit, taxis and monarchy. This is not simply to retain a means of describing our experience of the one God, but because the Trinity is the revelation and salvation of God. Emphasizing too much the illusory quality of the distinctions on the basis of an unqualified principle of inseparable operations, and losing sight of the gifts of the Son and the Spirit in order that we might know God precisely as Father, Son, and Spirit, runs the risk of the diminution of the content of the Christian faith.

Becoming Like the Son

Gordon Fee, writing on Paul's Trinitarian soteriology, notes that Paul, as a follower of Christ, "rephrases 'knowing' in terms of 'knowing Christ', for the surpassing value of which he has 'suffered the loss of all things' (Phil 3:8)." "Being found in him," he goes on, "has as its final goal 'to know him, both the power of his resurrection and participation in his sufferings, so as to be made like him in his death' (v.10)." Fee continues, "It is clear from any number of passages that for Paul 'knowing God' comes by way of 'knowing Christ' (cf. 2 Cor 4:6); and 'knowing Christ' comes by way of 'the Spirit's wisdom and revelation' (Eph 1:17)."[44] The Spirit brings us into a Christ-shaped existence and conforms us to the likeness of the Son in whom we relate analogously as sons and daughters in the Son and co-heirs of the Father. As Augustine writes, "In this respect too we will be like God, but only like the Son, who alone in the triad took a body in which he died and rose again, carrying it up to the heavenly regions." We will not be conformed to the image of the Father or the Holy Spirit "but only of the Son, because of him alone do we read and receive on wholesome faith that *the Word became flesh* (John 1:14)."[45]

Kathryn Tanner draws many of these themes together in her christologically oriented Trinitarian anthropology. She herself is committed to the

---

43. Coffey, "Proper Mission," 228.
44. Fee, "Paul and the Trinity," 71–72.
45. Augustine, *On the Trinity*, XIV.5.24.

principle of inseparable operations, but at the same time views the incarnation as the key to knowledge of God and participation in him. She draws on Barth, "we have always to remember that God's glory really consists in His self-giving, and that this has its center and meaning in God's Son, Jesus Christ, and that the name of Jesus Christ stands for the events in which man, and in man the whole cosmos, is awakened and called and enabled to participate in the being of God."[46] Barth himself precedes this with an emphasis on the Spirit as the one who draws and holds humanity in this existence. "If God is glorified through the creature, this is only because by the Holy Spirit the creature is baptized, and born again and called and gathered and enlightened and sanctified and kept close to Jesus Christ in true and genuine faith."[47] Tanner's christological anthropology maintains both the unity and distinction of the Divine life into which humanity is welcomed. The effect of this is not only that salvation is viewed through a Trinitarian lens in the light of a participatory ontology, but that by retaining the notion of taxis in concert with the inseparable operations, she paints a picture of humanity taken up into a life of God that is in motion. "If God shares God's triune life with us, that is a dynamic life, a life of action. Incorporated within the indivisible workings of the Trinity *ad extra* through Christ our lives are similarly set in motion."[48] This dynamic, I think, is lost unless we hold on to a real descent in the Godhead inviting a real ascent on the part of humanity drawn ever more Godward.

In sum, the doctrine of the Trinity, with all its technical terms and nuances is still at heart a doctrine in response to revelation and salvation. Trinitarian concepts and language were intended to be explicated and employed in the service of explaining and defending the gospel: that the Son and the Spirit are given to humanity so that we may know God and participate in his being, which is our salvation. Moreover, this revelation is not simply to do with *how* we might first come to know God, to be dispensed with in the fullness of time (as if the Son and the Spirit were simply a concession to our current human weakness), but is meaningful for *what* we know of him also in his very being. Thus, even if our knowledge of God and his ways remains partial and fragmentary for now, the Trinity still imparts to us the knowledge of God, reveals to us how we might be drawn to the Father through and in the Son and the Spirit, and gives us the means to become partakers of the divine nature.

---

46. Barth, *Church Dogmatics*, II/1, 670 cited in Tanner, *Jesus*, 37.
47. Barth, *Church Dogmatics*, II/1, 670.
48. Tanner, *Jesus*, 69.

Bibliography

Athanasius, St. *On the Incarnation*. Translated and edited by A Religious of C.S.M.V. New York: St. Vladimir's Seminary, 1944.

Augustine. *The Trinity*. Translated by Edmund Hill. New York: New City, 2010.

Ayres, Lewis. *Nicaea and Its Legacy: An Approach to Fourth-Century Trinitarian Theology*. Oxford: Oxford University Press, 2009.

Barth, Karl. *Church Dogmatics*. Translated by G. W. Bromiley and T. F. Torrance. Edinburgh: T. & T. Clark, 1957.

Blocher, Henri. "Immanence and Transcendence in Trinitarian Theology." In *The Trinity in a Pluralistic Age*, edited by Kevin J. Vanhoozer, 104–23. Grand Rapids: Eerdmans, 1997.

Boff, Leonardo. *Trinity and Society*. Maryknoll, NY: Orbis, 1988.

Coakley, Sarah. "'Persons' in the 'Social' Doctrine of the Trinity: A Critique of Current Analytic Discussion." In *The Trinity: An Interdisciplinary Symposium on the Trinity*, edited by Stephen T. Davis, Daniel Kendall, and Gerald O'Collins, 123–44. Oxford: Oxford University Press, 1999.

Coffey, David M. "A Proper Mission of the Holy Spirit." *Theological Studies* 47 (1986) 227–50.

Del Colle, Ralph. *Christ and the Spirit: Spirit-Christology in Trinitarian Perspective*. New York: Oxford University Press, 1994.

Eco, Umberto. *Semiotics and the Philosophy of Language*. Bloomington: Indiana University Press, 1984.

Farrer, A. *Words for Life*. Edited by Charles Conti and Leslie Houlden. Eugene, OR: Wipf and Stock, 1993.

Fee, Gordon. "Paul and the Trinity: The Experience of Christ and the Spirit for Paul's Understanding of God." In *The Trinity: An Interdisciplinary Symposium on the Trinity*, edited by Stephen T. Davis, Daniel Kendall, and Gerald O'Collins, 49–72. Oxford: Oxford University Press, 1999.

Gregory Nazianzen. *Theological Orations*. Translated by Charles Gordon Browne and James Edward Swallow. Edited by Philip Schaff and Henry Wace. Nicene and Post-Nicene Fathers, 2nd Series, Vol. 7. Buffalo, NY: Christian Literature, 1894.

Gregory, of Nyssa, Saint. *Ad Ablabium*. Translated by H. A. Wilson. Edited by Philip Schaff and Henry Wace. Nicene and Post-Nicene Fathers, 2nd Series, Vol. 5. Buffalo, NY: Christian Literature, 1893.

Grudem, Wayne. *Systematic Theology: An Introduction to Biblical Doctrine*. Grand Rapids: Zondervan, 2000.

Hilary of Poitiers. *On the Trinity*. Translated by E. W. Watson and L. Pullan. Edited by Philip Schaff and Henry Wace. Nicene and Post-Nicene Fathers, 2nd Series, Vol. 9. Buffalo, NY: Christian Literature, 1899.

Holmes, Stephen R. *The Holy Trinity: Understanding God's Life*. Milton Keynes, UK: Paternoster, 2012.

Keener, Craig, S. *The Mind of the Spirit: Paul's Approach to Transformed Thinking*. Grand Rapids: Baker Academic, 2016.

Kilby, Karen. "Is an Apophatic Trinitarianism Possible?" *International Journal of Systematic Theology* 11 (2010) 65–77.

―――. "Perichoresis and Projection: Problems with Social Doctrines of the Trinity." *New Blackfriars* 81 (2000) 432–45.

Louth, Andrew. *Maximus the Confessor*. New York: Routledge, 1996.

Maximus Confessor. *Selected Writings*. Translated by George C. Berthold. New York: Paulist, 1985.

McFarland, Ian A. *The Divine Image: Envisioning the Invisible God*. Minneapolis: Augsburg, 2005.

Moltmann, Jürgen. *The Trinity and the Kingdom of God*. London: SCM, 1981.

Sanders, Fred. *The Triune God*. Grand Rapids: Zondervan, 2016.

Tanner, Kathryn. *Jesus, Humanity and the Trinity: A Brief Systematic Theology*. Minneapolis: Fortress, 2001.

Van den Brink, Gijsbert. "Social Trinitarianism: A Discussion of Some Recent Theological Criticisms." *International Journal of Systematic Theology* 16 (2014) 331–50.

Vidu, Adonis. "Trinitarian Inseparable Operations and the Incarnation." *Journal of Analytic Theology* 4 (2016) 106–27.

Weinandy, Thomas G. *The Father's Spirit of Sonship: Reconceiving the Trinity*. Edinburgh: T. & T. Clark, 1995.

CHAPTER 5

The One Divine Nature

WILLIAM HASKER

The Problem

According to the doctrine of the Trinity there are three Persons—Father, Son, and Holy Spirit—each of whom is fully divine, fully God. There is, furthermore, a single concrete divine nature—a single trope or instance of Godhood—that is the nature of each of the three Persons. As an analytic theologian, my task is to explore whether these two statements make sense together. In analytic circles, some theologians believe that it is impossible to make sense of three fully divine Persons and one single instance of Godhood. Keith Yandell, for example, refers disparagingly to "what appears to be a self-contradictory doctrine to the effect that the Trinitarian Persons all have the *concrete* divine nature."[1] In his own account of the Trinity, Yandell abandons this doctrine, holding that each Person has all of the essential divine attributes but denying that they have between them a single instance of Godhood, a single concrete divine nature. In this essay I will show that what appears self-contradictory to Yandell is not, in fact, self-contradictory, and that the doctrine he proposes to abandon is an important, indeed essential, part of Trinitarian doctrine. First I discuss a few texts that make the case that the one concrete divine nature is indeed part of the historic

---

1. Quotations from Yandell, unless otherwise noted, are taken from his review of my *Metaphysics and the Tri-Personal God*, https://ndpr.nd.edu/news/metaphysics-and-the-tri-personal-god/.

Trinitarian doctrine of the church. I then go on to argue that this part of the doctrine is vital if we are to give a satisfactory account of the unity of God. I explain why the traditional answer to this problem, in terms of the doctrine of divine simplicity, is an answer we cannot accept. Next, I provide examples that make the case that the doctrine is not, as claimed, self-contradictory. I conclude by offering a metaphysical account of the doctrine in terms of the theory of material constitution.

A brief note is called for concerning the nature of the Trinitarian Persons. I use "Persons," with an upper-case "P," to denote the Trinitarian Three without being committed to a more definite account of what divine personhood amounts to. My own sympathies lie, as will become apparent, with social Trinitarianism. That is, the Three are persons in something like the everyday sense of the term. I believe, however, that the issues concerning the divine nature remain much the same regardless of the answer to this question, *provided that* the Persons are seen as objectively existing realities, and not merely aspects or ways of speaking about what is ultimately an undifferentiated divine reality. We shall return briefly to this topic at the end of this essay.

The Tradition

It would be difficult to deny that the doctrine of a single concrete divine nature, common to all of the three Persons, is an integral part of Trinitarian doctrine in the later Western church. Yandell notes Aquinas's assertion that "among creatures, the nature of the one generated is not numerically identical with the nature the one generating has. . . . But God begotten receives numerically the same nature God begetting has."[2] This same view is held by Augustine; I cite here a couple of texts from his book on the Trinity. Consider his objection, in book 6, to the idea that the Trinity is "triple, or three by multiplication."[3] Here we may contrast the Trinity with a group of three men—say, Abraham, Isaac, and Jacob. In such a group we have three individuals sharing a common (abstract) nature, but given the three of them there is "three times as much manhood" as in Abraham alone—in our terminology, three instances or tropes of human nature. But no such multiplication can exist in the case of the Trinitarian Persons; unlike the "three men" case, those Persons have only one trope of divinity between them, which is why "the Father alone or the Son alone or the Holy Spirit

---

2. Aquinas, *Summa Theologiae* Ia.39,5 ad 2.245a; translation by Brian Leftow.
3. Augustine, *Trinity*, bk. 6, 212–13.

alone is as great as Father and Son and Holy Spirit together."[4] Another telling passage occurs in book 7:

> If however being [*essentia*] is a species word like man, and those three which we call substances or persons have the same species in common, as Abraham, Isaac, and Jacob have in common the species which is called man; and if while man can be subdivided into Abraham, Isaac, and Jacob, it does not mean that one man can be subdivided into several single men—obviously he cannot, because one man is already a single man; then how can one being be subdivided into three substances or persons? For if being, like man, is a species, then one being is like one man.[5]

This requires some unpacking; both the syntax and the thought are complex. What I think Augustine means is this: While "man" is a species-word, and the species man can be subdivided (that is, exemplified multiple times), it does not follow that *an individual man* can be so divided. But then, neither can *an individual being* (in the divine case) be subdivided into three "substances[6] or persons." The argument has force precisely because Augustine assumes that the divine being (*essentia*) is individual and concrete, like a man, and not an abstract universal like "manhood." (Otherwise, just as "man can be subdivided into Abraham, Isaac, and Jacob," it would follow that "God can be subdivided into Father, Son, and Holy Spirit.") The divine *essentia*, in other words, consists of a single trope of Godhood or divinity.

Sometimes it is claimed that the Cappadocians, in particular Gregory of Nyssa, were in disagreement with Augustine on this point. The impression that this is the case gains plausibility from the fact that Gregory specifically invites us to apply to the Trinity the relationship between *hypostasis* and *ousia* as we understand it in the case of human beings: "If now you transfer to the doctrine of God the principle of differentiation between *ousia* and *hypostasis* that you acknowledge on the human level, you will not go astray."[7] However, Gregory understands this relationship in the human case in a way that is truly surprising. Gregory admits that "Peter, James, and John, being in one human nature, are called three men."[8] Why then are not

---

4. Augustine, *Trinity*, bk. 6, 212.

5. Augustine, *Trinity*, bk. 7, 232–33.

6. This disjunct is included because Augustine is going along, at this point, with the Greek use of *hypostasis* for the Trinitarian Persons, and he accepts the linguistic equivalence of *hypostasis* and *substantia*. However, he goes on to argue against the propriety of saying there are "three substances" in God (bk. 7, p. 231).

7. The quotation is from Basil of Caesarea, Epistle 38, 70. This epistle is now generally believed to have been written by Gregory rather than Basil.

8. Gregory of Nyssa, "On 'Not Three Gods,'" 331.

Father, Son, and Holy Spirit, who share the one divine nature, three Gods? Gregory's response here is that it is actually a mistake, a "customary misuse of language," to call Peter, James, and John "three men." When referring to the plurality of individuals we ought to do so by some designation peculiar to them (for instance, by their names), rather than by the name of their common nature. To refer to them as "men," in the plural, suggests that there are "many human natures," which we know to be false.[9] No doubt Gregory fails to convince us that it is really a mistake to refer to "men" in the plural. But what we need to attend to is his reason for insisting on this. He seems to think of the common essence of humanness as a *real unity* that somehow exists *as a whole* in each individual human being.[10] But what sort of unity is this? To "divide" an abstract nature in the sense that it is exemplified multiple times does not pose any problem. If on the other hand we think of the *ousia* as a concrete property-instance—in our terminology, as a trope—then it seems perfectly plausible to suppose that there is a distinct trope for each individual human being. Gregory, however, needs to resist this precisely because *he intends to transfer to the Trinity the relation between ousia and hypostasis that obtains for human beings*. Having stated (perhaps unwisely) that the distinction between *hypostasis* and *ousia* can be transposed directly from the human case to that of the Trinity, Gregory now has to interpret (we might rather say, to distort) the human situation in order to render it parallel with the conclusion he wants to draw concerning the Trinity. To make sense of all this, we have to recognize that for him the divine *ousia* is not merely an abstract set of properties, but rather something concrete and individual.

Before leaving this topic it is appropriate to remark that the notion of a fundamental difference over the doctrine of the Trinity between the Cappadocians and the Eastern tradition, on the one hand, and Augustine and the West on the other, has been largely discredited among patristic scholars. The possibility of appealing to the Cappadocians in order to show that there is not a united tradition on the point in question has little credibility.

---

9. Christopher Stead remarks, "Gregory needs to convince us that Moses, Eunomius, and Cleopatra are 'all one man'!" (Stead, *Philosophy in Christian Antiquity*, 184.)

10. "[Y]et their nature is one, at union in itself, and an absolutely indivisible unity, not capable of increase by addition or of diminution by subtraction, but in its essence being and continually remaining one, inseparable even though it appears in plurality, continuous, complete, and not divided with the individuals who participate in it" (*Ad Ablabium*, 332).

The Cost of Rejection

Having documented the place held in the Trinitarian tradition by the notion of a single concrete divine nature, we now proceed to consider the theological costs if this doctrine is rejected. These costs will differ, however, depending on the acceptance or rejection of another element of traditional Trinitarian doctrine, namely the doctrine of "processions in God," in other words the eternal generation of the Son and the eternal procession or spiration of the Holy Spirit. We consider briefly the views of two philosophers, who between them take both of the available options.

If one rejects both the single concrete divine nature and the derivation of the Son and Spirit from the Father, the problem is to retain any adequate affirmation of the unity of God. Keith Yandell proposes as a solution "the doctrine that the Father depends for existence on the Son and Holy Spirit, the Son depends for existence on the Father and Holy Spirit, and the Holy Spirit depends for existence on the Father and the Son." In this way he replaces the one-sided derivation of Son and Spirit from the Father, postulated by the doctrine of processions, with a mutual dependence. But what sort of dependence is this? It cannot be causal dependence, according to Yandell, because the essential divine attribute of aseity is the property, *existing without being caused by anything else*. If the Persons are caused to exist by each other, then none of them exists *a se*, as Yandell insists that they must. The dependence, then, must be logical rather than causal. But it is difficult to see how this can work. If the Son's existence logically presupposes the Father's existence, then the Father's existence must be logically prior to that of the Son. But then, since the dependence relation goes both ways, it follows that the Father's existence logically presupposes the Son's existence, and so it seems that it must be the Son's existence that is logically prior—but obviously, both cannot be true. Perhaps, then, what is necessary is the entire complex of Father plus Son plus Holy Spirit. That is to say:

N1.   Necessarily, (Father + Son + Holy Spirit) exists.

This situation, however, is logically indistinguishable from the following:

N2.   Necessarily, the Father exists, *and*,

N3.   Necessarily, the Son exists, *and*,

N4.   Necessarily, the Holy Spirit exists.[11]

---

11. Yandell affirms N2–N4 in "Most Brutal and Inexcusable Error," 204.

Indeed, (N1–N4) seems to be precisely what Yandell has in mind; in a more recent article, he leans heavily on the claim that the Trinity is a "logically inseparable triad" as guaranteeing the divine unity.[12] Contrary to what Yandell seems to think, however, (N1–N4) *completely fails* to secure any meaningful dependence relationship between the three divine Persons. Nothing whatever can exist if a necessary being fails to exist: If the number 37 is a necessary being, then it is impossible that you or I should exist and that number fail to exist—but this, of course, says nothing whatever about any meaningful dependence relation between each of us and that number. Indeed, the number 37, the mean distance between the earth and Mars, and the smell of avocado form a logically inseparable triad! (Even if there were no planets or avocados, the properties in question arguably are necessary existing abstract objects.) Similarly, (N1–N4) are consistent with the proposition that each of Father, Son, and Holy Spirit is an *ultimate source of being*; each possesses a necessity that is in no way derived from any other being, and whatever further relationships may exist between them are subsequent to the existence of each Person, an existence which is not in any significant way bound up with the existence of either of the other Persons. If this is not tritheism, it comes far too close to that for comfort. But if both the unitary concrete divine nature and the processions are denied, it is hard to see how this conclusion can be avoided.

Our example of a philosopher who rejects the unitary concrete divine nature but affirms the processions is Richard Swinburne. In retaining the doctrine of processions, Swinburne rules out the possibility that each divine Person is an ultimate source of being. But how are we to understand the derivation of Son and Spirit from the Father? In an early article, Swinburne provides an interesting answer to this question: "If it is an overall best act that a solitary God share his essential almightiness, the only way in which this can be done is if he creates as a separate God what is God anyway, i.e., if he divides himself. The creation being everlasting, this is to be read as: he creates as a separate God what, but for his creative action, would be himself."[13] This asserts that what the Father communicates to the Son is not the entire concrete divine nature (as the tradition held), but rather a *part* of that nature, a part that, "but for his creative action, would be himself." The event in which God "divides himself" cannot, however, be a temporal event, since all three Persons must be eternal (that is, everlasting). Rather, the Father from all eternity brings it about that *two parts of the divine nature distinct from himself exist*, not as the Father's own nature (as they would be,

---

12. Yandell, "Doctrine of the Trinity," 162.
13. Swinburne, "Could There Be More," 232.

apart from the processions), but rather as the natures of the Son and of the Holy Spirit.

Interestingly, this explanation of the processions does not reappear in Swinburne's *The Christian God*, which otherwise incorporates a great deal of the content of the earlier article. This means, however, that in that book the question about the nature of the processions remains unanswered. Fortunately, Swinburne has clarified this topic in correspondence. He states, "in chapter 8 of *The Christian God*, I dropped the claim that the Son and the Spirit can only be 'created' if the Father 'divided himself.' I can't see any need for that requirement, and in any case I doubt that it makes any sense to talk of a non-physical being dividing itself—division only applies to extended and so physical substances."[14] He also says, "I avoid talk of the Father 'creating' the other members of the Trinity in the book, in deference to the normal usage of the fathers and scholastics that 'creates' only applies to the bringing about of something finite by an act of will." Does this mean, then, that the Son and the Spirit are brought into being *ex nihilo*? In response to this question, Swinburne states, "I'd prefer to say that the Son and the Spirit were 'brought about, but not brought about out of anything,' rather than that they were 'brought about from nothing.' The phrase '*ex nihilo*' caused a lot of trouble in the Middle Ages, when creation of the universe *ex nihilo* was understood by some as if being brought about from some pre-existing thing, 'nothing.'"

Swinburne's clarification is carefully hedged with qualifications, but it does clearly imply that both Son and Holy Spirit are *created beings*, though no doubt very different from all the other beings that they, in company with the Father, have subsequently created. In my book, I objected to this, stating that "None of the ancient Fathers, I believe, would have accepted that a person could be both fully divine ("true God," as they would say) and created, even in the special sense in which, according to Swinburne, the Son and the Spirit are created."[15] In a forthcoming paper, "The Social Theory of the Trinity,"[16] Swinburne addresses this point. He partially accepts my claim, agreeing that "none of the ancient Fathers . . . would have accepted that a person could be both fully divine . . . and created" (ellipses in original). Obviously, the omissions from my statement are important: he does not agree that the sense in which his view holds that the Son and Spirit are "created" is a sense that the Fathers—and later orthodox Trinitarian theologians—would

---

14. This and the following quotations are from private e-mails; my thanks to Richard Swinburne for permitting me to use them here.

15. Hasker, *Metaphysics and the Tri-Personal God*, 154.

16. *Religious Studies*, forthcoming.

have objected to. The differences from the more ordinary sort of creation are that (1) the creation of Son and Spirit is necessary (since creating them is the overall best thing for the Father to do), rather than contingent; and (2) they are not created out of any pre-existing materials (not even "nothing"). I must confess to being unconvinced by this; I doubt very much either that the ancients would, or that we should, accept a view according to which *being uncreated* is not an essential divine attribute which must be possessed by any divine Person. Readers must make what they will of this disagreement. In any case, I believe the point has been made: denying the unitary concrete divine nature imposes serious theological costs, costs we might well prefer to avoid.

A Simple Solution?

For many theologians there is a relatively straightforward solution to the problem at hand, in terms of the doctrine of divine simplicity. The point is nicely illustrated by some thoughts about Augustine's view from patristic scholar Lewis Ayres: "The grammar of simplicity means that we must say that if God the Father is to generate another, a Son, both the generator and the generated must be wisdom and God in themselves: the grammar of simplicity allows us to say truly that 'the Father has given the Son to have life in himself' (John 5:26)."[17] So now we have the individual reality of both Father and Son (and, by implication, of the Spirit as well). "However, the language of divine simplicity enables and demands a further step. If the Son is wisdom itself, and the Father is wisdom itself, then we can go a step further and say that the Son's essence is identical with the Father's essence. There cannot, obviously enough, be two instances of wisdom itself."[18] Ayres sums up this process of thought as follows: "The Father generates the Son who is light from light, wisdom from wisdom, and essence from essence. The Son is an essence in Himself, not just a relationship: to talk of the person of the Son is to talk of the Son's essence. And yet, because the Father's and the Son's essences are truly simple, they are of one essence. . . . Thus, in using the grammar of simplicity to articulate a concept of Father, Son, and Spirit as each God, and as the one God, we find that the more we grasp the full reality of each person, the full depth of the being that they have from the Father, the more we are also forced to recognize the unity of their being."[19]

---

17. Ayres, *Nicaea and Its Legacy*, 378–79.
18. Ayres, *Nicaea and Its Legacy*, 379.
19. Ayres, *Nicaea and Its Legacy*, 379–80.

This is indeed an elegant intellectual structure, but a problem remains that Ayres seems not to have noticed—a problem that arises from the very concept of identity. Identity, as this notion is understood by logicians, is a transitive relation: if A is identical with B, and B with C, then A is identical with C. So if the Father is an essence in himself, and the Son also is an essence in himself, and yet their essences are identical, it follows inexorably that the Father is identical with the Son, a heretical conclusion that cannot possibly be accepted—and, of course, Augustine does not accept it. It does not help to point out at this juncture that Father and Son cannot be identical, because they are related by the "begetting" relation, a binary relation that a thing cannot have to itself. That is true enough, but it in no way cancels out the entailment noted from the concept of identity; it just brings out explicitly the contradictory character of the theological system so understood.

So far as I can see, there is no solution to this problem that is consistent with the strong doctrine of divine simplicity. It is tempting to point out that Augustine and the medievals did not have in mind the modern concept of identity, which in its fully articulated form is usually attributed to Leibniz. Perhaps they did not, but then the challenge for a contemporary scholar who wishes to defend their solution is to spell out the concept of identity which they were using, a concept which avoids the conclusion that each of the divine Persons is identical with each of the other two. *This challenge has not been met.* And I do not see how we could regard any concept of a relation that is not transitive as a concept of *identity*. In addition to all of its other deficiencies,[20] the strong doctrine of simplicity entails that the doctrine of the Trinity, which affirms a real distinction between the divine Persons, is false.[21]

Trinitarian Models

At this point I bring forward several models of the Trinity. These are not fully developed metaphysical accounts, but rather images or analogies that may help us in our thinking about Trinitarian matters. We begin with some ideas of William Craig. As an analogy for the Trinity, Craig cites the three-headed dog Cerberus from Greco-Roman mythology. We suppose that "Cerberus

20. I have identified some of these deficiencies in Hasker, "Is Divine Simplicity a Mistake?" 699–725.

21. To avoid misunderstanding, I should perhaps point out that there is a minimal concept of divine simplicity that should be accepted, and so far as I know is in fact accepted, by all theists. That concept is as follows: God is simple in that God is not assembled out of parts and cannot be decomposed into parts. Simplicity in this sense, however, does not provide a solution for the metaphysical problem of the Trinity.

has three brains and therefore three distinct states of consciousness of whatever it is like to be a dog."[22] Thus, we have a single being—a single organism—with three distinct states of consciousness. Craig proposes that "once we give up divine simplicity, Cerberus does seem to represent what Augustine called an image of the Trinity among creatures." However, there is a problem: "suppose Cerberus were to be killed and his minds survive the death of his body. In what sense would they still be one being? . . . Since the divine persons are, prior to the Incarnation, three unembodied minds, in virtue of what are they one being rather than three individual beings?"[23]

In order to resolve this problem, Craig invites us to reflect on the nature of the soul, which he takes to be an immaterial substance. He then reasons,

> Now God is very much like an unembodied soul; indeed, as a mental substance God just seems to be a soul. We naturally equate a rational soul with a person, since the human souls with which we are acquainted are persons. But the reason human souls are individual persons is because each soul is equipped with one set of rational faculties sufficient for being a person. Suppose, then, that God is a soul which is endowed with three complete sets of rational cognitive faculties, each sufficient for personhood. Then God, though one soul, would not be one person but three, for God would have three centers of self-consciousness, intentionality and volition, as social trinitarians maintain. . . . God would therefore be one being that supports three persons, just as our own individual beings each support one person. Such a model of Trinity monotheism seems to give a clear sense to the classical formula, "three persons in one substance."[24]

Craig later clarified his proposal with a pair of qualifications. First, it is infelicitous to suggest that God possesses "three complete sets of rational *cognitive* faculties," since this seems to exclude affective and volitional faculties, which is not what Craig intended. So the word "cognitive" should be omitted at that point. But secondly, it was not his intention to reify the faculties referred to, as is done in "faculty psychology." What is essential to the proposal is that it gives a model of God as a single being having "three distinct states of consciousness of whatever it is like to be God."

---

22. Moreland and Craig, *Philosophical Foundations*, 575–95, 593. (While the volume is coauthored, Craig is primarily responsible for the material on the Trinity.)

23. Moreland and Craig, *Philosophical Foundations*, 575–95, 593.

24. Moreland and Craig, *Philosophical Foundations*, 594.

We now move to a proposal from a different source, namely Brian Leftow. Leftow's proposal is embedded in a complicated story involving time-travel, but that story need not detain us here. His constructive explanation concerning the nature of the Trinitarian Persons is as follows:

> Suppose, then, that God's life has the following peculiar structure: at any point in our lives, three discrete parts of God's life are present. But this is . . . because God always lives His life in three discrete strands at once, no event of His life occurring in more than one strand and no strand succeeding another. In one strand God lives the Father's life, in one the Son's, and in one the Spirit's. The events of each strand add up to the life of a Person. The lives of the Persons add up to the life God lives *as* the three Persons. There is one God, but He is many in the events of his life.[25]

This proposal suffers rhetorically as a result of being separated from Leftow's longer story, but the intention should be clear: there is a single being, God—indeed, a single *person*; God for Leftow *is* a single person, in our modern sense of "person"—who lives simultaneously in three discrete life-strands, the life-strands respectively of the Father, the Son, and the Holy Spirit. Leftow is quite insistent on the distinctness of the three strands: the strands do not have in common "any events composing [God's] conscious life or involving His agency."[26] Furthermore, "God does not live save as Father, Son and Spirit. . . . God's life always consists of three other things which count as entire ongoing lives."[27]

Now, it is obvious that there are important differences between Craig's and Leftow's proposals. Craig is self-identified as a social Trinitarian, whereas Leftow is a leading critic of social Trinitarianism. We shall need to attend to this difference shortly. What should not be missed, however, is that each of them presents a picture in which a single being, God, has simultaneously three distinct life-strands, three self-contained series of experiences, belonging respectively to the Father, the Son, and the Holy Spirit. We can say, then, that they share in affirming the *Trinitarian Possibility Postulate*:

> *(TPP) It is possible for a single concrete divine nature—a single trope of deity—to support simultaneously three distinct lives, the lives belonging to the Father, to the Son, and to the Holy Spirit.*

---

25. Leftow, "Latin Trinity," 304–33; 312.
26. Leftow, "Latin Trinity," 30n22.
27. Leftow, "Latin Trinity," 312.

And now we must ask: *Is this in fact possible?* This question subdivides into two further questions: (1) Is this *logically or conceptually* possible, so that affirming it violates no constraints of logic or conceptual coherence? (2) Is this *metaphysically* possible, in the sense of being consistent with the ultimate nature of reality? Of these two questions, it is clearly the first that must occupy our attention here. If God is in fact a Trinity of the sort postulated, then the situation described by the possibility postulate is one that actually exists and *a fortiori* is also possible. If God is not a Trinity of this sort, then ultimate reality is inconsistent with the situation described by the postulate, which is therefore impossible. But since the nature of God as Trinity is precisely what is in dispute, neither conclusion on that point can be taken as a premise in order to answer our question as to the truth of TPP. What we need to consider here, then, is whether TPP is logically coherent and free from contradiction. This, we will recall, is precisely the challenge that was presented by Yandell, in his reference to "what appears to be a self-contradictory doctrine to the effect that the trinitarian Persons all have the concrete divine nature."

There is indeed one point at which the coherence of TPP has been questioned, and that point concerns the notion of "support" employed both in TPP and elsewhere. (Craig, we may recall, employed the same word in stating his own view.) I had stated that "'Support' here does not represent any obscure or technical notion; the term is used in the ordinary sense in which we can say that the human body/mind/soul . . . 'supports' the continuing conscious life of a human being."[28] Daniel Howard-Snyder, however, doesn't think "there is any such thing as 'the ordinary sense' of the term" in such a context. He surmises that "few of [Hasker's] peers, if any, will understand what he means by 'support.'"[29] Now, I am hopeful that Howard-Snyder is overly pessimistic. I hope, that is to say, that at least a good many readers will not have greeted the Trinitarian possibility postulate with blank incomprehension because of the allegedly unintelligible term "support." Nevertheless, a bit more discussion is in order. Among the online *Oxford English Dictionary*'s definitions for "support" some help is offered by 8b, "To maintain in being or in action; to keep up, keep going." This does seem to fit fairly well what I (perhaps naively) cited as the "ordinary sense" of the word in such a context. Even more helpful, however, is 8d, "Of a computer, operating system, etc.: to allow the use or operation with it of (a program, language, device, etc.)." I doubt that very many readers would express puzzlement if I were to say that my desktop computer supports word processing, whereas

---

28. Hasker, *Tri-Personal God*, 228.
29. Howard-Snyder, "Review of *Metaphysics*," 108.

my mobile phone does not. And this meaning seems to transfer very readily to my use of the word with regard to the brain's "supporting" a person's conscious life.

Another philosopher who finds the support relation puzzling is Dale Tuggy. Tuggy affirms that I "leave the meaning of 'supports' wholly unclear," but he thinks that in reality the implications of such a relation are clear enough—and damaging to my view. He explains the idea as follows:

> In addition to, and as it were, beneath a human life, there is the one whose life it is, whether this self be thought to be a soul, a union of soul and body, a whole organism, the body, or a part of the body (e.g., the brain). It's the doer of the actions in that life, the thinker of thoughts in that life, the experiencer of experiences in that life. What is this "supporting" relation which exists between the human self and his or her life? It would seem that this self is the substance/being common to those events.
>
> But then, for "the divine nature" to play the needed role, it must be a self. Only a self can do things like plan, strive, know, love, command, obey, etc. Hasker faces a dilemma here. If he says that this "divine nature" is a self, then he's got four selves in the Trinity.[30]

It is in order to avoid this unwelcome conclusion, according to Tuggy, that I leave the meaning of "supports" completely unclear. But on the contrary, as I am using "supports" it *does not follow* that what does the supporting must be a self. There is no self involved when a computer supports various functions (though admittedly the functions are "cognitive" only in an extended and analogical sense). Nor would I say that when, as we know to be the case, some tiny module of brain-tissue supports some kind of cognitive processing, the module in question is a "self." (For example, the human visual cortex comprises over thirty distinct processing sites, each of which supports a part of the process by which information is extracted from visual stimuli. Obviously, each site individually does not qualify as a "self"; nor does the visual cortex as a whole so qualify.) The notion that what supports mental life must be a self is one that Tuggy has constructed on his own, not one that he has derived from my usage of "supports." And since I have explicitly denied that the divine nature is a self or person, it seems inappropriate for Tuggy to assume that my usage of "supports" entails precisely what I have denied.

---

30. Tuggy, "William Hasker's *Metaphysics*."

Having said all this, I freely confess that I do not know, and am unable to describe in detail, exactly what happens when my brain/mind/soul supports the occurrence of some mental process; much less can I describe how the divine nature supports the mental life of a divine Person. But so far as I can tell, no one else knows these things either, so our talk about such matters retains an ineliminable element of vagueness, derived from the limitations of our knowledge of the world—and of God.

At this point I have to say that I am unaware of any further objections that pose a serious challenge to the logical and conceptual possibility affirmed by TPP. The situation as described by Craig and Leftow (that is, the situation with regard to what is common in their two proposals) seems clearly conceivable; no evident incoherence or contradiction stands out as one thinks about it. It is also worth noticing that, whereas neither of their proposals has escaped criticism, none of the other criticisms I am aware of is such as to call in question the conceptual coherence of the situation as they describe it. And there is an important additional point that can be made in favor of the proposal: there is significant evidence that *on the human level* the sort of situation depicted by the possibility postulated does on occasion obtain. I refer here to the evidence from "split-brain" or commissurotomy cases, as well as from cases of multiple personality. Both these sorts of cases provide significant evidence that, under special circumstances, human beings can have two or more distinct streams of consciousness occurring simultaneously. I have discussed this evidence elsewhere and will not rehearse it here.[31] The evidence remains controversial, but I believe the interpretation that allows for actual divided consciousness is better and more plausible than interpretations that seek to avoid that conclusion. Note, however, that I am *not* putting split-brain and multiple personality cases forward as models of the Trinity. Nevertheless, the fact that this apparently occurs among human beings under special circumstances does something to make it plausible that the sort of situation described by the TPP may be genuinely possible.

In view of all this, I assert that the logical possibility of a single concrete divine nature supporting three distinct personal life-strands can be affirmed; there is no known evident or plausible objection to this possibility. Admittedly, it would be desirable to have a more precise, well-developed metaphysical theory of the relation between the divine nature and the Trinitarian Persons. This question will soon be addressed, but I want to emphasize that the solution of the logical problem of the Trinity does not

---

31. See Hasker, "Persons and the Unity of Consciousness," 175–90; *Tri-Personal God*, 231–35; "Incarnation."

depend on such a developed metaphysical theory. That problem of logical consistency can now be put behind us, whatever further difficulties may still lie in wait.

We need, however, to address briefly the difference between Craig's model and Leftow's. The difference, we recall, concerns where in the picture personhood, in the sense of our modern conception of a person, is to be located. For Craig, each of the "three centers of self-consciousness, intentionality and volition" postulated by his model counts as a person in a robust sense: the divine Persons are persons. For Leftow, there is just one person, namely God; Father, Son, and Holy Spirit are names of the three "life-strands" through which the one person, God, lives his life. How shall we decide between the two?

Both views, it seems to me, are conceptually coherent and intelligible, even if a bit strange in terms of our ordinary ways of thinking. I doubt that either view has a major advantage in terms of naturalness or intuitive plausibility. (One's judgment on those points is likely to be strongly influenced by one's prior inclinations in Trinitarian theorizing.) I believe, however, that Craig's view has a large advantage with regard to coherence with the New Testament's witness to Jesus Christ. It is beyond question that the New Testament writings picture a rich relationship of personal interchange between Jesus and the Father. This relationship is, of course, conditioned by the Son's incarnate state, but it is considered by both Craig and Leftow, in agreement with the whole theological tradition, to be a relationship *between Trinitarian Father and Son.* Craig is able to understand this in a natural way, as a personal relationship in a perfectly straightforward sense—that is, as a relation between two persons, the Father and the Son. (This has always been the main point of appeal for social Trinitarianism.) For Leftow, things are not so simple. When Jesus prays, this for Leftow must in reality be *God praying to himself.* Especially poignant are the words of desolation from the cross: "My God, why have you forsaken me?" For Leftow, this apparently has to be read as, "Why have I-as-Father forsaken myself-as-Son?" In understanding this text, Leftow resorts to what I can only view as a desperate expedient: he suggests that, in his incarnate state, Jesus may not have been entirely clear about the nature of his relationship with the Father![32] Readers must judge for themselves the plausibility of that suggestion. But this disagreement between Craig and Leftow should not be allowed to obscure the agreement between them on other points, in particular about the Trinitarian possibility postulate.

32. "It should not seem odd to us that someone should feel that he had forsaken himself if he was not aware that it was he himself who (he felt) was doing the forsaking." (Leftow, "Time Travel and the Trinity," 322)

Trinitarian Metaphysics

Without doubt, it would be desirable to have a more explicit metaphysical account of the relation between the one concrete divine nature and the Trinitarian Persons. I have proposed a sketch of such an account, framed in terms of the metaphysical idea of constitution; this has proved to be one of the more controversial parts of my overall account of the Trinity. Now the very idea of constitution continues to be debated, and I cannot hope to settle that debate here. What I can do is render my application of the idea to the Trinity as clear as possible, and attempt to meet specific objections to that application. Those who are unpersuaded by the merits of the constitution relation will have to find their own solutions to the problems of Trinitarian metaphysics. Indeed, it may very well prove to be a good thing to have several different approaches competing in this arena, so that eventually whichever approach best illuminates the situation may prevail. In the meantime, I can only do my best. I begin with a general discussion of the need for, and the plausibility of, the constitution relation.

A classic example is that of a statue made of gold. We have, in this case, both a lump of gold and a statue. However, it is important to see that, contrary to what we might at first think, the lump of gold *is not identical* with the statue. If they were identical, they would need to have all of their properties in common, but this is not the case. The statue has the property, *being such that it would no longer exist if the gold were hammered into a different shape*, but the lump of gold lacks this property; hammering would leave it still the same lump of gold. So we say that the lump of gold *constitutes* the statue, but it is *not identical with* the statue; rather, it is *distinct from* the statue. The lump could exist without constituting a statue, but, given certain circumstances (including the fact that it has been shaped in a certain way by an artist), there is indeed a statue which coincides spatially with the lump, and yet is (as we have seen) distinct from it. Once we have the basic idea of constitution in hand, many examples become evident. A piece of cloth, dyed in a certain way, constitutes a national flag, given that there is a nation that recognizes objects with that color-pattern as its flag. A piece of paper, manipulated according to certain legal conventions, constitutes a marriage license. And so on.

Admittedly, the constitution relation is not the only way one could handle examples such as these. We might for instance say that the statue is not an object distinct from the lump of gold, but is rather the lump of gold itself, called a "statue" at the present time in virtue of its present possession of certain accidental properties (the "circumstances" noted above). This has the perhaps awkward consequence that hammering the statue into a different shape would not destroy anything, something art-lovers might find difficult to swallow. Even harder to accept is the implication that if, for example, a cat is run over by a car and killed, nothing has been destroyed in this case either; it is merely that a certain mass of cat-tissue has been rearranged. What needs to be recognized is that *any solution to these problems is going to be counter-intuitive in some way.* My own view is that the description of the situation in terms of constitution has decided benefits as compared with other options.[33]

We need, however, a more precise characterization of the constitution relation. I have proposed a definition of the relation based on the work of Lynne Rudder Baker. Her view of the relation makes essential use of two notions; the first is that of a *primary kind*. A thing's primary kind supplies the answer to the question, "What most fundamentally is x?"[34] The other notion required is that of *circumstances*, a general term that covers the answers, in different cases, to the question, "In virtue of what is y the kind of thing that it is?"[35] If x constitutes y, it does so in virtue of certain circumstances in which x finds itself; lacking those circumstances, x might exist without constituting anything having y's primary kind. "[I]t is in virtue of certain legal conventions that a particular piece of paper constitutes a marriage license; it is in virtue of the arrangement of molecules that something constitutes a block of ice; it is in virtue of its evolutionary history that a particular conglomerate of cells constitutes a human heart."[36] Given these notions of primary kind and circumstances, it is possible to give a definition of the relation of material constitution:

> Suppose x has F as its primary kind, and y has G as its primary kind. Then x constitutes y at time t just in case
>
> (i) x and y are spatially coincident at t;
>
> (ii) x is in "G-favorable circumstances" at t;

---

33. An elaboration of the golden statue case makes the point. Suppose a vandal has broken into the museum and has used a hammer to beat the statue into a formless lump. Fortunately, an exact impression had been made of the undamaged statue. A mold is prepared from that impression, and the lump of gold is recast using that mold, with a result that is indistinguishable from the undamaged statue. It seems that the anti-constitutionalist is obliged to say that the original statue (=lump) has survived; certain accidental properties of the lump were altered temporarily but have now been restored. But this seems clearly false; the original statue does not survive.

34. Baker, *Persons and Bodies*, 40.

35. Baker, *Persons and Bodies*, 40.

36. Baker, *Persons and Bodies*, 41.

(iii) necessarily, if an object of primary kind F is in G-favorable circumstances at t, there is an object of primary kind G that is spatially coincident with that object at t; and

(iv) it is possible for x to exist at t but for there to be no object of primary kind G that is spatially coincident with x at t.[37]

This however is *material* constitution, but the desired application is to the Trinity: specifically, kind F is to be *divine essence*, and kind G is to be *Trinitarian Person*. Since the essence and the persons are omnipresent, spatial coincidence is not relevant for this application. And since the relation in question holds always if at all, the time-reference can be suppressed. Following a suggestion from Baker, I will now substitute for the first clause of the definition, "(i) x and y are spatially coincident at t," the following: "(i*) x and y have all their parts in common." The same substitution should of course be made in the other clauses of the definition. There is, however, another problem. This problem arises from clause (iv) of the schema: "it is possible for x to exist at t but for there to be no object of primary kind G that has all its parts in common with x." Making the required substitutions, we have (iv*) "it is possible for the divine nature to exist but for there to be no divine trinitarian person that has all its parts in common with that nature." But *is* this possible? If we are speaking of metaphysical possibility, clearly not. If God is the Trinity, then the Trinity is an integral part of the fundamental structure of reality; there is no metaphysical possibility that there should not be the three Trinitarian Persons. What we must be asking about, then, is conceptual possibility. We are asking, is it *consistent with the concept* of the divine nature, that it should exist without sustaining the existence of any divine Trinitarian Person? Here, of course, everything depends on what concept of the divine nature we have in mind. If we are speaking of an explicitly Trinitarian concept of the nature, then once again the answer must be negative; the nature so understood is *by definition* the nature of the Trinitarian Persons. But this is not the only or, in this context, the most relevant concept that is available. We do have a general conception of the divine nature, describable in terms of Anselm's definition of God as "the being than which nothing greater can be conceived." There are disagreements about the specific attributes implied by this definition, but the definition itself is widely shared among theists, including non-Trinitarian theists. So what we should be asking is this: Is it logically possible that a divine nature so conceived should exist without sustaining a Trinitarian Person? To that question, I think the answer is Yes. If the answer were No, that would imply

---

37. Paraphrased from Baker, *Persons and Bodies*, 43.

that unitarians, and with them Jews and Muslims, are making a simple logical mistake, but this is implausible. To answer the question in the negative would imply that there is available something like an ontological proof of the existence of the Trinity—but I know of no such proof, and I very much doubt that one will be produced. Understood in this way, then, I believe we can indeed affirm condition (iv*)—but it will be well to make explicit that what we are affirming is conceptual possibility and not metaphysical possibility.

In view of this, we have a revised definition of constitution that can be applied to the Trinity:

> Suppose x has F as its primary kind, and y has G as its primary kind. Then x constitutes y just in case

(i*) x and y have all their parts in common;

(ii*) x is in "G-favorable circumstances";

(iii*) necessarily, if an object of primary kind F is in G-favorable circumstances there is an object of primary kind G that has all its parts in common with that object; and

(iv*) it is conceptually possible for x to exist but for there to be no object of primary kind G that has all its parts in common with x.

The constituted kind (G in the schema) is divine Trinitarian Person; the constituting kind (F in the schema) is divine mind/soul or concrete divine nature. Each Person is simple, in that it does not consist of separable parts; and so is the divine nature simple, so (i*) is satisfied. The divine nature constitutes the divine Trinitarian Persons when it sustains simultaneously three divine life-streams, each life-stream including cognitive, affective, and volitional states. Since in fact the divine nature does sustain three such life-streams simultaneously, there are exactly three divine Persons.

As has been noted, the constitution relation is controversial, and some philosophers will be inclined to reject my account out of hand. If so, they are welcome to propose their own accounts of the relation between divine nature and Trinitarian Persons; I cannot, of course, anticipate at this point what those other accounts might amount to. I can, however, address objections aimed specifically at my adaptation of constitution for Trinitarian metaphysics. Such an objection has been presented by Keith Yandell. His objection arises from my example (borrowed from Michael Rea), in which a single piece of marble constitutes at once a supporting pillar for a building and a statue of a person. Yandell observes that tropes are of different types, and the trope of marble in my example is a "stuff" trope. So if the example is to be extrapolated to heaven, then the divine essence must be a "stuff" trope. What "stuff" can it be? Of course, there can be no answer to that question: God, as a simple being, is not made of stuff. But if the divine essence is not a kind of stuff, Yandell concludes, the notion of constitution is the wrong way to make sense of the Trinity.

This is ingenious but a little too quick. No doubt it is true that God is not, literally, made of stuff, but it might be that the divine essence plays a role that is in some way analogous to that played by stuff in more mundane situations. Michael Rea suggests, in his own Trinitarian proposal, that the divine substance in the Trinity could "play the role of matter" in a form-matter compound, though, "It can't *really* be matter, since God is immaterial."[38] Rea does not develop the idea at length, but it might be worth a further look. But why the fixation on the pillar-statue example in the first place? I offered that example simply because it provided a case of a single entity constituting a plurality of entities; I never said, or meant to suggest, that this parallels the Trinity in any other way. Yandell admits that there can be other sorts of tropes than stuff tropes, so why not consider other options? Think again of Craig's model, in which the divine "soul" supports at all times three distinct states of divine consciousness. What sort of trope is the "soul" trope in Craig's model? I think it is clear that Yandell has failed to make his case.

Another objection made by Yandell can be disposed of more briefly. He notes that my constitutionalist view requires me to hold that "it is possible for the divine nature to exist but for there to be no divine trinitarian person that has all its parts in common with that nature."[39] He concludes that "the price of applying Constitutionalism to God is holding that the divine essence might 'some time or other'—and if some time or other, why not always?—exist without the Trinity existing!" Unaccountably, he overlooks or ignores my saying, in the very same context, that "we are not speaking here of real, metaphysical possibility. To repeat this once more: the divine Trinity is inherent in the ultimate structure of reality, so whatever is true of its nature is true of metaphysical necessity; contrary states of affairs are excluded by the fundamental nature of being. What we are asking about, then, is conceptual possibility"[40]—in other words, absence of logical contradiction. This objection depends on attributing to me a view I have explicitly denied.

38. Rae, "Trinity," 419.
39. Hasker, *Tri-Personal God*, 243.
40. Hasker, *Tri-Personal God*, 243.

Clearly, there are additional questions that could be asked here, and no doubt additional objections that could be raised. These ideas are not put forward as a completed theory, but more as what may be a promising line for future development. Alternative proposals are welcome, and may the best metaphysics win! At present, however, there is a shortage of viable alternative proposals.[41] As we have seen, the most widely held alternative, divine simplicity, cannot succeed in its present form, though one can't rule out the possibility of a revised version of simplicity that will do the job.

Coda: But What About the Hypostases?

Our discussion has been concerned primarily with the divine *ousia*, the essence that is common to the three divine Persons. But one cannot speak of the Trinity without speaking also of the hypostases, the Father, the Son, and the Holy Spirit. And of course, we have not refrained from speaking of the Persons; in fact we have done so, for the most part, in terms congenial to social Trinitarians, considering the three hypostases to be persons in something very like the ordinary, everyday sense of the term. (The main exception to this is Leftow's view, in which there are three distinct "strands of consciousness" which yet fail to qualify as persons, properly speaking.) This might with some reason be put down to a prejudice on the author's part. However, there is a noticeable lack of viable competitors among Trinitarian views that maintain a real, ontological distinction between the divine Persons. The dictum that the Persons are "subsisting relations" is just one more of the many unintelligible formulas that the doctrine of divine simplicity invites us to understand as transcendent wisdom. The view of Barth and Rahner, that the Persons are "modes of being" of the one God, is remarkably uninformative. The term is borrowed from the ancient Fathers, but not the meaning: for the ancients, the *tropoi hyparxeos*, the "modes of existing" of the Persons are the *personal properties* of "being begotten" on the part of the Son and "proceeding" on the part of the Spirit; the formula was not intended to tell us what a divine Person *is*. As things now stand, the formula "modes of being" stands for some sort of objective distinction within the deity that falls short of being a distinction of *persons*—but what such a "mode of being" might actually be is left wholly mysterious. The Anglican theologian Sarah Coakley, in a volume of theology devoted largely to the Trinity, says concerning the nature of Father, Son, and Spirit only that they are "personal entities so subtly distinguishable qua inherent relations that

---

41. Some philosophers hold that relative identity theories provide such an alternative. These theories are discussed in Hasker, *Tri-Personal God*, 119–38.

one can at best talk of each attracting the possibility of verb-forms, and then only in mutual 'co-inherence' with each other."[42] Make of that what you will! The social Trinitarian affirmation that the divine Persons *are persons* is not warmly received by everyone. It has, all the same, some claim to being the only game in town.

Bibliography

Aquinas, Thomas. *Summa Theologiae: Questions on God*. Translated by Brian Leftlow. Cambridge: Cambridge University Press, 2006.

Augustine. *The Trinity*. Translated by Edmund Hill. Hyde Park, NY: New City, 1991.

Ayres, Lewis. *Nicaea and Its Legacy: An Approach to Fourth-Century Trinitarian Theology*. Oxford: Oxford University Press, 2004.

Baker, Lynne Rudder. *Persons and Bodies: A Constitution View*. Cambridge: Cambridge University Press, 2000.

Coakley, Sarah. *God, Sexuality, and the Self: An Essay "On the Trinity."* Cambridge: Cambridge University Press, 2013.

Gregory of Nyssa. "On 'Not Three Gods,' to Ablabius." In *Nicene and Post-Nicene Fathers*, edited by Philip Schaff and Henry Wace, 331–36. 2nd series, vol. 5. Peabody, MA: Hendrickson, 1994.

Hasker, William. "Incarnation: The Avatar Model." In *Oxford Studies in the Philosophy of Religion*, edited by Jonathan L. Kvanvig, 118–41. Vol. 8. Oxford: Oxford University Press, 2016.

———. "Is Divine Simplicity a Mistake?" *American Catholic Philosophical Quarterly* 90 (Fall 2016) 699–725.

———. *Metaphysics and the Tri-Personal God*. Oxford Studies in Analytic Theology. Oxford: Oxford University Press, 2013.

———. "Persons and the Unity of Consciousness." In *The Waning of Materialism: New Essays*, edited by George Bealer and Rob Koons, 175–90. Oxford: Oxford University Press, 2010.

Howard-Snyder, Daniel. "Review of *Metaphysics and the Tri-Personal God*, by William Hasker." *Faith and Philosophy* 32:1 (January 2015) 106–15.

Leftow, Brian. "A Latin Trinity." *Faith and Philosophy* 21:3 (July 2004) 304–33.

———. "Time Travel and the Trinity." *Faith and Philosophy* 29:2 (July 2012) 313–24.

Moreland, J. P., and William Lane Craig. *Philosophical Foundations for a Christian Worldview*. Downers Grove, IL: InterVarsity, 2003.

Rae, Michael. "The Trinity." In *The Oxford Handbook of Philosophical Theology*, edited by Thomas P. Flint and Michael C. Rae, 403–29. Oxford: Oxford University Press, 2009.

Stead, Christopher. *Philosophy in Christian Antiquity*. Cambridge: Cambridge University Press, 1994.

Swinburne, Richard. "Could There Be More Than One God?" *Faith and Philosophy* 5:3 (July 1988) 225–41.

Tuggy, Dale. "William Hasker's *Metaphysics and the Tri-Personal God*: A Review Essay." *European Journal for Philosophy of Religion*, forthcoming.

---

42. Coakley, *God, Sexuality, and the Self*, 321.

Yandell, Keith E. "The Doctrine of the Trinity: Consistent and Coherent." In *Building on the Foundations of Evangelical Theology: Essays in Honor of John S. Feinberg*, edited by Gregg R. Allison and Stephen J. Wellum, 151–67. Wheaton, IL: Crossway, 2015.

———. "The Most Brutal and Inexcusable Error in Counting? Trinity and Consistency." *Religious Studies* 30 (1994) 201–17.

Zachhuber, Johannes. *Human Nature in Gregory of Nyssa: Philosophical Background and Theological Significance*. Leiden: Brill, 2000.

CHAPTER 6

On Whether or How Far We Can Know God

A Reflection on Epistemology, Language and Trinity in the Five Theological Orations *of Gregory of Nazianzus*

Claire Louise Wright

Through a set of late fourth-century sermons on the theology of God,[1] modern readers encounter the thought of one of the Fathers of the early church, known (among some exalted company) as Ὁ Θεόλογος[2]: preacher, poet, reluctant prelate, and self-confessed "lover of truth" (28:3).[3] But could we say that we "know" the man?

---

1. The *Five Theological Orations* by Gregory of Nazianzus. Since this title has no basis in the manuscript tradition, I will refer to the *Orations* simply as Sermons 27–31 (with a nod to the oral delivery which shapes their rhetorical style). All quotations from Scripture are taken from the NRSV translation, unless reproduced from elsewhere, or necessarily paraphrased in Anglo-Saxon.

2. For economy of reference, I will refer to Gregory of Nazianzus, or Gregory Nazianzen, simply as "Gregory"—not thereby to be confused with his Cappadocian colleague Gregory of Nyssa.

3. References in parentheses refer throughout to Gregory's *Orations* by number and section, in the edition entitled *On God and Christ: The Five Theological Orations and Two Letters to Cledonius.*

Through *Sermon 28*, Gregory seeks to argue (*contra* the Anomean movement) that although some facets of God's nature can be *ap*prehended by human reason—by analogy to, and as reflected by, the created cosmos—a transcendent God can never be fully *com*prehended.[4] For Gregory, therefore, we cannot truthfully say that we "know" God.[5]

My essay focuses on the nature of analogy, suggested by the argument of *Sermon 28*. The concept of analogy—summed up by the formula "as A to B, so C to D"—has long been used to wrestle through the problems of truthful human thought and language about God.[6] Among other themes, Gregory's Sermon 28 challenges us to ask: can there be any real analogy between God and the world? May we properly *argue* by analogy from what we know of the created order to the nature of the Creator? And when we talk about God, do we use *words* by mere analogy to our use of those same words to talk about God's creatures?[7] For me, the gap so carefully demonstrated by Sermon 28 between the known-by-analogy and the known-*per-se*—between objects related by correspondence and those related by shared substance—prepares the ground for Gregory's closely-argued theology of a three-person God, set out by Sermons 29–31.

My Thoughts Are Not as Your Thoughts

The Anomeans are generally remembered as opponents of (and, arguably, spurs to) the key creedal formulae developed by the late fourth-century church to cement the shared substance of Father and Son at the heart of orthodox theology: the nature of the Son as "true God from true God" and

---

4. The term "Anomeans" or "Anomoeans" ("dissimilarians") was used for the radical movement within the Arian movement, generally represented by its Cappadocian spokesman, Eunomius. It was derived from the strong position of their original leader, Aetius, that the Son of God was "completely unlike" the Father (*Anhomoios*)—although they preferred to be called Heterousiasts ("different essencers"): McGuckin, "Eunomius of Cyzicus," 127. Gregory never names the "Eunomians" in the *Orations*, and the heading commonly given to *Oration 27* ("An Introductory Sermon against the Eunomians"), though found in the manuscript tradition, is probably not Gregory's: Wickham, "Introduction," 25 n1. I shall therefore prefer the term "Anomean" throughout.

5. I am indebted for this summary of Gregory's position, which I find persuasive, to Beeley, *Gregory*. Beeley argues that Gregory's apophaticism is both atypically strong in *Oration* 28 and exaggerated by commentators even there (Beeley, *Gregory*, 99).

6. White, *Talking About God*. I am also indebted for my interest in analogy, and its foundational role in human thought processes, language, memory, and learning, to the work of Hofstadter and Sander, *Surfaces and Essences*.

7. White, *Talking About God*, 8.

"of the same essence as the Father."[8] The Anomean argument was that, however exalted as "Only-Begotten" and even truly "God," the Son was by nature "begotten" or generated by the Father and therefore *could* not be thought to be "of the same essence" as the Father, who was fundamentally Absolute and Un-begotten. A substance and the agency-and-effects-of-a-substance are not comparable, and should not be confused.[9]

Gregory and others of the orthodox party hotly rebutted each known apology for, and statement of, Anomean dogma.[10] Gregory's *Sermon 28*, however, represents not a head-on defense of the shared substance of Father and Son, but a prefatory—and perhaps more fundamental—challenge to the presumed *assurance* that underwrote the Anomean argument: the pretence that the nature of God *per se* can be fully known to human thought through accurate use of language.

The Anomeans argued that God was demonstrably both "one" uncompounded (ἀμερής, ἁπλοῦς) essence, and, as Source and Father, the "one and only" *un-begotten* (μόνος ἀγέννητος) essence. God's fundamental essence must, therefore, be unbegottenness (τὸ ἀγέννητον): the aspect of Godhead that encompasses all others. Moreover, they argued, names reveal essence: "Unbegotten" was not merely a human name for God, but one revealed by God to express God's own self-knowledge—and therefore able to express, accurately and fully, God's self-apprehended nature.[11] Of course, Gregory

---

8. The Nicene Creed, as amended by the Council of Constantinople in 381 CE. Wickham notes the way in which the Cappadocians (Gregory of Nazianzus, Basil of Caesaria and Gregory of Nyssa) used dialectic to develop the doctrinal positions that would shape and defend Nicene orthodoxy: "the Cappadocian doctrine of God ... is not explicable historically, nor indeed is really comprehensible, without reference to the Eunomians" (Wickham, "Introduction," 21).

9. Despite the title "dissimilarians," the Anomeans therefore did not teach the dissimilarity or "unlikeness" of Father and Son, merely the dissimilarity of *substance* between the unique Godhead (whose definition was ingeneracy) and the Only-Begotten (generated) Son (Wickham, "Introduction," 18).

10. Basil of Caesarea's *Adversus Eunomium* ("Against Eunomius"), and Gregory of Nyssa's *Contra Eunomium*, for example, were written as direct rebuttals to Eunomius's three *Apologies* and *Statement of Faith*: Wickham, "Introduction," 17. Similarly, the *Theological Orations* appear to be a direct response to the doctrines of Eunomius, "largely as a kind of ideal opponent whose views allow him to identify the problems in other positions as well" (Beeley, *Gregory*, 91).

11. "In order for our knowledge of God to be true, ... the names by which we know God must refer to him accurately, as he really is, with the same knowledge that God possesses of himself. ... Yet in this essentialist framework, Eunomius is not simply saying that God's essence is unbegotten, as one among many predicates that can be accurately attributed to God, but that God's unbegottenness is the primary definition of God's essence, superior to all others. ... Eunomius believes that his knowledge of God's essence as unbegottenness is both absolutely accurate and logically comprehensive"

wholeheartedly agreed that language must be used accurately to honor God properly: one need only see the careful way he later seeks to exegete the names of the Godhead—though only "so far as we can get to them" (30.18). And he agreed both that God was one uncompounded essence[12] and that God the Father alone had no source or cause.[13] What he could not stomach was the pretence that, from there, humans could presume to comprehend the nature of God accurately, fully, and exactly as God knows Godself.

The extended metaphor of Gregory's ascent of the mount, based on that of Moses (Exod 33), evokes and provokes the Anomean assurance that humans could ever know the essence of God completely. For a start, says Gregory, there's the problem of how we humans—dependent on our corporeal senses to process data about the world, and bounded powers of reason to extrapolate from there to the world of concepts—could ever *apprehend* a transcendent Godhead. Gregory portrays the soul's eager yet tremulous search to see God's face (28.2): he races upward to the peak, penetrates the dense cloud, detaches from the whole world of matter—and barely manages to see God's back (28.3). (Old Testament encounters seem ever thus: the bush that burns; the averted face; three messengers under a stand of oaks: shadows and types of Presence.) As corporeal and fallen humans, says Gregory, we can at best apprehend—not (*contra* the Anomeans) the full "nature . . . self-apprehended" of God,[14] but only the facets that God's mercy allows us: traces of the godhead "at furthest remove from God"; a grandeur and majesty feebly reflected by the created order, as rays reflected by water are all that can be seen by eyes too weak to gaze on the Sun. "Thus and thus only can you speak of God" (28.3), says Gregory: by analogy, and humbly.

Let's start afresh, then, he says (28.4). Undoubtedly, there's a language problem: forget the "grotesque and preposterous word-gamesters" who masquerade as advocates for accuracy (27.1)—*no-one* can presume to speak truthfully or reverently about a God who defeats all human powers of speech. Language can only be overwhelmed by all that God means. Even so—and

---

(Beeley, *Gregory*, 92–93, citing Eunomius *Apologies* 7, 8, and 11).

12. "Though there is numerical distinction, there is no division in the substance" (29.2).

13. "Only the Father is ingenerate" (29.11).

14. Gregory already identifies the "nature prime, inviolate, self-apprehended" specifically as *Trinity* (28.3). At the outset of the *Oration* (28.1), Gregory has declared his subject to be the Father, Son, and Holy Spirit; raised the paradox of a Triune Godhead "one in its distinctions and distinct in its connectedness"; and even sketched a mini-economy of *kerygma* (Father approving, Son aiding, and Spirit inspiring his sermon). However, he is thereafter mostly concerned to refer to "God" or "the divine"—in order to prepare the ground more thoroughly, on his opponents' own terms, for the full unveiling of the Triune God in *Orations* 29–31.

pace Plato—language may yet "show the known": not adequately, but at least somewhat (28.4). Our theology may, after all, *denote*—even as the words we use transcend themselves when we use them to refer to God.[15] But "mentally to *grasp* so great a matter"—fully to *comprehend* (καταλαμβανω: to grasp, master or "get one's head around") God, as the Anomeans presumed to be able to do—really cannot be done at all, even by "the very elevated and devout," to whom alone God reveals God's self (28.4).[16]

Fogged as we are by the "gloom" of our corporeal nature, after all, what could we truly know of God—and how (28.5)? The moon and stars surpass our power to understand them: how much more the Creator and Cause of all? We have no doubt *that* objects and persons are, but we can't know *what* they are. How much more must the same be true of our knowledge of God?[17] We know *that* all creatures have a Source—our eyes as well as natural law tell us so—but we can scarcely grasp the Power that "moves and safeguards" them (28.6). We can know God to be supremely great, lovely, and lofty—but God's greatness exceeds whatever we could connote by "greatness."[18] Whatever concepts human reason or fancy may formulate for God, they aren't—and can never be—the "real" God. And here, says Gregory, we see the Anomean's fundamental category error. As bounded, corporeal creatures, we could never comprehend a God who has no bound or body (28.7–8). Moreover, the "real, fundamental nature" of God cannot be encompassed by negatory aspects alone—whether the Anomean's "un-begottenness," or un-boundedness or freedom from change: as for any other object of knowledge, for the fullness of God's nature to be grasped, one would sooner or later have to be able not just to negate but to *assert* what the One named "ὅ ὢν" may actually *be* (28.9).

At worst, notes Gregory, we are led by an unassuageable hunger to know the Unknowable (28.13) to venerate created objects (28.14–15). At best, human reason—patterned, after all, on God's own Λογος—leads us upward from the beauty and order of the seen, by analogy, toward the Unseen (28.13); "leads us through them to what transcends them"; what made

---

15. Beeley, *Gregory*, 96.

16. The need for those who would seek the knowledge of God to be purified is a key theme in Gregory's work (Daley, *Gregory of Nazianzus*, 44). The ascent is only for the pure, with the unhallowed and unprepared relegated to the foothills (28.2). Gregory sums up the purpose of Sermon 27 as "using theology to cleanse the theologian" (28.1): preparing for the illumination of God in Christ by the power of the Spirit that will alone allow us to "know" the Divine properly.

17. "Conviction . . . of a thing's existence is quite different from knowledge of *what* it is" (28.5).

18. Beeley, *Gregory*, 95.

them, and orders and preserves them (28.16). But just as "you cannot cross your shadow, however much you haste" (28.12), reason can only take you so far; the Transcendent must always run beyond our grasp and our powers (28.13).[19]

What, then, about our godly human exemplars and sacred texts? Do they get us any further?[20] Barely. None of those who "knew God," as attested by the Old or New Testaments, had "full" knowledge—merely a "fuller" knowledge than our own (28.17).[21] From Enosh to Peter, whether through theophany or prophecy (28.18–19), "none saw, none told, of God's nature" (28.19). Even the (en)raptured Paul acknowledged that we know and prophesy only partly (1 Cor 13:9)—just as John wrote frankly of a truth beyond the present world's power to encompass (John 21:23). Solomon reels and Paul wonders at the "wealth and depth of God" (Rom 11:33). The Psalms "call God's judgements a 'great abyss' fathomless by sense" (Ps 36:6), and marvel at our human make-up as "too wonderful . . . too excellent . . . to be able to grasp" (Ps 139:6).[22] And so the search never ends. "There's always some truth left to dawn on us" (28.20).

And yet, for the same reason, says Gregory, our attempts to seek after God are not worthless; the ascent, not hopeless. God does not *resent* our knowledge (28.11). God sets the cloud between us only to ensure that we value the knowledge we have, to forestall arrogant assurance, and to preserve our future hope (28.12).

---

19. Note that Gregory values human reason (limited though it is) as analogous to (because derived from) the divine Logos (28.16). His hope is that "this God-*like*, divine thing, I mean our mind and reason, mingles with its *kin* when the *copy* returns to the *pattern* it now longs after" (28.17, emphasis added).

20. It may be anachronistic to impose a Wesleyan quadrilateral on a patristic theologian, but it seems to me that Gregory does systematically test reason, experience (from which reason works by analogy toward God), and Scripture, in *Oration* 28. Knowledge from tradition (notably the formulae of baptism, doxology, and prayer handed down by the church) will be crucial to Gregory's argument for the co-equal Godhead of the Son and Holy Spirit—as I hope to indicate later—but he does not deploy it at this preparatory stage.

21. So Gregory's memorable conviction that "our noblest theologian is not one who has discovered the whole—our earthly shackles do not permit us the whole—but one whose mental image is by comparison fuller, who has gathered in his mind a richer picture, outline, or whatever we call it, of the truth" (30.17).

22. It is worth noting here the way that allusions to, and quotations from, Scripture form the fabric of Gregory's thought and rhetoric: his argument of limited knowledge from Scriptural precedent by no means undervalues the role of Scripture itself, but merely admits the incompleteness of the revelation to our present state of enlightenment. Gregory is profoundly concerned to develop ways of talking about God as Trinity that do full and accurate justice to the biblical revelation: e.g., "How can justice be done to the *scriptural fact* that God pervades and fills the universe?" (28.8, emphasis added).

Job's Comfort

So Gregory takes us on a fresh journey of ascent, seen through a new and double lens: God both utterly confounds and exceeds all that we can know—*and* draws and enables us to know more.[23]

We have learned that we can never fully comprehend the nature of God by analogy to the created order—but hang on, says Gregory: can we even say we "know" *that*? Let's start close to home: what do we really know even about our own selves; our own nature; the mystery of our speech and senses, movement and memory, sleep and dreams, anger and urges (28.22)? Then let's move on to the thousand creatures of earth, water, and sky (28.23–24): we can only marvel at the Creator's works! The labor of some creatures show what can only be called "cleverness," though they lack "thought": traces of Λογος everywhere we look (28.25). Or let's ponder the beauty and usefulness of plants, and all the other wonders of "mother earth": are these, perhaps, the clearest and most complete mark of God's hand at work (28.26)? What about the sea, and the marvellous way that God's command forms "a fence for the face of the waters" (28.27)? (Let's note here that the latter phrase references Job 26:10. Although Gregory's challenges to the hearer/reader are drawn from a number of texts, e.g., the Psalms, they feature a clear cluster of echoes of, or quotes from, YHWH's unanswerable challenges to Job.[24]) Eventually, Gregory leads us beyond the stratosphere—and the bounds of human reason—where we can only embrace mystery (28.28–29).[25] Surely the Sun, "noblest we can see," leads us by analogy to God, "noblest we can know by thought" (28.30)—but no: God "counts the number of the stars and calls them all by name" (Ps 147:4). At last, as we "transcend sense" al-

---

23. Beeley, *Gregory*, 103—*contra* Wickham, who sees in Gregory (unlike the Eunomians) a "reverent willingness not to know" ("Introduction," 23). Gregory does present God *primarily* as unknowable here, in the context of rebutting the Eunomians, but elsewhere he insists that God has revealed Godself to us in Christ by the Holy Spirit, and particularly emphasizes the need to grow increasingly toward the knowledge of the Trinity, as the unfolding self-revelation of God in the age of the church (Beeley, *Gregory*, 105–6).

24. E.g., Job 38:36 (LXX) "Who gave to women skill at weaving cloth?" (cf., *Orations*, 28.24); Job 38:22 "What of the storehouses of the snow?" (28.28); Job 38:28 "Who gave birth to the dewdrops?" (28.28); Job 38:29 "From whose womb did the ice come forth?" (28.28); Job 38:31 "Do you know what binds the Pleiades or what fences Orion in?" (28.30).

25. "Faith rather than reason shall lead us—if, that is, you have learned the feebleness of reason to deal with matters quite close at hand and have acquired enough knowledge of reason to recognize things which surpass reason" (28.28). Cf., the earlier challenge to the Eunomians of 28.7: "What can your conception of the divine be, if you rely on all the methods of deductive argument?"

together, the angel ranks unabashedly "bear the shape . . . of God's beauty" and hymn God's majesty (28.31).

One by one, from the nearest to the most remote, the realms of the created order we have presumed to know well have proved too much for us to grasp. Yet they have also drawn us step by step up the scale of greatness, toward—at least, *toward*—the transcendent grandeur of the Creator. And on that ascent, we also have traced the path of the human soul—that "dear return voyage"—back toward the Source from Whom we came, and fell.[26]

As noted above, Gregory's unanswerable challenges clearly echo YHWH's response to Job's demand to understand God and God's ways (Job 38–41): "What on earth can you know of Me? What do *you* know about the cosmos and how the world was made?" And here, by the parallel to the story of Job, we reach at last the threshold of Gregory's theology of God. We dare not presume to speak about God correctly: as Job does, we must confess that we speak what we do not understand, matters too wonderful for us (Job 42:3). Yet God chooses to *reveal* God's self to us. We have heard of God, spoken and speculated about God—but now, our eyes *see* (Job 42:5). God chooses to reveal God's self to us not just by analogy—but by encounter.[27]

And for Gregory, as a result of encounter, from now on "when we say God, we mean Father, Son and Holy Ghost."[28]

From (Re)semblance to (Con)substance

So Gregory has demonstrated the poverty of reason and analogy as means to know God, to "level off the face of the ground" (28.1). Cured of arrogance, alerted to category error, we are now ready to learn properly of God.

Three key consequences flow from Gregory's argument so far: the fact that God's true nature can only be self-revealed ("top down" knowledge of God *per se*, rather than "bottom up" knowledge by analogy to the created order); the way the Old and New Testaments, the economy of the Godhead

---

26. "We, being so far fallen from the great God, cannot make our dear return voyage without a struggle": Gregory of Nazianzus, "Poem 1.1.8 De Anime," in Gilbert, *On God and Man*, 67. Gregory's ascent (28.22–31) appears deliberately to reverse the order of creation (Gen 1), as if drawing us "back" toward a context in which the Godhead is conspicuously and foundationally Trinitarian: Creator, co-creative Word and hovering Spirit (Gen. 1:1–3).

27. Peter Gilbert affirms that, for Gregory (as expressed particularly in his theological poetry), "within Christianity, God, who is tri-personal, can be experienced only in a personal way—can be known only by communion with the living God in Jesus Christ" (by the Holy Spirit). Gilbert, "Introduction," 21.

28. Meredith, *Cappadocians*, 102.

and the observances of the church all enable us to encounter God as three Persons; and the need for the Son and Holy Ghost to be of the self-same substance as the Father, for *any* of the above to be effectual.

Humans can only know whatever of God's nature or essence God chooses to reveal. And God has chosen to reveal God's self, not just reflected at one remove by the created cosmos, but personally and by presence. A babe at the breast, a hug offered to a leper, a labored breath on a cross, breakfast on a beach, tongues of flame across an upper room.... For Gregory, the Son and the Holy Ghost are so central to the self-revealed nature of God that one can only speak of the Godhead as three Persons, though One. Early on, he touched on the Son's revelatory role as the one by whom alone, as the Rock of shelter, he was allowed to see God on the mount (28.3): the one whom Beeley calls "the necessary and permanent focus of the knowledge of God."[29] All knowledge of God comes through the Son, the Word that utters God's thought,[30] and the Πνευμα, the breath of that utterance.[31] The Son alone allows us, corporeal as we are, to see and touch and know God—and to have the full empathy of God for our humanness—as the human Jesus, Word made flesh.[32] The Paraclete alone "searches out and knows God's depths" and teaches us all truth (28.6). No one has ever seen God—but the one and only Son, close to the Father's heart, has made God known to us (John 1:18), as attested by the Πνευμα, by whom we, too, may cry "Abba, Father!" (Rom 8:15–16).

God as One-and-Three alone has explanatory power for the church's sense of the Godhead. All three persons are revealed partly (through theophany and typology) by the Old Testament, and clearly (as enfleshed Emmanuel and effectual Paraclete) by the New.[33] All three are encountered as part of God's economy (the master story of God's plans to form, govern, redeem, and restore the cosmos, from the "ἐν ἀρχη" to the new heavens and

---

29. Beeley, *Gregory*, 115.

30. For Gregory, Christ is named Word "because he is related to the Father as word is to mind . . . the concise and simple revelation of the Father's nature" (30.20).

31. Cf., John 20:22. This is a common analogy in patristic exposition of the Trinity. Meredith, *Cappadocians*, 107.

32. "He bears the title 'Man' . . . with a view to being accessible through his body to corporeal things—being in all other respects inaccessible" (30.21).

33. Typology is a feature of Gregory's Old Testament exegesis: Christ seen in the cleft rock of Sinai (28.3), foreshadowed by Abraham's sacrifice of Isaac (28.18). While New Testament allusions permeate Gregory's prose, the full Scriptural revelation of Christ awaits *Oration 29*, particularly the extraordinary passages on the paradoxes of Christ's dual nature (29.19–20). Gregory acknowledges that the Spirit is not named explicitly as "God" in the Bible, but only because, in God's progressive revelation, "light shines on us bit by bit" (31.27).

new earth): each, looked at severally, properly known as Creator, Redeemer, or Perfecter—yet all at work throughout.³⁴ All three are known to the church, by encountered presence—and reverent address by the threefold Name—at font, and sacrament, and prayer; the church throughout the ages has known, loved, taught and venerated God as One-and-Three.³⁵ And only so, after all, may we gradually become purer of body and soul (27.3), and accustom our eyes to glory, for our own ascent of the mount, so that—though for now we can only "grasp what we can and pray to grasp the rest"³⁶—we may at last hope to see God face to face, and to know fully, even as we are fully known (1 Cor 13: 12).³⁷

But for any of the above to make sense, the Son and the Holy Ghost must be part of the Godhead not merely by analogy, correspondence or resemblance to the Father, but as self-same substance.³⁸ And here, of course, we come to the crux of the matter for fourth-century theology: for God to restore a wounded cosmos, the Son must be fully and truly God as well as fully and truly human—for (as Gregory famously argued) "what has not

34. Daley argues that Gregory's theology of the Trinity is not something we believe "about God" but "a creed: a summary of what Christians find revealed in the one long narrative of Israel's history, the life and death and resurrection of Jesus, and the church's continuing life in the power of his spirit as Christ's body" (Daley, *Gregory*, 49).

35. In terms of the "Wesleyan quadrilateral," Gregory has shifted focus from reason and experience (which limit us to knowing the Transcendent by analogy to the knowable creation) to Scripture and tradition (understood as means by which the Transcendent makes Itself known).

36. Gregory of Nazianzus, *Oration 20*: 12. Beeley highlights Gregory's doctrine of purification as the way of Christian life entered by baptism, by which we are "increasingly illuminated by Christ within the light of the Trinity" (Beeley, *Gregory*, 100).

37. "We count it a high thing that we may perhaps learn what (the being of God) is in the time to come. . . . Yes, this is what men, who purify themselves for it, must think of and hope for" (29.11). For Gregory, this hope is linked with his larger conception of salvation as θέωσις: the "transforming participation of the human person in the being and life of God" (Beeley, *Gregory*, 117). "Although the vision of the Trinity will not be complete until the world to come, nevertheless through faith it begins now, in baptism and in the Christian life of on-going discipleship and deification" (Beeley, *Gregory*, 231).

38. I am, of course, seeking to invoke the famous distinction in late fourth-century theology between the terms ὁμοιούσιος ("of like substance") and ὁμοούσιος ("of self-same substance"), to refer to the Father and the Son, and by extension, the Holy Spirit. John Anthony McGuckin notes that ὁμοιούσιος was a flawed word in its day: not featured in the Bible and too "material" for the Godhead, among other objections. However, it did explain the import of the creedal confession of Christ as "God from God" rather than, as for the Arians, "a god from The God" (McGuckin, "Trinity in the Greek Fathers," 63n38). Sameness of substance is also germane to Gregory's argument against category error: it is not as if Father and Son can belong to the same "class of things" to which the name "God" is given; they must be of the self-same (unique) substance (McGuckin, "Trinity in the Greek Fathers," 64).

been assumed has not been healed."[39] Once more, Gregory counters the Anomeans (among others), who asserted that Son and Holy Ghost, as generate, could not be of the same substance as the absolute, ungenerated Godhead.[40] For the cosmos to be redeemed depends on a shared self-same substance, says Gregory—or else broken humanness has not been assumed by the Godhead. The prayer and sacraments of the church attest to that truth—or else she venerates mere creatures.[41] And reason and theology must accommodate that truth—or else we subject the Godhead to "number" or "place" or "whenness" (29.3) and attempt to make the Persons "plural" or separate" as we use those terms by analogy to created objects.

Gregory's sermon sequence thus moves gradually, by a hard-won and relentlessly careful use of words, toward the full-blown language of one substance and three hypostases: both absolute oneness of essence[42] *and* a mutual relatedness of three unconfounded persons.[43] Gregory has groped for

---

39. "Letter to Cledonius" (*Letter* 101.5). The same thought is expressed in the *Orations*: "(Christ) bears the title, 'Man' . . . with the aim of hallowing Man through himself, by becoming a sort of yeast for the whole lump" (30.12).

40. Gregory asserts the fully divinity of Son and Spirit, and their co-equality with the Father, against a range of opponents, including the homoian (insisting on a relation "of similar substance"), heterousian ("dissimilar" substance) and pneumatomachian (denying the divinity of the Spirit) (Gilbert, "Introduction," 21). However, he counters the specifically Eunomian argument that "the ingenerate and the generate are not the same. If that is the case, the Father and the Son cannot be the same thing." "It goes without saying," responds Gregory, "that this argument excludes either the Father or the Son from the Godhead. . . . Make your choice of alternative blasphemies. . . . Still, what are your grounds for denying that ingenerate and generate are the same? . . . It is in the nature of an offspring to have a nature identical with its parent's" (29.10). In "Poem 1.1.2 De Filio," Gregory writes pithily, "The terms/'unbegotten' and 'begotten of the Father' do not make/two kinds of Godhead" (Gregory of Nazianzus, *On God and Man*, 40).

41. "If (the Holy Spirit) is a creature why do you believe in him, why are we baptized in him?" (31.7)

42. The oneness "produced by equality of nature, harmony of will, identity of action and the convergence toward their source of what springs from unity. . . . Though there is numerical distinction, there is no division in the substance" (29.2). Elsewhere, Gregory locates the unity of God in the Father as Source and Cause, without implying hierarchy. "We must recognize one God, the Father, without source and unbegotten, and one Son, begotten of the Father, and one Spirit, which takes its existence from the Father and which, while yielding unbegottenness to the Father and begetting to the Son, is however in all other respects equal to them in nature, dignity, glory and honour" (*Oration* 32.5, cited by Beeley, *Gregory*, 194).

43. "The aim is to safeguard the distinctness of the three hypostases within the single nature and quality of the Godhead. The Son is not the Father; there is *one* Father, yet he is whatever the Father is. The Spirit is not Son, because he is from God; there is *one* Only-begotten. Yet whatever the Son is, he is. The three are a single whole in their Godhead and the single whole is three in personalities. Thus there will be no Sabellian

an adequate explanatory analogy for the concept—source, stream, and flow (31.31); sun, beam, and effulgence (31.32)—but at last says goodbye to all such "shadows," as fundamentally flawed. At the end, he resolves henceforth just to persuade all people to let God be God, to adore Father, Son, and Holy Ghost as one Godhead and power, to whom belong all glory and honor for ever and ever (31.33). Amen.

Creed and Coda

The church has become so accustomed, as settled and sacrosanct orthodoxy, to the creedal formulae that name Son and Holy Ghost as part of the Godhead—not merely by analogy, correspondence, or resemblance, but as a matter of very essence, "true God from true God." One cannot help but honor the work of theology and word care that brought Gregory, and other Fathers of the Church, across that desperately contested ground to the concept of three unconfounded Persons who nevertheless share the self-same substance: a leap not easy to make, as the heated debates show. As we watch Gregory struggle to express the unspeakable paradox, through these sermons, we can trace the hard-won emergence of the most profound Mystery of our *Credo*: the threefold Godhead of the One God; the movement from (re)semblance to (con)substance, from analogy to theology, that has permanently changed the landscape of thought about God—and made more than its iota of difference to us all.

~

Afterword: Dotting Some I's

So the game is up: my essay is a lipogram—although for reasons that may now be obvious, I couldn't say so in the text. Although the "game" of writing a text without an "i" was the original stimulus for this piece—justified, I hope, as a small joke about the "iota of difference" between the terms *homoiousios* ("of like substance") and *homoousios* ("of self-same substance") in relation to the being of Christ—I was genuinely committed to the content I was trying to convey, and didn't want to distract the reader with self-conscious nudges and winks. ("Due to a confluence of factors beyond my

---

'One', no (Arian) three" (31.9). In the succinct explanation of Rosemary Radford Ruether, Sabellianism unified both persons and substance, while Arianism divided the substance as well as the persons (Ruether, *Gregory*, 68).

control, Gregory cannot—for now—be more accurately named"? "Note that references have been made to the 'Holy Ghost,' rather than the more common nomenclature, as the relevant vowel would currently be taboo for reasons of orthography"? "Memo to self: get a Thesaurus"?) For the same reason, many clarifying arguments, supporting references, and direct quotations had to be pushed into the footnotes: I do apologize . . .

In my reflection, I've tried to make a fairly simple point about the difference, in Gregory's *Second Theological Oration*, between knowing something by "like substance" (or analogy) and knowing the substance of the thing *in se* (by what I've called encounter), and the way in which, for Gregory, this distinction encourages both an epistemic humility (the Divine surpasses all human words and concepts) and a hopeful aspiration (God nevertheless draws us to know God more and better), which allow us to be open to what Gregory saw as the educative, progressive, and unfolding self-revelation of God—as Trinity. By framing the epistemological issue in terms of "substance," I've also hoped to align it with Gregory's core affirmation that the Son and Holy Spirit are indeed "very God" by substance—not by mere analogy or likeness of being to the Godhead—and that the Godhead can truly be *known* as the Father self-revealed in the Son through the Holy Spirit.

Even so, all this may seem a rather tenuous justification for an essay written without an "i"—with the gratuitous hardships it imposes on both writer and reader—even if one is inclined to indulge it as an extended orthographic metaphor for the missing iota in "*homoousios*." So perhaps I might add some brief comments on form and content: how the process of writing in this way became an integral part of my reflection on how one thinks and writes about a Triune God.

A lipogram (from the Greek λειπογράμματος, "lacking a letter") is a piece of text written under the self-imposed constraint of systematically excluding the use of one or more letters of the alphabet. The game has a very long history, but E. V. Wright's novel *Gadsby* (1939) and Georges Perec's *La Disparition* (1969) exemplify the modern tradition in what Douglas Hofstadter cheerfully dubs "Anglo-Saxon" (English without the letter "e") and "Gallic" (French, ditto).[44]

One particular genius of lipography is the mental discipline and vigilance imposed by the constraining of what can legitimately be written. Writing text without an "i"—having to find circumlocutions and synonyms, constantly testing expressions for adequacy—made me wonder: is this how "doing theology" was for Gregory, and other fourth-century theologians, in

---

44. Hofstadter, *Le Ton Beau*, 107.

their trial-and-error search for a disciplined language with which to speak of a Triune God? The struggle toward Nicene orthodoxy surely required its own rigorous orthography: keeping within self-imposed bounds defining what could and could not legitimately be said.

I resisted drafting my essay in English and translating it into Anglo-Saxon: I wanted to experience in my own process of composition the kind of frustration, flow, and redirection of thought by constraints of orthography that I found at the heart of Gregory's rhetorical style—and at the heart of theology's struggle with language and its limits. "These are the replies," Gregory says of Orations 27 and 28, "that one can use to put a brake upon this hasty argumentativeness, a hastiness which is dangerous in all matters, but especially in discussions about God" (29.1). Gregory's own language is endearingly self-monitoring ("I eagerly ascend the mount—or to speak truer, ascend in eager hope matched with anxiety for my frailty," 28.2) and rigorously discriminating. What are the implications if we call God *this* . . . or *this* . . . or *this* (28.8)? The term "x," though granted, doesn't do justice to . . . (28.9). And what are we really *thinking* about when we use the word "y" (28.13)? Why not say then instead . . . ? (29.5). No, if we are sober, we make a distinction, I think, between . . . (29.6). "This," says Gregory, "is why we limit ourselves to Christian terms" (29.2). This is why we submit our expressions and our analogies to examination, testing their truth and adequacy (31.31–33).

I wonder if we exercise such word-care in our writing or preaching. I wonder if we deliberate over every term—the connotations of a name or epithet, the relationships implied by a preposition—placing a brake upon hasty argumentativeness, ensuring that we limit ourselves to Christian terms. The most important part of "writing (and speaking) Christian" may be what is not said—or not *easily* said.[45] And as Gregory's colleague Basil of Caesarea challenged us, "Which theological word is so small that the right or wrong understanding of it does not have great weight in both instances? For, if one iota . . . of the Law will not pass away, how is it safe for us to pass over even the smallest matters?"[46]

Another genius of lipography is the way in which it intentionally disrupts our habits of language and written style, resisting colloquialism and

---

45. Hauerwas, *Working with Words*, 88.

46. Basil the Great, *On the Holy Spirit*, ch. 1.2, 28–29. Basil writes to Amphilochius, Bishop of Iconium, "I delight very much in the carefulness and sobriety of your idea that not one of the words that are applied to God in every use of speech should be left uninvestigated" (Basil the Great, *On the Holy Spirit*, 1.1). Basil himself exuberantly exemplifies attention to theological and liturgical language (especially prepositional relationships).

cliché. Effortful and "unnatural" both to write and to read, lipogrammatic writing makes us all slow down; makes us consciously aware (by absence and surprising/dissonant substitution) of our otherwise unexamined "off-the-shelf" linguistic formulae. Gregory seems to have sought a similar discipline in the constraints of metrical poetry—as others have, no doubt, in sonnet or sonata form. "I wished," he writes in his poem *In Suos Versos*:

> So to subdue my own unmeasuredness;
> Indeed, though I write, I don't write much
> When toiling on the meter.[47]

It is difficult for us to "unlearn" the facility and familiarity we have developed with the orthodox formulations of Trinity: "in the name of the Father, and of the Son and of the Holy Spirit"; "begotten, not made, of one being with the Father"; "with the Father and the Son he is worshipped and glorified." Writing an essay on the Trinity without "i's"—being forced to find alternatives to apparently non-negotiable words like "Trinity" and "Triune," "divine," and "deity," "Christ" and (perhaps most conspicuously) "Spirit"— reminded me that all this language was originally hard-won and *far* from "natural" speech. And that perhaps it still is—or should be. "Trinitarian speech," notes Daley, "is language with rules of signification that have been permanently altered, bent beyond the shape and contours of normal use, to point to the ineffable."[48]

I wonder if we are always mindful of how irreducibly *odd* it is to speak of a Triune God—or of how reductive our linguistic habits can be, for example, in regard to gender.

And herein lies, perhaps, the third genius of lipography. It is, precisely and paradoxically, the self-imposed constraints—the rules defining what can and cannot legitimately be written—that challenge the writer to *less* bounded, *less* habitual thinking.[49] Within the strictures and structures of the game—one's "rule of faith," as it might be—one is forced to enrich one's vocabulary, to experiment with new grammatical constructions, to question and explore connotations, to allow incongruities, and to develop intuitions. And in the process, one discovers all kinds of new insights and joyous serendipities.

Being orthographically unable to use words like "Trinity," "Christ," or "Spirit" forced me to grope after different titles, economic roles and

---

47. "In Suos Versos" (2.1.39) in Gregory of Nazianzus, *On God and Man*, 154.

48. Daley, *Gregory*, 45.

49. Reflecting on the process of writing his commentary on the Gospel of Matthew, for example, Stanley Hauerwas recalls, "In order to force myself to write, and thus to think, differently, I gave myself certain rules" (Hauerwas, *Working with Words*, 107).

analogies, some of which offered surprising fruit for reflection—but there were also far deeper implications for my prose style. Inability to use "is" statements frustrated the most simple—as well as simplistic or dogmatic— assertions, pushing my sentences toward more tentative, exploratory constructions, moods and tenses, in a way that (in retrospect) rather happily echoes Gregory's resistance of Eunomian certainties. For the same reason (both "it" and "is" being orthographically taboo), unities tended to edge toward pluralities in a very Trinitarian way. Our thought naturally shapes our linguistic practices. But our linguistic practices also shape our thought.

The inherent playfulness of lipographic writing unsettles, provokes, and revivifies formulaic language with its incongruities and unfamiliarities. As a form of translation from one medium to another (from English, as it might be, into Anglo-Saxon), it insists on the complexity and surplus of meaning in words and texts, demanding our respect for the multiple facets of the original—and our alertness to the way in which meanings inevitably change in translation: promoting the very kind of rigorous word care, coupled with epistemic humility, that Gregory advocates. It requires constant risk-taking, experimentation, adjustment, and evaluation—encouraging insight and discovery. As Hofstadter notes, "the imposition of any reasonably sharp set of constraints will force a writer to explore and discover pathways in semantic space that would otherwise have been left entirely unexplored."[50]

For me, the theological work of Gregory of Nazianzus embodies just this kind of mutually dependent discipline and playfulness, constraint and exploration, the earning of freedom within the bounds of care. In challenging the Eunomians's claim to a logically rigorous and reverent use of language, he takes them on at "the game" (29.7). In pyrotechnic passages like the one in *Oration* 29 on the paradoxes of Christ's human-and-divine nature—"He hungered—yet he fed thousands. . . . He was tired—yet he is the 'rest' of the weary" (29.20)—Gregory himself seems to *play* his way through linguistic and exegetical precision to theological insight.[51] "Despite his cautions about the limits of language," as Daley affirms, "Gregory is creative, even bold, in plotting out the semantic boundaries within which the Church's faith may rightly and safely be articulated."[52]

"Our noblest theologian," writes Gregory, "is not one who has discovered the whole—our earthly shackles do not permit us the whole—but one

50. Hofstadter, *Ton Beau de Marot*, 135.

51. Several scholars note Gregory's love of word-plays and puns ("talk of God's body has no solid body to it," 28.8) among other rhetorical and poetic devices. See, for example, Ruether, *Gregory*, 65.

52. Daley, *Gregory*, 45.

whose mental image is by comparison fuller, who has gathered in his mind a richer picture, outline, or whatever we call it, of the truth" (30.17). I wonder if, in our own struggle with language and its limits in speaking about a Triune God, we still make room—within (and even, perhaps, in the service of) the disciplined semantic boundaries of "Christian terms"—to be creative, even bold, even perhaps playful.

In any case, I've enjoyed "taking the game on." I think Gregory would have approved—as long as I've also done some justice to the content of his argument, upon which so much rests. The iota really does make all the difference.

Bibliography

Basil the Great. *On the Holy Spirit*. Translated by Stephen Hildebrand. New York: St. Vladimir's Seminary, 2011.

Beeley, Christopher A. *Gregory of Nazianzus on the Trinity and the Knowledge of God*. Oxford: Oxford University Press, 2009.

Daley, Brian E. *Gregory of Nazianzus*. New York: Routledge, 2006.

Gilbert, Peter. "Introduction." In *On God and Man: The Theological Poetry of Gregory of Nazianzus*, translated by Peter Gilbert, 1–36. New York: St. Vladimir's Seminary, 2001.

Gregory of Nazianzus. *On God and Christ: The Five Theological Orations and Two Letters to Celdonius*. Translated by Frederick Williams (Oration 27) and Lionel Wickham (Orations 28–31). New York: St. Vladimir's Seminary, 2002.

———. *On God and Man: The Theological Poetry of Gregory of Nazianzus*. Translated by Peter Gilbert. New York: St. Vladimir's Seminary, 2001.

Hauerwas, Stanley. *Working with Words: On Learning to Speak Christian*. Eugene, OR: Cascade, 2011.

Hofstadter, Douglas, and Emmanuel Sander. *Surfaces and Essences: Analogy as the Fuel and Fire of Thinking*. New York: Basic Books, 2013.

Hofstadter, Douglas R. *Le Ton Beau de Marot: In Praise of the Music of Language*. New York: Basic Books, 1997.

McGuckin, John Anthony. *The SCM Press A–Z of Patristic Theology*. 2nd ed. London: SCM, 2005.

———. "The Trinity in the Greek Fathers." In *The Cambridge Companion to the Trinity*, edited by Peter Phan, 49–69. Cambridge: Cambridge University Press, 2011.

Meredith, Anthony. *The Cappadocians*. New York: St. Vladimir's Seminary, 1995.

Ruether, Rosemary Radford. *Gregory of Nazianzus: Rhetor and Philosopher*. London: Oxford University Press, 1969.

White, Roger M. *Talking About God: The Concept of Analogy and the Problem of Religious Language*. Farnham, UK: Ashgate, 2010.

Wickham, Lionel. "Introduction." In *On God and Christ: The Five Theological Orations and Two Letters to Cledonius*, 9–23. New York: St. Vladimir's Seminary, 2002.

CHAPTER 7

"From His Fullness We Have All Received"

Reflections on Divine Agency, Time, and the Experience(s) of Salvation[1]

CHRIS E. W. GREEN

Introduction

In the Christian theological tradition, God has been understood as altogether immutable. In St. Thomas's words, God is "pure act" (*actus purus*),[2] that is, absolutely identical with his own act of being.[3] God is infinite and simple, entirely without potential: his deity is always already fully realized.[4] He is not, therefore, moved or changed in any way by anything outside of himself. Unequivocally and comprehensively perfect, God lacks no excel-

---

1. Thanks to Jason Goroncy, Daniel Castelo, Matt Emerson, and Robb Blackaby for their remarks on earlier drafts of this paper, which made it possible for me to think through what I actually wanted to say in the first place.

2. Aquinas, *ST* I.9.

3. Championing this position, Thomas Weinandy ("God and Human Suffering," 99–116) argues that "the very character of the act of creation reveals and so demands that God be 'being itself' and so 'pure act,' for any other mode of existence, one which by necessity would possess self-constituting potential within its own actuality, would be incapable of performing such an act."

4. As Scripture insists; see e.g. Mal 3:6 and Jas 1:17.

lence of any kind.⁵ He does not experience anything previously unknown to himself, or, over time, become a better or worse God than he would have been otherwise. In brief, creation does not make God, God; and it cannot keep God from being God.

Assuming all the above is true—that God in fact is pure actuality and categorically free from all that is not God—how do we think about God's works in and upon creation? What sense, if any, does it make to talk about God acting within history? And how does that matter for his life and for ours? Taking Scripture seriously requires us to raise these questions; because, as Rowan Williams has said, the God witnessed in Scripture "is a god whose identity is consistently clarified in terms of what he has done and whom he has known, called or spoken to." We cannot speak faithfully about God as he is in himself without considering what it means for God to be God with and for us in the ways the Scripture and the saints declare that he is. In the biblical tradition, "God is the god of the 'fathers' even before he is the 'I am' of the great self-declaration."⁶

Before moving on, let me pause to explain why I am drawn to these questions and why I would risk answering them. I was raised in a classical Pentecostal church, which means, among other things, that I learned early on to expect God to work in my life. Faith, in my tradition, was a passionate expectancy for divine "outpouring," a desire for encounters with God that would dramatically alter our lives for the better.⁷ We talked in every service about desiring God's presence, and we expected regular (if unpredictable and uncontrollable) divine "interventions" and supernatural "manifestations," not only in the goings-on of our worship liturgies but also in the course of our day-to-day routines.⁸ Eventually, however, I realized that I had no way of making good sense of what my experiences—or the apparent lack of such experiences—meant for me or for God.⁹ And that realization not only spurred me to critical theological reflection then, but continues to press me ever more deeply into it.

---

5. Aquinas, *SCG* I.28.
6. Williams, "God," 77.
7. See Asamoah-Gyadu, "'You Shall Receive Power,'" 45–66.
8. See Menzies, *Spirit and Power*, 23.
9. As Daniel Castelo ("What if Miracles Don't Happen?" 237) argues, "the Pentecostal/charismatic worldview raises the theodical stakes in both the spiritual life and theological endeavoring since healings and miracles are understood as available at the level of quotidian existence." What is more, "the Pentecostal worldview, as typically formulated and propagated, cannot account—either conceptually or practically—for those cases in which healings and miracles do not occur." For Castelo's articulation of the classic view of impassibility, and what he think it means and could mean for Pentecostalism, see his "An Apologia," 118–26.

Jamie Smith has characterized Pentecostal spirituality as an affective and imaginative "construal of the world" marked, above all, by "a radical openness to God and, in particular, to God doing something differently or new" in the world.[10] And Veli-Matti Kärkkäinen has argued that openness to and expectation of divine intervention—especially in the form of miracles, signs and wonders, and charismatic manifestations (e.g., speaking in tongues, prophecy, dreams, and visions)—are crucial to the extraordinary growth of Pentecostal movements worldwide.[11] In keeping with these views, Amos Yong has attempted to vindicate Pentecostal expectations for the "palpable, tangible, and kinesthetic encounter with the living God." He has done so by suggesting a theological/philosophical frame of reference that he hopes can render such expectations and encounters intelligible.[12] While I share most of his concerns and have learned much from his proposals, I want to make a case in more explicitly traditional terms, providing a dogmatic account of how we experience God and why. What follows in this essay, therefore, is one attempt to provoke further reflection and construction, not only for Pentecostals but also for Christians of whatever tradition.[13]

Pentecostal Expectancy and the Coming/Going of God

Like Yong, Smith, and Kärkkäinen, among others, I want to affirm this Pentecostal expectancy, at least in some form.[14] In fact, I believe it is a gift Pentecostals are called to share with their Christian sisters and brothers in other ecclesial traditions—and with those outside the faith, as well. But I have found that this expectancy is far too often rooted in disastrous and disastrously fragmentary misapprehensions of both divine being/agency and creaturely responsibility. This expectancy usually entails the assumption, not always acknowledged, that God is only sometimes active—usually

---

10. Smith, *Thinking in Tongues*, 32.

11. Kärkkäinen, "Pentecostalism and Pentecostal Theology," xiv–xv.

12. Yong, *Spirit of Creation*, 73. See also, Smith and Yong, *Science and the Spirit*; Yong, *Spirit Renews*; Vondey, "Passion for the Spirit."

13. As Yong ("On Divine Presence," 183) argues, to claim that God is active in the world "without providing some explanation of how that happens is theologically vacuous."

14. Not least because it is so resonant with the biblical tradition. As Smith and Yong (*Science and Spirit*, 74) says, "Most pentecostal Christians expect God's ongoing intervention in the same manner as such divine action was displayed in the lives of the earliest Christians."

"spontaneously"[15] and always only in events that seem otherwise inexplicable. As if God is most at work where creaturely reality is least understood.

God, in such accounts, exists exclusively in the "gaps" of our knowledge, gaps generated by a common-sense "modernist" grasp of reality.[16] What is worse, such accounts often, if not always, arise from the seedbed of something like "ontological pelagianism," a construal of reality in which God is responsive to our initiatives so that we are finally personally responsible for the making of our own fortunes.[17] Even in such construals, believers are expected to collaborate with God, of course, and with the resources that obedience to God affords. Still, the life of faith, so conceived, is more a (Babelian) "making be" than a (Marian) "letting be."[18] As if God is mostly *in*active, stationed at an inspective remove, waiting to be moved to action by the intensity of desire or the audacity of an act of faith.

Pentecostals are not alone in holding such assumptions about God, of course. Under the influence of various post-Enlightenment sociocultural forces, both secular and religious, many if not all Protestant traditions in the West have lost touch with how to think astutely about God and God's present-tense work in the world. By and large, our attention has been focused on so-called "practical" concerns. But speaking the gospel faithfully requires thinking faithfully about the God of that gospel. If we hope as Christians to speak intelligibly and gracefully about God and God's work in the world, then we have to think and speak about God in ways more recognizable in the light of the gospel and more resonant with Scripture's broad witness. The truth is, if God is just one being among other beings, one agent among other agents; if God is always coming and going, swayed one way or another by our desire or by our faithlessness; if God is sometimes active, sometimes inactive, waiting to respond to our initiatives; then God just cannot be the God the gospel promises.[19]

How God Happens

What, then, are we supposed to say? How should we speak about God's involvement in our lives and the experience(s) of our salvation? We should,

---

15. That is, in ways not planned for or intended by worshippers.

16. See Smith and Yong, *Science and the Spirit*, 75.

17. Schindler, "America's Technological Ontology." Schindler sees this "ontological pelagianism" as peculiarly "American," but I would argue that it is more capitalist/consumerist.

18. Schindler, "America's Technological Ontology," 438–39.

19. See Williams, "God," 83.

first, affirm that God is immutable. But we should then immediately insist that this immutability is not static: God's actuality is *lively*.[20] In the language of Scripture, the true God—as opposed to all false gods—is the "living God."[21] I find Jenson's way of putting it particularly helpful: "the one God is an *event*."[22]

> Events, of course, happen *to* something. What the event of God happens to is, first, the triune persons. The fundamental statement of God's being is therefore: God is what happens between Jesus and his Father in their Spirit. But . . . we may also say: God is what happens to Jesus and the world. . . . God is the event of the world's transformation by Jesus's love, the same love to which the world owes its existence.[23]

This should not be taken to mean that God is made to be God by the world's existence.[24] The creator/creature distinction must be upheld.[25] God does not actualize himself through his actions within history. Just the opposite, in fact: God actualizes history by freely enacting his own life for us. God decides not to be God without us, and so we exist.[26] God decides to save us from sin and death, and so we come to share in his life. God happens—that is why there is anything at all, rather than nothing.

But it is not enough to say *that* God happens. We must move to say *how* God happens. Only in that way can we bear witness to his character, and, when all is said and done, God's character is what makes the gospel the magnificent news that it is. Again, I find Jenson's description instructive: God happens as "a structure of relations."[27] To be clear, this does not mean that God is the communion of three existents. God is not a being, much less a corps of beings. God is "the ground of being" just as a trinity of persons-in-relations.[28] In Aquinas's terms, "the persons are the subsisting relations

---

20. See Jenson, "Ipse Pater Non Est Impassibilis," 117–26.

21. See e.g. Ps 42:2; Isa 37:17; Matt 16:16; Acts 14:15; 2 Thess 1:9; 1 Tim 4:10; Heb 10:31.

22. Jenson, *Systematic Theology*, 221. Here, Jenson is following Barth (*KD* 2/1, p. 288).

23. Jenson, *Systematic Theology*, 221.

24. As Thomas Weinandy, George Hunsinger, and David Bentley Hart, among others, have taken Jenson to mean.

25. Without it, all accounts of salvation and all forms of the Christian life fall into one form or another of self-justification

26. See Rom 8:31–33.

27. Jenson, *Systematic Theology*, 218. See also Jenson, "Once More," 130–33.

28. See Aquinas, *ST* I.3.

themselves. Hence it is not against the simplicity of the divine persons for them to be distinguished by the relations."[29] Or, again in Jenson's phrasing, "the 'relations' are not static collocations but mutual actions."[30] Notice what is claimed: there are not existent persons existing at the end of each relation; the "persons" simply *are* the relations. The Father *is* the begetting and sending of Jesus, the Son. Jesus *is* the begotten and the sent. The Spirit *is* the breathed forth and the poured out. All there is to God, we might say, is the event of these relationships. There isn't a divine being (much less three divine beings!) that sometimes decides to act but usually simply observes and waits. God's being *is* act. God's essence is "event"—in particular, the event of "irresistible Possibility" and "encompassing Faithfulness."[31]

What do we gain from this sort of description? First, we see that our relationship to God, whatever it is, must be categorically unlike our relationships with anyone or anything else. God is not one kind of thing and creatures another kind of thing. We are what we are just because God is not a thing at all, but (because he is in himself beyond all that is) the very condition of our existence.[32] "God is not an object competing for attention"—not even the greatest, most powerful object.[33] God is not another person in our lives; God is our life.[34] Recognizing this, we see, second, that there is no conflict or competition between God and us. Indeed, God is and makes the reality within which we can be truly ourselves. God being God is what makes it possible for us to be the creatures we are. Said another way, God's inviolable will does not impinge on our freedom: it constitutes it.[35] And this means, third, that we are free to go about our lives precisely because we are participating in God.[36] God includes us in his life, and thereby creates us and redeems us in freedom.[37]

---

29. Aquinas, *ST* I.29 and I.40.
30. Jenson, "Logic of the Doctrine," 247.
31. Jenson, "Logic of the Doctrine," 247.
32. Jenson, *Systematic Theology*, 224–25.
33. Williams, "God," 77.
34. See Col 3:1–3.
35. See Jenson, "Bride of Christ," 1–5.
36. See Jenson, *Systematic Theology*, 224–36.
37. On these lines, see Kathryn Tanner's pathbreaking account of participation and the image of God in *Christ the Key*.

God With, Within, and Without Us

The question remains, however: how does God, as the immutable event that he is, participate in *our* lives? Speaking the gospel requires us to say that God, by his own decision, is within the creation's reality as surely as it is within his. The God of the gospel is an actor in our stories as well as the author of them as a single story. Jenson is right, I believe, to contend that our existence has the shape it has because of the character and nature of the God who happens to it.[38] Creation is what it is, and bears some analogy to God's own life, because God is an event with a (perichoretic and eternal) "beginning," "middle," and "end."[39] And given that time is constitutive of creation's being, we can speak of the one God as creator only insofar as we say that God acts without, upon, and within time.

This needs to be articulated in explicitly Trinitarian terms, and it might be done like this: the Father, the unbegotten and begetting "principle who proceeds from no other,"[40] is God acting *without* time; Jesus, the eternally begotten one sent in the fullness of time, is God acting *within* time; the Spirit, the *nexus amoris*, is God acting *upon* time.[41]

---

38. As Tanner (*Christ the Key*, 145) insists, "There are no new movements of the trinity represented by the mission on which the one Jesus calls Father sends the Son and Spirit. The persons of the trinity just keep doing what they are always doing, but now with humanity along for the ride."

39. In Jenson's own words ("Creation as a Triune Act," 34–42), "God can be both the Beginning and the End of time in that he within time reconciles the Beginning and the End. God is the Father, the sheer Given for all time. God is the Spirit, the time-giving Goal of time. And he is both not by being a Father-Spirit—i.e., *not* by being anything like the average God—but by being the Son, the one who *in* and *through* time reconciles the given world to its goal. The triune God is in himself Given, Goal, and Reconciliation; Purposer, Purpose, and Word; Start, Finish, and History. His being is the Life among the Three. And if the triune God is the real God, then time is the *accommodation* this life makes in itself for the particular History that the Son in fact and freely is, Jesus's history with what is not God."

40. Bonaventure, *Breviloquium* I.3.

41. As Augustine says (*Confessions* VII.15), "All spaces of times, both those which have passed and those which shall pass, neither go nor come except through your working and abiding presence." And as Jenson (*Systematic Theology*, 222) puts it, "What happens to the world with Jesus has three identities that are the origin of time, the goal of time, and what within time is what time is about; the three bracket time and occupy time and just so reach through time."

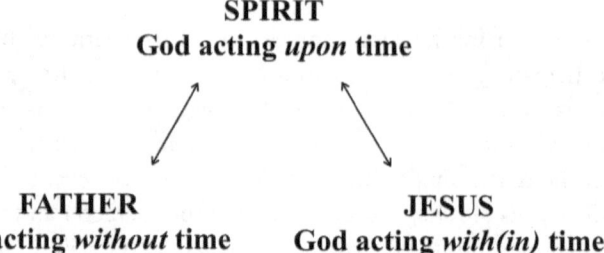

But for this model to work, we need to acknowledge a distinction between the *act* that is God's way of being and the *works* of God that constitute and direct all things to their end. For God, of course, there is no separation between the divine being-event and his works. As Rowan Williams makes clear, "action is predicated of God only in the category of *ousia*."[42] God's eternal activity and the activity whereby he makes himself known, in reality, are inseparable. The "works" of God are simply "the diverse ways in which his single *actus essendi* is present to us."[43] They only *seem* to be distinct "because the conditions of created existence are such that we apprehend the latter as a sequence of apparently discrete operations."[44] God's being-act comes to us in time as works, because in coming to us God's life mercifully takes up created realities so we may know the unknowable and unapproachable one who has drawn near.

In the life of Jesus, the event of God's being and God's works are identical. As Williams insists, Jesus's life is not a life "episodically inspired by God, let alone interrupted by God at moments of crucial importance."[45] God is not an element or factor in Jesus's story, but what Jesus's entire life expresses or communicates.[46] The very fullness of God dwells in Christ bodily, Scripture says, which means that everything Christ is and does brings God to bear truly in the world.[47] The humanity of the Word shares a unique relation both to the rest of creation and to God.[48] God happens in him—"without measure."[49] And this is so that through him all creation might share in his

---

42. Williams, "Philosophical Structures," 31.
43. Williams, "Philosophical Structures," 40.
44. Williams, "Philosophical Structures," 31.
45. Williams, "God," 79.
46. Williams, "God," 79.
47. Col 2:9.
48. See Aquinas, *ST* III.26.1–2.
49. John 3:34.

intimacy with the Father, which is just another way of saying that through him all creation might be filled with his Spirit.[50]

Given that Jesus is God, we of course cannot suggest that the Father's and the Spirit's works for him are somehow not also his. We have to affirm at least some form of the doctrine of inseparable operations. Jesus does not do what is necessary to move God to act. Jesus *is* God's act.[51] So, why and how should the works of God *in* him be distinguished from the works of God *for* him? First, because God truly does receive from God: God's life is a life of gift, given in fullness and received in fullness, from glory to glory. And we should not forget that in Christ the divine and human "natures" are eternally at-one-ed, which means, among other things, that his human will is in perfect, transparent communion with the divine will. By incorporating us into his body, then, Christ draws our wills into alignment with his humanity. And how does he draw us? By his perfect openness to the Father and the Spirit in their witness to him: that relational openness, after all, is just who he *is*.

Apart from the ministry of Jesus, the works of God are *not* identical with God's being-act. So, we need another pair of distinctions: first, between the divine-human works *of* Jesus and the works of Father and Spirit *for* Jesus; and second, between the works that happen *in* time and the works that happen *to* time. In these ways, God works perichoretically (as Father) to constitute the structures of creation, (as Spirit) to open those structures for Christ as the fullness of the presence of God, and/or (in Christ) to move creation toward its promised end.[52] This is true not only of our redemption, but creation itself, which the New Testament insists came into being in Christ, by his agency, and for his glory.[53] And it is true of the consummating eschaton, as well. Scripture promises that when Christ appears in his glory—an appearance the Spirit effects for the Father's sake—creation will be thrilled into God and so transformed into its own fullness.[54] In this time between his ascension and creation's eschatological "end," Christ's incarnational ministry continues in and through the church's charismatic, diaconal, and sacramental life as the Spirit's temple.

50. See Macchia, *Baptized in the Spirit*, 128–29.

51. See Tanner, *Christ the Key*, 257–58.

52. I include the "and/or" because I am suggesting a distinction between the Spirit's and Son's works in moving creation toward its purpose. To be clear, I am assuming the doctrine of inseparable operations, but contending that within those operations, distinctions remain critical. Also, I am rejecting the doctrine of appropriations, following the reasoning of T. F. Torrance, *Christian Doctrine of God*, 200–201.

53. See, e.g., John 1:3; Eph 3:9; Col 1:16–17; Heb 1:2.

54. See, e.g., 1 Cor 13:12; Rom 5:2; Col 3:3; 1 John 3:2.

A few examples should help make the point: (a) creation and eschaton are both the works of Jesus and works of the Spirit and the Father for him, and they happen not in time, but to it. These works, like the ministry of Jesus within time, are most transparently grounded in the being-act of God, although of course they remain distinct from it. The difference between the creation and eschaton is that the first establishes the condition for our existence, and the latter effects the full realization of that existence as a share in the life that God creates in and through what happens with and for Jesus of Nazareth, Mary's son;[55] (b) Jesus's death, resurrection, and ascension are works of the Father and the Spirit for Jesus, and they happen both in time and to it; these works are the primary ways in which God opens creation for its promised future; or, in the language of Scripture, in these works God makes "new creation";[56] (c) the Eucharist is the work both of Jesus (as head of the *totus Christus*) and of the Father and the Spirit for him, and these works happen not to time but in it; we can get at this reality by asking, "Who gives what to whom in Communion?"; (d) Jesus's Sermon on the Mount was the work of Jesus for God's sake and ours, and happened not to time but in it; Matthew's account of that sermon, however, is given within time as the work of the Spirit for Jesus's sake and ours; (e) Peter's sermons about Jesus, as well as Luke's account of those sermons, both happen within time, not to it, and are not the work of Jesus himself but are inspired by the Spirit for Jesus's sake, as witness to him and his work.

Faith to Faith, Grace to Grace, Glory to Glory

Let me pause to summarize the central claims that I have proposed to this point: (1) we need to affirm God's immutability, but (2) we also need to insist that immutability is lively; (3) because God's actuality is in the structure of the triune relations, not only can we participate in God's life but also he can participate in ours; (4) God's creaturely participation comes in the works of Jesus and/or the works of the Father and the Spirit for Jesus; (5) and those works happen to time and/or in it, either by constituting creaturely reality, opening it up for God's presence, or directing it toward its constitutive end; (6) eschatologically, the works of God and the being-act of God are

---

55. As Tanner (*Christ the Key*, 144–45) puts it, "The incarnation is for the purpose of humanity's entrance into trinitarian relations. In enabling that entrance, the Word's becoming incarnate is for our sake rather than its own."

56. In Tanner's words (*Christ the Key*, 256–57), "Humanity is at one with the divine in Jesus. This is true of the cross as much as everywhere else in Jesus's life and that is what is saving about it. . . . God is taking saving action from the very first [moment of incarnation]."

at-one-ed for all things in Christ, so that creatures may be brought to the full realization of their being in God as "all in all."[57] In this final section, I want to make a last, and I believe equally crucial, claim: (7) the works of God come throughout our lives in an array of styles, all created to prepare us in Christ for eschatological transfiguration into the being-act of God.

In my judgment, we need distinctions like these if we hope to make sense of our lives with God and with one another in this time between Jesus's "going away" and his "coming again." What already has happened to Jesus in his resurrection—a reality we grasp by faith as we are grasped by it in hope—has not yet happened to us and to the rest of creation.[58] We stand convinced that everything that happens takes place within the providential unfolding of the will of God, and that nothing that happens takes place outside or in violation of that unfolding. And we believe that when God's will is finally fully realized, all things will be put right. Until then, all kinds of things happen, fortunate and unfortunate, good and evil, significant and insignificant, meaningful and absurd, and only some of them are works of God. Of course, even those things that are not God's doing take place within God's will, and so remain apt for God's use. Not all things are God's doing, but God nonetheless is at work in all things for our good.[59] That is why what others mean for evil—or do not mean for us at all—God can turn to our blessing. As a result, we will go on praying as Christ taught us to pray, acknowledging that God's will is not yet done "on earth as it is in heaven." And we will go on anticipating Christ's advent as the answer to that prayer, because the Spirit has promised that his appearance will effect finally and once for all the redemption, sanctification, and Spirit-baptism of all creation. Through the Spirit's intercession, Christ's appearance happens not in time but to it.[60] As the Spirit acts upon time in fullness, all creation will be made to see Christ within time as the fullness of the Father who is beyond time—just in that way creation will be transfigured into its own fullness.

That said, we must remember that we will rarely, if ever, be able to distinguish what God is doing from everything else that is happening to us. Truth be told, attempts to do so are very likely to end in either presumption or despair. This may sound like bad news, but I do not believe it is. As a friend once said to me, we are called to live from faith to faith, not from experience to experience. And rather than wondering if God is acting in

57. 1 Cor 15:28.
58. See, e.g., Heb 2:5–9 and Rom 8:18–25.
59. Rom 8:28.
60. Perhaps Jesus's prophecy (Matt 24:14) that the gospel of the kingdom must be proclaimed in the entire world as witness to all nations is fulfilled in this way?

any particular moment, we have only to ask how to respond faithfully to our circumstances so that God's work can form God's character in us in anticipation of our eschatological transfiguration.[61] In Pauline language, Christ is formed in us as we are being changed by the Spirit "from one degree of glory to another." By grace, we are being moved toward the actualization of our creatureliness in communion with all things.[62] In Johannine language, we are receiving grace from Christ's fullness in a dynamic and manifold movement that carries us from one grace to another.[63] For example, one grace brings us into being; another holds us in being; another brings us across the threshold of death. One grace endows us with gifts; another grace shapes our character by strengthening us to bear our lack of giftedness worthily. One grace comes as light; another as darkness. One grace moves us into a promised land of experiences in prayer; another leads us into the wilderness. These many graces, whatever their character, and however they come to us, are the works of God—that is, either the works of Jesus or the works of the Father and the Spirit on his behalf—transforming our lives for the sake of the kingdom.

We need not adopt medieval schemas of nature and grace to see that God brings about all kinds of good in an astonishing array of modes. Simply put, not all of God's works bear the same weight. For example, Rublev's icon is glorious, and I am confident that God was at work in his painting; and yet it is not glorious in the same way as Paul's letter to the Romans. These works are differently "inspired." Similarly, every sermon that makes the gospel heard is a work of God, as is every encounter with the beautiful (say, in rapturous song or architectural wonder). But, again, God is at work in them differently, effecting different graces. Some of God's works might be described as "miraculous" or "supernatural," while others might be called "natural." Some are "common"; others are "special." What matters, finally, is that all God's works have the same telos: to conform creation in its entirety to Christ's character and his divine-human share in the being-act of God.[64] And that end will come as God works within, upon, and without time to bring all things into perfect alignment with his own act-of-existing, God as God is in himself.

---

61. See Williams, "Philosophical Structures," 41.
62. 2 Cor 3:18.
63. John 1:16.
64. See Rom 8:29.

Conclusion

In conclusion, let me say a few words about how the model I have just sketched matters for me in the light of my Pentecostal upbringing. I certainly continue to expect God to work in my life—more than ever, in fact. But I make a radically different sense of that work now, and especially in relation to my "experiences." I am convinced that none of God's works, however powerful, deliver us out of faith and into sight.[65] As the Scriptures insist, in this present age we never see "face to face," but always only "through a glass darkly."[66] Whatever God does for us and whatever happens to us, we remain at every turn a people of *hope*—"and hope that is seen is not hope."[67] What does that mean for how we live and what we expect from God? We should pray for God to heal the sick. But we should know that a healed body is no closer to a resurrected body than a sick body is.[68] We should expect charismatic manifestations in our service to God and in our care for our neighbors. But we should remember that those manifestations are no truer God's doing than simple words offered in thanks for our food, a cup of water given to a stranger, or a visit to the sickbed of a neighbor.[69] After all, the "supernatural" is no more or less God's creation than the "natural," and God is no more present, and no more transformatively at work, in dramatic mystical experiences and dramatically miraculous incidents than in seasons of dryness and what St. John of the Cross calls "the dark night." We should remember this, too: even though God is at work in myriad ways in our lives, calling us to respond more and more faithfully, we are no nearer to God awake than asleep, in strength than in weakness, in faith than in doubt, in success than in failure, in mercy than in judgment. Because Christ shares our humanity of his own initiative and not in response to our decisions or even our desire, we are free to live with radical openness to and transparency before God and neighbor. Because Christ has been raised from the dead, translating his humanity and ours into the divine communion, we are free, like Mary, to make room in our lives for what only God can do. Because Christ has poured out the Spirit on "all flesh," we can be sure that as we are pouring ourselves out in attentive care of others, God is happening to and in and through and around us, empowering us to bear Christ's burden with

---

65. 2 Cor 5:7.

66. 1 Cor 13:12–13.

67. Rom 8:24.

68. Besides, a "healed" body remains "sick" in other ways, and obviously is no less mortal.

69. See Matt 10:40–42.

him.[70] Just in that way, we are moved by the Spirit from faith to faith by grace upon grace, primed and readied for our eschatological transformation into the triadic fullness of God.

Bibliography

Asamoah-Gyadu, J. Kwabena. "'You Shall Receive Power': Empowerment in Pentecostal/Charismatic Christianity." In *Pentecostal Mission and Global Christianity*, edited by Wonsuk Ma, Veli-Matti Kärkkäinen, and J. Kwabena Asamoah-Gyadu, 45–66. Regnum Edinburgh Centenary Series 20; Eugene, OR: Wipf & Stock, 2014.

Castelo, Daniel. "An Apologia for Divine Impassibility: Toward Pentecostal Prolegomena." *Journal of Pentecostal Theology* 19 (2010) 118–26.

———. "What if Miracles Don't Happen? Empowerment for Longsuffering." *Journal of Pentecostal Theology* 23 (2014) 236–45.

Jenson, Robert W. "The Bride of Christ." In *Critical Issues in Ecclesiology: Essays in Honor of Carl E. Braaten*, edited by Alberto L. Garcia and Susan K. Wood, 1–5. Grand Rapids: Eerdmans, 2011.

———. "Creation as a Triune Act." *Word & World* 2.1 (1982) 34–42.

———. "Ipse Pater Non Est Impassibilis." In *Divine Impassibility and the Mystery of Human Suffering*, edited by James F. Keating and Thomas Joseph White, 117–26. Grand Rapids, Eerdmans, 2009.

———. "The Logic of the Doctrine of the Trinity." *Dialog* 26.4 (Fall 1987) 245–49.

———. "Once More the Logos Asarkos." *International Journal of Systematic Theology* 13 (April 2011) 130–33.

———. *Systematic Theology*. Vol. 1, *The Triune God*. New York: Oxford University Press, 1997.

Kärkkäinen, Veli-Matti. "Pentecostalism and Pentecostal Theology in the Third Millennium: Taking Stock of the Contemporary Global Situation." In *The Spirit in the World: Emerging Pentecostal Theologies in Global Contexts*, edited by Veli-Matti Kärkkäinen, xiii–xxiv. Grand Rapids: Eerdmans, 2009.

Macchia, Frank. *Baptized in the Spirit: A Global Pentecostal Theology*. Grand Rapids: Zondervan, 2009.

Menzies, William, and Robert Menzies. *Spirit and Power: Foundations of Pentecostal Experience*. Grand Rapids: Zondervan, 2000.

Schindler, David L. "America's Technological Ontology and the Gift of the Given: Benedict XVI on the Cultural Significance of the Monastic *Quaerere Deum*." *Radical Orthodoxy* 1 (Sept. 2013) 426–53.

Smith, James K. A. *Thinking in Tongues: Pentecostal Contributions to Christian Philosophy*. Grand Rapids: Eerdmans, 2012.

Smith, James K. A. and Amos Yong, eds. *Science and the Spirit: A Pentecostal Engagement with the Sciences*. Bloomington: Indiana University Press, 2010.

Tanner, Kathryn, *Christ the Key*. Cambridge: Cambridge University Press, 2010.

Torrance, T. F. *The Christian Doctrine of God: One Being, Three Persons*. London: T. & T. Clark, 2016.

---

70. See Castelo, "What If Miracles Don't Happen?" 236–45.

Vondey, Wolfgang. "A Passion for the Spirit: Amos Yong and the Theology of Science Dialogue." In *The Theology of Amos Yong and the New Face of Pentecostal Scholarship*, edited by Wolfgang Vondey and Martin Mittlestadt, 180–197. Leiden: Brill, 2013.

Weinandy, Thomas. "God and Human Suffering: His Act of Creation and His Acts in History." In *Divine Impassibility and the Mystery of Human Suffering*, edited by James F. Keating and Thomas Joseph White, 99–116. Grand Rapids: Eerdmans, 2009.

Williams, Rowan. "God." In *Fields of Faith: Theology and Religious Studies for the Twenty-First Century*, edited by David F. Ford, Ben Quash, and Janet Martin Soskice, 75–89. Cambridge: Cambridge University Press, 2005.

———. "The Philosophical Structures of Palamism." *Eastern Churches Review* 9.1–2 (1977) 27–44.

Yong, Amos. "On Divine Presence and Divine Agency: Toward a Foundational Pneumatology." *Asian Journal of Pentecostal Studies* 3 (2000) 167–88.

———. *The Spirit of Creation: Modern Science and Divine Action in the Pentecostal-Charismatic Imagination*. Grand Rapids: Eerdmans, 2011.

———, ed. *The Spirit Renews the Face of the Earth: Pentecostal Forays in Science and Theology of Creation*. Eugene, OR: Pickwick, 2009.

CHAPTER 8

Restlessly Thinking Relation
Robert Jenson's Theological Uses of Hegel

STEPHEN JOHN WRIGHT

What does a doctrine of God conditioned by the gospel entail? Like forked lightning, this question has struck modern theology in numerous locations with great intensity. Revisionist theologians such as Wolfhart Pannenberg and Jürgen Moltmann have suggested that the events of history occur within the life of God. At this site of impact, the drama of Christ's travail to the cross is the drama of God's own life; God's very divinity is risked in the event of Christ's death and resurrection.[1] Elsewhere, the impact is felt in the work of figures such as David Bentley Hart, who champion a renewed commitment to divine impassibility as the most coherent vision of divine being according to the gospel; God draws close by being entirely unaffected by history's threats.[2] Modern theological projects tend to position themselves in relation to Hegel, who is regularly identified as the first great modernizer to collapse God's eternal being into history. In Trinitarian theology, these two points of impact are described by various configurations of the relation between the "immanent Trinity" and the "economic Trinity." At stake here is the identification of God's eternal life with the life that goes to the cross. The so-called historicizing and Hegelian

---

1. Pannenberg declares that "the Father made his deity dependent upon the success of the mission of the Son." Pannenberg, *Systematic Theology*, 2:391.

2. See, for example, Hart, *Experience of God*.

theologies of figures like Moltmann argue for an utter identity between the two, while the so-called classical theologies of theologians such as Hart employ distancing strategies such as analogy to open up a space between them. Both approaches operate with one eye looking back to the creeds to determine whether they are capacious enough to accommodate such proposals.

The American Lutheran Robert Jenson's particular way of abiding by creedal orthodoxy manifests itself in the theological task of working through the gospel-logic of Christianity. This entails a thinking-with, and not merely a thinking-after, the logic of the creeds. It would be a grave misreading of Jenson to suggest that his theology rests in perfect alignment with the preceding Western theological tradition. To do so would be to ignore his clearly stated intent to interrogate the metaphysical presuppositions that have so far dominated Western theology by the logic of the gospel, and to furnish his own proposals for metaphysical revision in order to evangelize fully our concepts and language.

Jenson's revisions have led to some theological proposals that induce a degree of consternation in readers who feel that Jenson has abandoned the safe harbors of Augustine and Aquinas for the putridly toxic bay of Hegel. It is now not uncommon to hear dismissive descriptions of the "Hegelian" character of his theology. And yet, the precise nature of Jenson's "Hegelianism" rarely receives attention. Something is afoot in Jenson's theology that whiffs of Hegel, and that something might just be his construal of time. From his doctoral thesis onwards, Jenson has railed against timeless divinity. God's eternity, he maintains, cannot be thought of as the mere negation of time. In his 1969 volume, *God After God*, Jenson identifies God with time, claiming that "time is the form of God's life with and for us."[3] Dissatisfied with Barth's attempt to relate God's time to ours, Jenson proposes that we think of God's relation to our time with respect to futurity. God's "time" is our future. Does Jenson mean to say that God's being is achieved through the progress of time? Does God start as pure potentiality that is actualized through history, so that God is *actus purus* only at the end? Has Jenson resolved all differences between God and creation into a pernicious univocity? These questions and more have been prompted by Jenson's denial of divine timelessness, which for many of his critics brings him dangerously close to Hegel.

In this essay, I set out to examine the "Hegelian" critique of Jenson's theology by looking first to the critiques of Jenson, then to the character of Hegel's own thinking, and then examining Jenson's explicit use of Hegel. I will argue that Jenson's theology does not follow the logic of a metaphysics

---

3. Jenson, *God After God*, 128.

of identity with creation, even if God is identified "by and with" his acts in history. Instead, Jenson's theology is ordered by a series of dialectical relations that do not culminate in a bland identity.[4] In this, there is indeed a certain Hegelian logic on display in Jenson's theology, but it is not the "pantheism" or "panentheism" for which Hegel has gained theological notoriety. I will thereby show that the numerous critiques of Jenson fail to take into full account his revision to eternity, tending to see his denial of eternal timelessness as a collapse of God into creaturely time. By overlooking Jenson's insistent rejection of the idea that God is subject to time, they fail to recognize the simultaneously dialectical[5] character of Jenson's proposed revision.

Theologians contra Hegel

It seems to have been Hegel's fate to be deplored by theologians. When working at the University of Berlin, Hegel found his entry into the Academy of Sciences blocked by his colleague, Friedrich Schleiermacher.[6] The advertised reason for this intervention in Hegel's career was the lack of need for speculative philosophy in the academy—an argument supported by August Böckh, who stated that since speculative philosophy is "self-contained" it "has no need of collegial work"[7]—though one might reasonably wonder if this explanation masked a set of deeper divisions between Hegel and Schleiermacher. Hegel suspected Schleiermacher of over-dependence upon Kant, and Schleiermacher distrusted Hegel's philosophical systematizing.[8] Moreover, the affable Schleiermacher commanded a popularity that the polarizingly awkward and difficult Hegel struggled to match. But whatever personal, philosophical, and theological differences they had, the exclusion from the academy intensified the dissonance between the two great figures to an irresolvable interval.

---

4. One could apply this reasoning to an entire series of interrelated instances of difference-in-relation in Jenson: the relations to the Trinity, the relation of God to creation, the relation of the church to Christ, the relation of the world to the kingdom, etc. Throughout, Jenson avoids reducing these to antithetical positions.

5. Jenson's theology is also, at times, deeply analogical.

6. Schleiermacher claimed that Hegel's work did not fit within the purview of the academy. Hegel returned the favor by establishing his own philosophical society, to which Schleiermacher was never admitted. The authoritative account of their time together in Berlin is Richard Crouter's article, "Hegel and Schleiermacher."

7. Crouter, "Hegel and Schleiermacher," 33.

8. Harnack claims that Schleiermacher at least wanted the academy to be free of the "despotism" of Hegel's system: "Schleiermacher fürchtete die Despotie der Hegel'schen Philosophie: wenigstens die Akademie sollte frei von ihr bleiben." Harnack, *Geschichte*, 735.

Numerous theologians and religious scholars today sympathize with Schleiermacher's misgivings about Hegel, although now the dissatisfaction lies with Hegel's reputed lack of theological orthodoxy. It is commonplace in many theological circles to say that Hegel's philosophy amounts to theogony. For Hegel, we hear, God becomes God through the course of history; Spirit self-actualizes through a process of alienation and return (*Aufhebung*); at the end of history, all creaturely differentiation is superseded into a new divine reality. As a result, history tells the story of God's life and forms the very basis of God's life. Not only can God not be thought of apart from the world, but God can have no reality apart from the world. Finally, then, according to this account, Hegel struggles to maintain the distinction between God and creation, establishing a form of dialectical pantheism. We find various renditions of this account among the theologians.

Lewis Ayres concludes his illuminating, historically meticulous, and rigorously argued work on pro-Nicene theology with something of a jeremiad against modern theology's incautious dabbling with Hegel.[9] In Ayres's account, the Hegelian legacy continues in modernity's resistance to premodern epistemology and hermeneutics, both of which have been allegedly overcome by later scholarship. Ayres argues that Hegelian epistemological progressivism produces ironically ahistorical theological engagement with the early Christian tradition, anachronistically "liberating" the creeds and doctrines into new metaphysical paradigms provided by modernity and underwritten by the forgetting of ancient models of knowledge. This allows Hegel and his readers to smuggle "not only difference but also anguish and suffering" into the life of God.[10] Hegel's chief legacy is found in the ever-closing space between divine and human experience.

David Bentley Hart picks up a similar line of argumentation, claiming that Hegel closes the gap between God and creation, allowing only a bland identity between the two at the cost of genuine difference. The dialectical union of apparent polarities renders necessary the relation of violence to peace, so that there can be no final perfect peace, but only a persistent "inevitable violence" and its "capricious god for whom creation and destruction are as one."[11] According to Hart, Hegel binds God to creation with a twofold necessity: the necessity of creation for God's own life, and the necessity of suffering as internal to the life of God. Hart contrasts Hegelian "totality" with Christian infinity, viewing the former as inimical to authentic difference, requiring all differences to be resolved into "the Same" in a grand

---

9. Ayres, *Nicaea and Its Legacy*, 384ff.
10. Ayres, *Nicaea and Its Legacy*, 406.
11. Hart, *Beauty of the Infinite*, 38–39.

cosmic *Aufhebung*.¹² Sympathetic with Hart's critique, D. Stephen Long identifies Hegel's chief theological legacy as the transposition of theology into theogony.¹³

Cyril O'Regan's scrupulous study of Hegel's theology elaborates on the awkward fit between Hegel's constructive theological proposals and orthodox Christian theology. Interestingly, O'Regan does not attempt simply to place Hegel outside of Christianity, but acknowledges Hegel's indebtedness to the theological tradition and Hegel's self-understanding as a Christian philosopher.¹⁴ O'Regan's more recent work focuses on the ways in which Hegel's thought was resisted by Hans Urs von Balthasar, as it "troubles Christian discourse, twists it, even twists it inside out" by carrying forward the "ancient ghosts" of theological options left behind by Christian orthodoxy.¹⁵

Theologians contra Jenson

What catches our interest in our present examination is the way that critiques of Hegel are extended to other later Christian thinkers—in particular, Robert Jenson. Sometimes, when reading the secondary sources, one might be forgiven for thinking that Hegel was Jenson's chief theological inspiration.¹⁶ Much of the discourse surrounding the allegedly Hegelian character of Jenson's theology appears to stem from George Hunsinger's highly critical 2002 review essay on Jenson's two-volume *Systematic Theology*. Despite many of the chief claims of Jenson's theology remaining settled since the late 1980s, negative discussion of Hegel in relation to Jenson prior to Hunsinger's essay is difficult to find.¹⁷ Hunsinger attempts to demonstrate that key moments of Jenson's system are determined by heretical influences. Jenson, Hunsinger claims, takes his cues from Socinius, Arius, and Hegel. "All the mistakes in Jenson's theology are the same. When they do not confuse what

---

12. Hart, *Beauty of the Infinite*, 137–38.
13. Long, *Perfectly Simple Triune God*, 385.
14. O'Regan, *Heterodox Hegel*.
15. O'Regan, *Anatomy of Misremembering*, 51.
16. For instance, Ayres trots out a list of modernizing theologians, with Jenson leading the pack, and Hart presents Jenson as a victim of Hegel's thorough systematizing of the God/world relation. Ayres, *Nicaea and Its Legacy*, 406.
17. Only two exceptions come to mind, both published in the same year as Hunsinger's review: Molnar, *Divine Freedom*; and Sholl, "On Robert Jenson's Trinitarian Thought."

ought to be kept distinct, they separate what ought to be kept as one."[18] If Jenson's God is baptized, the baptism "was administered by Hegel."[19] Despite Hunsinger's claim that "it is Hegel, more than any other, who determines Jenson's view of the Trinity," Hunsinger does not seem to be suggesting that Jenson relies directly on Hegel for his insights, but that he adopts a panentheistic metaphysics that leads to an irregular vacillation between identity and difference in which identity eventually wins out.[20] Jenson's system, in Hunsinger's view, establishes such clear identity between God and creation that "God is metaphysically conditioned by something other than God, that God cannot be God apart from the world, that God must be conceived in fundamental dependence upon his creation."[21] If Hunsinger's charge is correct, then Jenson does have some questions to answer. His critique has colored numerous subsequent works on Jenson.

In the revised form of his doctoral thesis, Scott Swain provides one of the most robust critical engagements with Jenson's theology ever produced. Swain divines a pernicious Hegelianism in Jenson, and locates a closure between God and creation in the alleged historicizing of divine being. To interrogate the extent to which Jenson ties God to history, Swain confidently navigates a host of material from theological history—spanning the range from patristics to theological modernity. Ultimately, he finds Jenson radicalizing a lightly Hegelian theology mediated to him by Barth.[22] For Swain, the dialectical logic of Hegelianism entails collision and overcoming. The original peacefulness of the triune relations perishes under the violent logic of Hegel who requires antithetical tensions that are overcome in synthesis. In Jenson, Swain reads this as the inability to "effect communion between . . . peacefully related dualities. . . . Jenson's revision is ironic because it ultimately reveals a failure to excise a false, contrastive view of the God-world relation from his theology. He has instead *dramatized* this false view, making it a moment in the story of God and creation, a moment that the Spirit must *transcend*. But *Aufhebung* is not the same thing as the

---

18. Hunsinger, "Robert Jenson's *Systematic Theology*," 162.

19. Hunsinger, "Robert Jenson's *Systematic Theology*," 175.

20. Hunsinger, "Robert Jenson's *Systematic Theology*," 175. Hunsinger's critique is notably short on textual evidence for his claims about Jenson's debt to Hegel. Texts that he presents as proving that Jenson considers God to be dependent upon the world do not hold up to scrutiny. On these, see Wright, *Dogmatic Aesthetics*, 102–19; and Wright, "Precise Mystery."

21. Hunsinger, "Robert Jenson's *Systematic Theology*," 176.

22. "Jenson's quest for a theological ontology appropriate to the gospel's God belongs to the historicizing family of approaches to the doctrine of God that emerged in the wake of Barth's theology." Swain, *God of the Gospel*, 63.

Spirit's *koinonia*."²³ Swain's critique follows the textbook Hegelian accounts of violence begetting new modes of being by the eradication of difference. He reads Jenson as claiming that God becomes God in the throes of history, with the contrastive difference between God and the world being overcome in the eschaton. Much of Swain's argument will be called into question in what follows.

Less moderately than Swain, Paul Molnar voices his full agreement with Hunsinger's critique of Jenson, claiming that Jenson's "Hegelianized version of Christianity" carries overt "adoptionist and Arian overtones" with a touch of "subordinationism and 'perhaps tritheism'" (which is quite a remarkable collection of heresies to execute in a single system).²⁴ Molnar rehearses familiar critiques of Jenson's Hegelianism, and its "making God in some sense dependent on the world for his own existence and inevitably confusing time and eternity."²⁵ This final point is telling, as the logic of Molnar's critique succeeds only if one takes for granted the very construal of time that Jenson attempts to revise. If one tries to reconcile Jenson's account of the incarnation with a conventional pairing of linear creaturely time with divine timeless eternity, then undoubtedly a confusion will arise. In line with the other "Hegelian" critiques of Jenson that tend toward theogony, necessity, or identity, Molnar spends very little time with the internal logic of Jenson's account.

Under the limitations of the present task, we will condense these charges to a set of themes common to these critiques of Jenson's theology: 1) that Jenson collapses the distinction between the immanent and the economic in a way that renders God's relation to creation necessary for God's own being; 2) that God becomes triune/divine through the course of history; and 3) that the distinction between God and the world collapses into perfect identity.

Many of these critiques involve a reconstruction of Jenson's arguments, which is then used as a mirror of Jenson's theology and is judged as a representation of his views. But Jenson does not see himself in these mirrors. Among these critics, Hart alone owns up to this rhetorical device, concluding his critique with, "Of course, Jenson says and intends none of this" only to proceed to reiterate his concerns.²⁶ Jenson questions the faithfulness

---

23. Swain, *God of the Gospel*, 202–3.

24. Most of the greatest heretics only managed to perform a single heretical theological move in their lives. Molnar, "Perils of Embracing," 461.

25. Molnar, "Perils of Embracing," 462.

26. Hart, *Beauty of the Infinite*, 166.

of these readings to his thought. Replying "abruptly"[27] to Molnar, Jenson writes, "If a reader takes [standard] metaphysics as unchallengeable, and assumes that the writer also must at bottom depend on it, he will, of course, discover the most horrid consequences and absurdities. But to the elucidation of the book or to the critique of its claims, these discoveries will be neither here nor there."[28] Similarly, of Hunsinger's critique, Jenson finds himself "loathe" to respond line-by-line to Hunsinger's reading.[29] So little does Hunsinger's rendition of Jenson's theology resemble his own intentions in the authoring of the *Systematics* that he quips that Hunsinger has seen his task as uncovering "what the text must 'really' say," taking cues from his reconstruction of the text rather than the text itself: "It has been suggested that the review before us may be the pioneering—if inadvertent—postmodernist review of a theological work."[30]

When called upon to review Hart's *The Beauty of the Infinite*, Jenson felt it proper to open with a disclaimer, since "Hart does me the honor—and I mean that straightforwardly—of spending eight prominent pages deploring my theology."[31] In Hart's narrative, Hegel presents one of the most pressing dangers to modern theological integrity, and he "needs a case study of a trinitarian theologian misled by Hegel."[32] Again, we see Jenson here distance himself from the Hegelian construction presented as a summary of his theology: "I think he [Hart] seriously misrepresents me."[33]

Perhaps the strongest response can be found in Jenson's comments upon Thomas Weinandy's critiques of his theology in the collected proceedings of a conference on impassibility. To the claim that God self-actualizes in history according to Jenson's theology, Jenson replies, "I have not said any such pseudo-Hegelian thing, nor do Weinandy's citations from my work entail the proposition."[34] Embedded within this defense rests a two-fold denial: Jenson distances himself from theogony, but his use of "pseudo" means he implicitly dismisses the idea that Hegel advocates a historicized theogony as well. In other words, neither the "Jenson" nor the "Hegel" targeted in these critiques rings true for Jenson. For this reason, he has never felt com-

---

27. This is how Jenson describes his earlier two-paragraph reply to Molnar in his "Response to Watson and Hunsinger," 225.
28. Jenson, "Reply," 132.
29. Jenson, "Response to Watson and Hunsinger," 230.
30. Jenson, "Response to Watson and Hunsinger," 232.
31. Jenson, "Review Essay," 235.
32. Jenson, "Review Essay," 235.
33. Jenson, "Review Essay," 235.
34. Jenson, "*Ipse Pater non est Impassibilis*," 117.

pelled to offer a robust defense of his alleged binding of God to creation. In Jenson's opinion, it seems, if Hunsinger's critique is right, then it is only God-according-to-Hegel-according-to-Jenson-according-to-Hunsinger who is condemned; Jenson's actual theology remains unscathed.

In what follows, I intend to explore whether Hegel and Jenson are "Hegelian" in the way these critics contend. To do so, we must first turn to the Hegel specialists.

Hegel among the Philosophers

Perhaps the two features of Hegel's philosophy that all interpreters can agree on are that it is brilliantly grand, and grandly difficult. Beyond this consensus, things get a little controversial. Hegel-interpretation splintered rapidly into left- and right-wing factions. These continued to fragment as Hegel's system was denounced (Kierkegaard) and inverted (Marx).

Some recent scholarship has paid more attention to the dynamics of Hegel's logic, and tends to critique the old standard accounts of his grandiose systematizing. David Kolb, in his careful study of Hegel and Heidegger, suggests that Hegel's logic cannot be discarded readily without damaging the intelligibility of his entire project. Hegel's logic provides "a study of the necessary structure of thought" and in this sense presents a metaphysics—not as a consuming ontology, but as an "analysis of the categories of thought."[35] Hegel's logic is metaphysics, Kolb explains, only in the manner of Kant's *Metaphysics of Morals*. In itself, this insight might not provide much relief for the theologians who worry that the defect lies in Hegel's dialectical logic that eradicates difference through sublation into new realities. For if the critics are right and the engine of Hegel's thought produces identity from difference, then we will inevitably end up with some form of pantheism or panentheism, as Hunsinger and others fear. However, this familiar critique provides only a very crude account of Hegel's logic.

Hegel's logic resists a neat separation of thinking and being, as though we could in Kantian fashion posit an encompassing world beyond our thinking about the given world. We cannot situate ourselves beyond the scope of our own thought to derive categories to make sense of reality which we then apply. "In this sense Hegel never makes ontological claims."[36]

The Kantian critique of the ontological argument, Hegel observes, requires a division between abstract concept and concrete reality. Kant essentially argues that "being" is not a predicate and therefore adds nothing

---

35. Kolb, *Critique of Pure Modernity*, 41.
36. Kolb, *Critique of Pure Modernity*, 87.

to the concept of "God." In his response, Hegel employs his distinction between representation [*Vorstellung*] and concept [*Begriff*]. What Kant treats as a concept of God is actually a mental representation of God. Hegel's *Vorstellung* does not entail being as a determination, but the *Begriff* does, though only in the case of God. This is not because we move from an interior "concept" to exterior "reality"—this would be the image-thinking of representation—but rather it is because representation finds itself in the concept, which entails being while remaining distinct from being.[37] This curious and difficult piece of dialectics accomplishes a logic of relation, where "being" and "thinking" falter as independent ideas, but gain content within their mutual determinations. In Kolb's summary, "Hegel says that his logic can be read as an extended version of the ontological argument for God. But this does not mean that the logic develops a set of categories and then proves they exist in reality as well as in the mind. . . . Rather, he is elevating our awareness of our own existence to an awareness of our full necessary conditions and context. There is no move from inside to outside."[38] For Hegel, Kant's critique of ontological arguments fails because it treats only the representation of God, and ignores the true concept without which the representation cannot truly be thought.

If we cannot order our knowing by a movement from interior thinking to exterior reality (or vice versa), can we order it temporally—from past to future, so that there arrives at the end of history a grand knowing subject? A glance at the table of contents for the *Phenomenology* might produce such an opinion. If we read the *Phenomenology* first as a lavish metaphysical system describing the emergence of Spirit from the detritus of history, then we will understand the concluding "absolute knowing" as the arrival of this final subject, who has finally fully transcended the inert externality of reality. However, if we read the *Phenomenology* within the context of the logic, then we can see with Kolb that "absolute knowing" presents "not some last and largest horizon of interpretation within which we see the true content of the world. . . . It is rather the transparency of the motion of pure thought that is the event of having a world."[39]

Despite a recent trend among some Hegel scholars such as Robert Pippin[40] to deny any metaphysics in Hegel, Kolb comes short of such a claim. Stephen Houlgate, in deep disagreement with Pippin's non-metaphysical reading, goes further than Kolb in presenting the *Logic* as metaphysics,

---

37. Hegel, *Lectures on the Philosophy of Religion*, 181–88.
38. Kolb, *Critique of Pure Modernity*, 87.
39. Kolb, *Critique of Pure Modernity*, 88.
40. See Pippin, *Hegel's Idealism*.

while still seeing a drastic revision in Hegel's metaphysics along the lines indicated above: thinking and being occur simultaneously. The *Logic* "does not suddenly shift from being an account of what there is to being an account of our own mental activity but remains throughout an account of the basic categories of thought and of the basic forms of being."[41] Houlgate interprets absolute knowing as a "self-critical openness to being," ruling out any "absolute closure."[42] Hegel's primary aim, therefore, is not the attempt to construct a metaphysical account of history within the emergence of "a wondrous new superentity,"[43] but the working of logic within the world. Hegel's system entails metaphysics, but is not driven by it.

This manner of rendering Hegel's system provides quite a different picture to that driving the critiques of Jenson offered by the theologians listed above. To see what promise this different account of Hegel might have for theology means looking to the theologians who admire Hegel.

Hegel among the Theologians

Somewhere in the late 1980s Rowan Williams appears to have undergone a Hegelian conversion from the old critiques to a new appreciation. This was undoubtedly in part due to the influence of Gillian Rose who revealed to him a Hegel shorn of teleology through a new attentiveness to Hegel's logic. "According to Rose, the most spectacular misunderstanding we could have of Hegel's *Phenomenology* is to suppose that it is an account of how consciousness absorbs its objects," and instead it "keeps us uneasy" about accounts of knowing and being, which pivot on the coming upon an inert world by an active consciousness.[44] Hegel troubles thinking.

The dialectical logic that Hegel champions refuses settled equivocations, because its underlying contention amounts to the conviction that all knowledge occurs within relations. As such, there could not be two self-contained realities about which to equivocate, and this simultaneously rebuts anything like what Thomas called univocity, since meaning is found in true difference. Hegel's work does not suggest that "thinking gets better by stages" but his "absolute" thinking amounts to "thinking of what is entailed in its own relatedness, in the fusion of interior and exterior, subject and object."[45] In Williams's interpretation of Hegel, thinking presents no "final

---

41. Houlgate, *Opening of Hegel's Logic*, 116.
42. Houlgate, *Opening of Hegel's Logic*, 58.
43. Kolb, *Critique of Pure Modernity*, 43.
44. Williams, "Between Politics and Metaphysics," 9.
45. Williams, *Edge of Words*, 192.

structural scheme" for the world, instead leading us into "a process of discovery in which there is always more otherness to encounter, the otherness of new perspective and new requirements for 'negotiation.'"[46]

Williams finds himself drawn to Hegel's logic of mediated knowledge, and does not seem to find it totally incompatible with Christian orthodoxy. That an object cannot be thought apart from its determination by another—by its being this and not that—might seem to render God's relation to the world necessary. But Williams attempts to show that Hegel's logic "yields" divine predicates such as simplicity, rather than presuming them.[47] Our concept of simplicity remains flawed, in Hegel's logic, while we think of it "as the pure negation of complexity and thus think the divine predicates in a static, discrete or world-dependent way."[48] Hegel's logic is restless, and provokes one to refuse tidy resolutions of conceptual tensions. Williams shows how Hegel will not allow us to think God as contained within the world, nor as merely a power that acts from outside the world, but "God's difference from the world is too radical to be expressed by any formulation that rests content with some version of 'God *and* the world', whether it is the world that determines God or God who defeats and overcomes the world."[49]

The dialectical movements are quite brisk and elaborate, but Williams points to the way in which Hegel situates logic within theology, as thinking occurs "within an infinite relatedness."[50] Since thinking itself depends upon the infinite grounding of God's life, Williams discerns strong resistance to pantheism and a compatibility with aseity in Hegel. But because of the dialectics, aseity can never settle into a safe grounding for the rest of our theological thinking. To think of God as either dependent upon or reposing apart from the world would be a breakdown in thinking.

All of this might make the theologian wary of a creeping dependency being written into the God-world relation. Can God be God without the world? Williams replies, "Hegel simply refuses us the vocabulary and conceptuality to put such a question intelligibly."[51] As we will see, we find here a strong affinity between Williams's reading of Hegel, and Jenson's theological system.

Williams gets us part of the way to seeing how Hegel's system might not necessarily bear all of the faults that his theological critics presume of

---

46. Williams, *Edge of Words*, 193.
47. Williams, "Logic and Spirit in Hegel," 39.
48. Williams, "Logic and Spirit in Hegel," 39.
49. Williams, "Logic and Spirit in Hegel," 39.
50. Williams, "Logic and Spirit in Hegel," 38.
51. Williams, "Logic and Spirit in Hegel," 47.

it. But it is the theologically bold proposal of Nicholas Adams that might provide the set of grammatical provisions and analogies we need to help us move forward. Like Williams, Adams chooses to focus on Hegel's logic, and indeed believes that one can make a formal distinction between this logic and Hegel's own material theological proposals.[52]

Adams's book commends Hegelian logic to theologians. In this task, Adams proposes that theologians understand Hegel's logic as "Chalcedonian."[53] At the level of logic, Adams holds that Hegel's philosophy presents a heavy reliance on doctrinal theology. Chalcedon stipulates a particular logic for understanding the incarnation; Christ's identity consists of two natures "without confusion, without change, without division, without separation; the distinction of the natures being in no way annulled by the union, but rather the characteristics of each nature being preserved and coming together to form one person and substance." Doctrinal error emerges when this logic is forgotten, as a quick survey of the christological heresies illustrates.[54] Arian theology treats divinity and humanity as occupying an oppositional relationship; Eutychian theology performs a false sublation in which difference is erased to create a new synthesis.

Hegel's "Chalcedonian logic" can be contrasted with a dualistic (binary) "Manichean logic," which understands all differences as situations of opposition.[55] This contrast provides a new vocabulary for the distinction between *Vorstellung* and *Begriff*. The Manichean oppositional logic is what Hegel calls *Vorstellung*, or "representation." And Adams's Chalcedonian logic expresses Hegel's *Begriff*, or "concept." The vocabulary Adams gives us might lead some readers to think that Chalcedonian logic is always to be preferred, but Adams argues that *Vorstellung* operates constructively in most cases. Cooking, for example, requires the oppositional choice between "cooked" or "not cooked."[56] In Adams's formulation, *Begriff* expresses "a non-oppositional logic that guides thinking about subject and object, or thinking and being," and therefore functions within specific circumstances.[57] Employing Hegelian dialectic does not provide one with a singular path from question to answer. Hegel's logic is not oriented toward outcomes.

Adams memorably likens reading Hegel to listening to Beethoven: the scale and majesty of the developments are not incidental to the work. To

---

52. The latter of which Adams finds to be a bit questionable.
53. An idea he adopts from Martin Wendte. Adams, *Eclipse of Grace*, 21.
54. And Adams rightly provides such a survey. Adams, *Eclipse of Grace*, 6–7.
55. Adams, *Eclipse of Grace*, 23.
56. Adams, *Eclipse of Grace*, 24.
57. Adams, *Eclipse of Grace*, 31.

ask only after Hegel's conclusions "is as crass as to press fast forward on the remote during a Beethoven symphony."[58] Hegel performs his dialectic. Like a piece of music, its sensibility lies in its extension over time.[59] A lack of attentiveness to this insight results in the oversimplified accounts of Hegel bandied about in much theological discourse. The third moment in the dialectic—the sublation—functions within an ongoing process, and is not the goal and outcome of the logic. Relations define knowledge and direct thinking.

Thinking operates precisely when it relates *Vorstellung* to *Begriff*, so that the thinker refuses to settle for Manichean oppositions. Seen this way, we can understand Hegel's entire system as a series of thinking difference within relation in a manner akin to the two-natures Christology of Chalcedon. Hegel thinks difference in a way that is open to being (Houlgate) and so disrupts standard Manichean oppositions by situating them alongside other relations. Sublation [*Aufhebung*] does not eradicate difference, but situates differences within relation. Manichean difference does not merge into a Eutychian conflation, but a Chalcedonian inseparable relation "where terms retain their distinctness."[60]

A More Hegelian Jenson

This path of inquiry through dialogue with Hegel specialists moves the discussion of Jenson forward quite considerably. Ironically, it appears that the concerns raised by Jenson's critics will be alleviated by a more thoroughly Hegelian reading of his thought, which pays closer attention to the contours of dialectical logic, moving beyond the textbook accounts that misread *Aufhebung* as an erasure of difference.

We glimpse moments of implicit Hegelian logic—Adams's "Chalcedonian logic"—in numerous areas of Jenson's thought. Given that the critiques of Jenson outlined above center on claims of reductive identity between God and creation, of particular interest for our discussion is the relation of difference and identity. The three themes of critique outlined above—making creation necessary to God's being, the self-actualization of God through history, and the collapse of the distinction between God and the world—all rest on the question of what *Aufhebung* does in Jenson's theology. Is sublation

---

58. Adams, *Eclipse of Grace*, 14.

59. Williams points out that, for the logic, this temporalizing need only be metaphorical—a "transcription" into the language of history—rather than a collapsing of God into history.

60. Adams, *Eclipse of Grace*, 99.

the eradication of difference into a new totality, or does it maintain difference in relation?

For example, Swain critiques Jenson on two fronts, suggesting both: 1) that for Jenson God's eternal life is identical with the events of history; and 2) that Jenson's theology is fundamentally composed out of a logic of opposition and conflict. For both of these charges, Swain directs our attention to Jenson's dabbling with Hegel. But, as we have seen from Adams and Williams, Hegel's dialectical logic maintains difference in relation. The opposite of incommensurable alterity is not identity, but precisely this kind of dialectic. If this is also true of Jenson, then it undermines both of Swain's points of critique.

Our task here will be to look for the function of *Aufhebung* in Jenson's theology, to see if it maintains difference-in-relation. If it does, then his mode of Hegelian engagement would be closer to Williams and Adams than the theogony defined by his critics. By his own account, Jenson was largely ignorant of Hegel prior to his arrival in Heidelberg for his doctoral studies. While there, he undertook instruction in German philosophy under the direction of a young Wolfhart Pannenberg. He learned from Pannenberg that Hegel cancels out all of history with one final sublation, and so undoes all of his attentiveness to the particularity of history's developments. Jenson found Hegel disappointing.[61] He would proceed to critique Hegel in his early theological writing, arguing in *God after God* that an "anti-historical drive" permeates Hegel's system, due to the "cancellation of all finite things in infinity" in the self-actualization of Spirit.[62] *Aufhebung*, at this point, is seen by Jenson as the "self-overcoming of contradiction" and is best left alone. However, Jenson soon left this caricature of Hegel behind.

In *The Triune Identity*, published in 1982, Jenson makes positive— though not uncritical—use of Hegel. Here, Jenson contrasts Hegel with Schleiermacher. The doctrine of the Trinity in Schleiermacher's *The Christian Faith* serves as a memory tool to keep God's presence in Christ fixed firmly in our minds.[63] What the doctrine cannot do, Schleiermacher teaches, is provide a coherent doctrine of God. In this regard, Jenson prefers Hegel. With a newfound appreciation for Hegel, Jenson now sees that the German thinker makes a synthesis out of Greek rationality and biblical history to say that "history makes its own kind of sense, which is the sense not of a merely beholding and sense-describing mind, but of the living and sense-creating

---

61. Jenson, "Theological Autobiography," 49.
62. Jenson, *God After God*, 34–35.
63. Jenson, *Triune Identity*, 133.

spirit."⁶⁴ This new formulation arises from the bringing together of two alternatives into a unique rational union, but Jenson modifies Hegel on two points: he translates *Aufhebung* as "reconciliation" rather than "negation" or "sublation," and he makes this "reconciliation" the act of Christ rather than the universal logic of created history.

This latter move is more overt in a subsequent piece of writing on the Holy Spirit for a two-volume dogmatics intended for Lutheran classrooms.⁶⁵ In this piece, Jenson famously—notoriously?—claims that Hegel can be redeemed: "To reclaim Hegel's truth for the gospel, we need only a small but drastic amendment: Absolute consciousness finds its own meaning and self in the *one* historical object, Jesus."⁶⁶ Commenting on this claim, Hart warns that "we flirt here with calamity," for lurking behind this seemingly evangelical substitution lies the brutal mechanism of Hegel's dialectical machine which will tie God to the world in a relation of necessity.⁶⁷ But Hart elides the logic of Jenson's revision of Hegel. Jenson's revision lies not in a mere substitution, but in a complete subversion and subjugation of the dialectic to the Lordship of the risen Christ. "The specific Lordship of Christ outside the church occurs when and where the miracle of Hegelian 'synthetic' creativity actually occurs."⁶⁸ As such, Jenson adapts Hegel's basic insight—history has a certain logic—and makes it the logic of Christ's intervening freedom in history. Jenson's Hegelian talk of "Spirit finding its object in Christ" here is merely positing the identity of the one who makes sense of history by bringing conflicts to resolution.⁶⁹ Here we have Jenson operating according to a modified metaphysical "big entity" reading of Hegel, but instead of the "big entity" being the outcome of dialectical history, this entity is the freedom and possibility of that history—what Christians tend to call "providence."

In exceptionally candid moments when Jenson suspends his regular rhetorical reserve, he comments directly on his reading of Hegel's logic. "It may be noted that I am—if any kind of Hegelian—a 'right-wing' one, in that

---

64. Jenson, *Triune Identity*, 135.
65. Jenson, "Holy Spirit," 101–78.
66. Jenson, "Holy Spirit," 169.
67. Hart, *Beauty of the Infinite*, 157.
68. Jenson, "Holy Spirit," 2:169.

69. Jenson acknowledges throughout this rendering how he is willfully avoiding asking whether this is Hegel's own account, and instead asserts it as his new modification of Hegel. Williams presents a similar rendition of Hegel's logic, though in less dogmatic terms: "To think what is real, in the *Logic*, . . . is to affirm the thinkable character of contingent particulars, and, precisely in so doing, to think what is not any particular but that which 'holds' the flow of one particular into another." Williams, "Logic and Spirit," 39.

in my judgement the attainment of a *Begriff* does not leave the *Vorstellung* behind, indeed the *Begriff* does not function in actual thought without its *Vorstellung*."[70] Here, Jenson appears to be in explicit agreement with Hegel specialists who posit that Hegel's dialectic maintains rather than eradicates difference. Like Adams, Jenson also observes a distinction between Hegel's theology and Hegel's logic. Indeed, he finds Hegel's metaphysics distressing, and so engages Hegel at the level of logic. He warns that theology cannot merely adopt Hegel's "whole doctrine of spirit and history."[71] At one point he finds himself driven to describe Hegel as a "theological disaster."[72] Nevertheless he is drawn to Hegel's account of making "sense" of history. That is, Jenson identifies with Hegel's description of thinking.

Jenson Thinking Relation

This provides us with enough background to return to those passages in Jenson's system that have proved to be the most distressing to his critics. Swain's critique that "*Aufhebung* is not the same as the Spirit's koinonia" becomes more difficult to maintain when one pays close attention to Jenson's deployment and revision of Hegelian logic. Or, at the least, it will require a bit more argument to become compelling. Jenson's account of Christ's transcendence over history by bringing about its consummation—framed in the Hegelian logic of *Aufhebung*—refuses the kind of inevitable pseudo-Hegelian supersession that Swain seems to have in mind. With this observation we also see that Jenson does not appear to be advocating the narrative of modern epistemological triumph that troubles Ayres.

Hunsinger and others have expressed concern that Jenson's theology collapses the distinction between God and creation by historicizing the being of God. Hunsinger claims that Jenson frequently implodes essential distinctions and bifurcates necessary unions. Hunsinger appears to be struggling against Jenson's appropriation of Hegel's "Chalcedonian logic" of difference in relation. With particular strength, Jenson does indeed claim that "God himself is identified by and with the particular plotted sequence of events that make the narrative of Israel and her Christ."[73] What Jenson does not suggest here is that God *becomes* God through this history. Indeed, he makes recourse to Barth to claim that God chooses to be God in this

---

70. Jenson, *On Thinking the Human*, 1n1.

71. Jenson, "Anima Ecclesiastica," 64n14. See also, Jenson, *On Thinking the Human*, 78: "Hegel himself is finally no help."

72. Jenson, "Great Transformation," 40.

73. Jenson, *Systematic Theology*, 1:60.

history.⁷⁴ And yet this does not alleviate the apparent offense. For it appears that this view introduces an ontological fickleness into God's being. Jenson attempts to secure both the transcendence and contingency of God's life by saying that God could have been "the same God . . . other than Jesus the Son and his Father and their Spirit" but "what that would have been like, we can know or guess nothing whatsoever."⁷⁵ Hart finds this account intolerable: "If God could be God otherwise, then he already is God otherwise."⁷⁶ But Hart's critique—as with Hunsinger's, Swain's, and Molnar's—attempts to critique Jenson's thought by translating its logic into a different metaphysics. A more thoroughly Hegelian reading of Jenson will distance him from historicizing Hegelianism.

As was observed through Williams, Hegel's logic resists our asking questions of God's identity apart from the world. We do not have access to a thought-world of discrete objects where persons and things become susceptible to speculation in isolation. In the case of theology, we are on dubious ground whenever we attempt to abstract from the world to God, because if we cannot think God in relation then we cannot think God at all.⁷⁷ Like Hegel, Jenson resists an opposition between thinking and being. "God's knowability cannot be understood in isolation from other ways in which being is openness to participation."⁷⁸ In Jenson's theology, therefore, God provides the conditions of human thinking. He does indeed speak of God as thinkable only in Christ, but he partners this affirmation (thesis) with the claim that God would be God apart from the world (antithesis), without resolving the tension in either direction. To imagine God apart from the Christ would be to have a *Vorstellung*, but God only enters thought as this relates to a *Begriff* in the affirmation that God is known through difference in relation.

Since we are thinking of relation to God, the relation cannot be merely symmetrical. Just as Williams summarizes Hegel, "God's difference from the world is too radical" to be captured by pairing "God and the world,"⁷⁹ Jenson writes that it would be an "error" to "think of God as simply one thing and creatures as another, and then inquire how the second, given its capabilities, can know the first, given its characteristics."⁸⁰ The critiques suppose that

74. Jenson, *Systematic Theology*, 1:140.
75. Jenson, *Systematic Theology*, 1:141.
76. Hart, *Beauty of the Infinite*, 162.
77. Which is, of course, the terminus of much modern liberal theology.
78. Jenson, *Systematic Theology*, 1:225.
79. Quoted above.
80. Jenson, *Systematic Theology*, 1:224. On God's "knowability" in Jenson, see

Jenson must be operating according to the distinction between thinking and being, so that he is establishing the conditions for God's reality, rather than expounding the gospel-logic of God's revelation in history.

This point appears in quite stark relief in an earlier work. Here Jenson appears at his most radically Pannenbergian: God's "identity with himself must truly be at risk as Moses and the Pharaoh struggle or as Jesus dies."[81] Can God's life be so very historically contingent as to be susceptible to risk? On the very next page Jenson disrupts this collapse of God into history: "the resurrection of Jesus could not be believed in advance but afterward is plainly the only thing that could have happened."[82] As with Williams, "we can't think necessity forwards without falling into fantasy."[83] Jenson's use of dialectic becomes visible in his refusal to treat these twin affirmations as antithetical, rather they are dialectically related and therefore dialectically compatible.

Jenson's resistance to theogonic readings becomes more pronounced once we begin to appreciate the subtly dialectal character of many of his claims. For instance, Hart and Hunsinger question Jenson's rendition of Barth's doctrine of election: that God is God-for-us as a self-determining act of election. Hunsinger infers typical Hegelian theogony here, asserting that for Jenson, "only in the course of history does the trinity work out its own self-actualization."[84] In Hunsinger's view, Jenson claims that God becomes triune through the processes of history, and this provides an explanation for Jenson's persistent denial of the *logos asarkos*.[85] The centrality of Jenson's revision of divine time becomes visible when such questions are raised.

From the beginning of his theological career, Jenson has dismissed the idea that eternity equates to divine timelessness. To determine God's relation to time as antithesis to creaturely time would be crudely equivocal—a point that one suspects should evoke sympathy from theologians of analogy. For Jenson, to suggest that God either must be timeless or subject to time amounts to a false opposition—an instance of Adams's "Manichaean logic." The denial of timelessness invites us to the difficult theological work of thinking God's relation to creation. For Jenson, this means also avoiding "plotting the triune life on a time line," where "before" and "after" would be univocally predicated

---

Wright, "Precise Mystery."

81. Jenson, *Unbaptized God*, 140.
82. Jenson, *Unbaptized God*, 141.
83. Williams, "Logic and Spirit," 48.
84. Hunsinger, "Robert Jenson's *Systematic Theology*," 172.

85. It should be noted that Jenson, in his doctoral writings, critiqued Barth for his denial of the *logos asarkos*, but quickly changed his mind on the matter. For details, see Wright, *Dogmatic Aesthetics*, 21–23.

of creatures and of God.[86] Jenson refuses the introduction of sequence within God's life. God's relation to creaturely time is presence, not duration or subjection. "Nothing in God recedes into the past or approaches from the future."[87] Having made these moves, Jenson makes the final affirmation that one would expect to arise out of these dialectics: "It indeed better suits the gospel's God to speak of 'God's time' and 'created time,' taking 'time' as an analogous concept, than to think of God as not having time."[88] This move is simultaneously Thomistic and Hegelian; the appeal to analogy serves to establish a positive relation between God and time, rather than a pure denial of such a relation. *Aufhebung* maintains the analogical distance between the two *Vorstellungen* to allow *begrifflich* thought. For Jenson, the God revealed in Christ is evoked in theology only through the thinking of these relations and the avoidance of all lazy equivocations and univocities.

Any critique that suggests that Jenson argues that God becomes God through a sequence of events over the passage of time fundamentally misunderstands Jenson's most central theological revision. It is because his logic articulates a theological vision of difference in relation that Jenson concludes his system with a sounding of musical harmony: God is a great fugue. Jenson's musical imagining of God's life enfolding ours depicts not the loss of creaturely difference, but harmony *establishes* this difference as we are drawn into the difference-in-relation of God's own triune life. Throughout this account, Jenson maintains the asymmetry of the relation of creatures to God, and his manner of articulating participation follows in patristic footsteps by speaking of union with Christ. In fluent Hegelian he affirms that the eschatological vision—the final "reconciliation [*Aufhebung*]"—will establish harmony by maintaining difference: "He will give us each other's differences as the very opportunities of solidarity."[89]

Conclusion

It has been my contention in this essay that Jenson's critics who have attempted to dismiss him by associating him with Hegel have not treated

---

86. Jenson, *Systematic Theology*, 1:140. Jenson, of course, does not use this Thomistic language in this argument.

87. Jenson, *Systematic Theology*, 2:35.

88. Jenson, *Systematic Theology*, 2:35. Jenson's developing accounts of impassibility should also be read through this logic, rather than simplifying his account into Moltmannian passibility (which he explicitly denies). Jenson, "*Ipse Pater non est Impassibilis.*"

89. Jenson, *Story and Promise*, 64.

Jenson as Hegelian enough.[90] Once the dialectical (Chalcedonian) logic is uncovered, we see that Jenson's rendition of the God/world relation does not collapse God into history, but maintains that Christ is the Lord of history, bringing resolution to conflicts and drawing all of our differences into a future kingdom of peaceable relation.

According to Jenson, theology must maintain the twin affirmations that God's identity is intimately tied to the events of history and that God transcends that same history. Any other formulation risks falsely confident comprehension of God's life. Jenson's theological project avoids the historicizing of Moltmann, but also the safely analogical theology of Hart. Theological reasoning is a dangerous enterprise, with all of our theological constructions liable to be undermined by the reality of God.

Bibliography

Adams, Nicholas. *The Eclipse of Grace: Divine and Human Action in Hegel*. Malden, MA: Wiley-Blackwell, 2013.
Ayres, Lewis. *Nicaea and Its Legacy: An Approach to Fourth-Century Trinitarian Theology*. Oxford: Oxford University Press, 2004.
Crouter, Richard. "Hegel and Schleiermacher at Berlin: A Many-Sided Debate." *Journal of the American Academy of Religion* 48 (1980) 19–43.
Harnack, Adolf von. *Geschichte der königlich preussischen Akademie der Wissenschaften zu Berlin*, I/2. Berlin: Reichsdruckerei, 1900.
Hart, David Bentley. *The Beauty of the Infinite: The Aesthetics of Christian Truth*. Grand Rapids: Eerdmans, 2003.
———. *The Experience of God: Being, Consciousness, Bliss*. New Haven: Yale University Press, 2013.
Hegel, Georg Wilhelm Friedrich. *Lectures on the Philosophy of Religion: The Lectures of 1827*. Edited by Peter C. Hodgson. Translated by R. F. Brown, P. C. Hodgson, and J. M. Stewart. One-volume ed. Oxford: Clarendon, 2006.
Houlgate, Stephen. *The Opening of Hegel's Logic: From Being to Infinity*. West Lafayette, IN: Purdue University Press, 2006.
Hunsinger, George. "Robert Jenson's *Systematic Theology*: A Review Essay." *Scottish Journal of Theology* 55 (2002) 161–200.
Jenson, Robert W. "Anima Ecclesiastica." In *God and Human Dignity*, edited by. R. Kendall Soulen and Linda Woodhead, 59–71. Grand Rapids: Eerdmans, 2006.
———. *God After God: The God of the Past and the God of the Future as Seen in the Work of Karl Barth*. Philadelphia: Fortress, 1969.
———. "The Great Transformation." In *The Last Things: Biblical and Theological Perspectives on Eschatology*, edited by Carl E. Braaten and Robert W. Jenson, 33–41. Grand Rapids: Eerdmans, 2002.
———. "The Holy Spirit." In vol. 2 of *Christian Dogmatics*, edited by Carl E. Braaten and Robert W. Jenson, 101–78. Philadelphia: Fortress, 1984.

---

90. Or Hegel, for that matter.

———. "Ipse Pater non est Impassibilis." In *Divine Impassibility and the Mystery of Human Suffering*, edited by James F. Keating and Thomas Joseph White, 117–26. Grand Rapids: Eerdmans, 2009.

———. *On Thinking the Human: Resolutions of Difficult Notions*. Grand Rapids: Eerdmans, 2003.

———. "A Reply." *Scottish Journal of Theology* 52 (1999) 132.

———. "Response to Watson and Hunsinger." In *Scottish Journal of Theology* 55 (2002) 225–32.

———. "Review Essay: David Bentley Hart, *The Beauty of the Infinite*." *Pro Ecclesia* 14 (2005) 235–37.

———. *Story and Promise: A Brief Theology of the Gospel about Jesus*. Philadelphia: Fortress, 1973.

———. *Systematic Theology*. 2 vols. New York: Oxford University Press, 1997–99.

———. "A Theological Autobiography, to Date." *Dialog* 46:1 (Spring, 2007) 46–54.

———. *The Triune Identity: God According to the Gospel*. Philadelphia: Augsburg Fortress, 1982.

———. *Unbaptized God: The Basic Flaw in Ecumenical Theology*. Minneapolis: Fortress Press, 1992.

Kolb, David. *The Critique of Pure Modernity: Hegel, Heidegger, and After*. Chicago: University of Chicago Press, 1986.

Long, D. Stephen. *The Perfectly Simple Triune God: Aquinas and His Legacy*. Minneapolis: Fortress, 2016.

Molnar, Paul. *Divine Freedom and the Doctrine of the Immanent Trinity: In Dialogue with Karl Barth and Contemporary Theology*. London: T. & T. Clark, 2002.

———. "The Perils of Embracing a 'Historicized Christology.'" *Modern Theology* 30 (Oct. 2014) 455–80.

O'Regan, Cyril. *The Anatomy of Misremembering: Von Balthasar's Response to Philosophical Modernity*. Vol. 1, *Hegel*. New York: Herder and Herder, 2014.

———. *The Heterodox Hegel*. Albany, NY: SUNY Press, 1994.

Pannenberg, Wolfhart. *Systematic Theology*. Vol. 2. Translated by Geoffrey W. Bromiley. Grand Rapids: Eerdmans, 1994.

Pippin, Robert. *Hegel's Idealism: The Satisfactions of Self-Consciousness*. Cambridge: Cambridge University Press, 1989.

Sholl, Brian K. "On Robert Jenson's Trinitarian Thought." *Modern Theology* 18 (2002) 27–36.

Swain, Scott R. *The God of the Gospel: Robert Jenson's Trinitarian Theology*. Downers Grove, IL: IVP Academic, 2013.

Williams, Rowan. "Between Politics and Metaphysics: Reflections in the Wake of Gillian Rose." *Modern Theology* 11 (January 1995) 3–22.

———. *The Edge of Words: God and the Habits of Language*. London: Bloomsbury, 2014.

———. "Logic and Spirit in Hegel." In *Wrestling with Angels: Conversations in Modern Theology*, edited by Mike Higton, 35–52. Grand Rapids: Eerdmans, 2007.

Wright, Stephen John. *Dogmatic Aesthetics: A Theology of Beauty in Dialogue with Robert W. Jenson*. Minneapolis: Fortress, 2014.

———. "A Precise Mystery." In *The Promise of Robert Jenson's Theology: Constructive Engagements*, edited by Chris E. W. Green and Stephen John Wright, 9–28. Minneapolis: Fortress, 2017.

CHAPTER 9

Trinitarian Science?
Torrance, Polkinghorne, and McGrath on a Christian Interpretation of the Natural World

GIJSBERT VAN DEN BRINK

You could not get a more fundamental theory than that which Trinitarian theology offers to us.[1]

1. Introduction

In a recent paper Canadian biologist and theologian Denis Lamoureux criticizes theologians like T. F. Torrance, Alister McGrath, and John Polkinghorne who argue that constructing a natural theology or theology of nature should be done from a Trinitarian perspective.[2] Being unable to find out how Torrance, Polkinghorne, and McGrath actually integrate Trinitarian thinking in their reflections on theology and science, Lamoureux concludes that "[t]his all strikes me as being merely fashionable Christian rhetoric."[3] In this essay, I will investigate whether Lamoureux has a point here. In doing

---

1. Polkinghorne, *Science and the Trinity*, 90.
2. Lamoureux, "Do the Heavens Declare," 36n19.
3. Lamoureux, "Do the Heavens Declare," 36.

so, I don't have any strong preexisting opinions in one direction or the other. On the one hand, "Trinitarian" has indeed become a buzzword in certain parts of contemporary Christian theology, and Lamoureux's reservations on this point are shared by other theologians who have come to criticize the recent "Trinitarian renaissance."[4] On the other hand, intimations in Torrance, McGrath, and Polkinghorne that a Christian evaluation of nature could only be appropriately developed along Trinitarian lines may be more convincing than Lamoureux wants to concede. In what follows, I will explore whether that is the case by asking what difference the doctrine of the Trinity might make for our view on the scientific study of nature. In doing so, I follow up a heuristic suggestion that is implicit in the work and life of Colin Gunton, namely that the entire business of theology—and even Christian thought more generally conceived—should proceed from a Trinitarian perspective.[5]

So what has the Trinity to do with science? I will first discuss the relationship between Trinitarian doctrine and the calling of the sciences according to Thomas F. Torrance (1913-2007) (§2). Next, I will turn to John Polkinghorne's views on the topic (§3), in order to then discuss Alister McGrath's position (§4). Of course, these three thinkers have much in common, since both McGrath and Polkinghorne can be considered pupils of Torrance. Still, as we shall see, there are also significant differences between them. I will end up with a brief evaluation (§5).

2. An Unresolved Tension: Thomas Torrance on the Trinity and the Sciences

This is not the place to review Torrance's elaborate views of the relationship between what he called "theological science" and the natural sciences. Instead, I will focus on how these views hang together with the thoroughly Trinitarian character of Torrance's theological thought. In his landmark analysis of Torrance's theology, Paul Molnar sets out to show that "Torrance's thinking is deeply structured around his understanding of the triune God."[6] Indeed, Torrance considered the doctrine of the Trinity

---

4. Stephen R. Holmes's plea for a much more sober and reticent Trinitarian theology along (a number of) patristic lines is a case in point here. See most extensively his *Quest for the Trinity*.

5. Cf. Metzger, "Introduction," in Metzger, *Trinitarian Soundings*, 6. For one example of how Gunton himself developed this basic idea, see his still impressive study *The One, the Three and the Many*. One may wonder whether the recent Trinitarian renaissance would have declined so suddenly as it did if Gunton had survived until today.

6. Molnar, *Thomas F. Torrance.*, 2; cf. 31: "For T. F. Torrance, the doctrine of the Trinity is the central doctrine around which all other Christian doctrines gravitate and

as the ultimate ground of theological knowledge of God, the basic grammar of theology, for it is there that we find our knowledge of God reposing on the final Reality of God himself, grounded in the ultimate relations intrinsic to God's own Being, which govern and control all knowledge of him from beginning to end.[7]

At the same time, Molnar rightly notes that Torrance "is perhaps the most widely known for his study of science and Christian theology."[8] This raises the question that concerns us here: how, if at all, did the central place Torrance attributed to the doctrine of the Trinity in his thinking affect his work on the relationship between theology and the sciences? Molnar definitely sees an analogy between both, in that according to Torrance both theology and science must conform themselves to the unique objects of their respective inquiries, namely the God who reveals himself as triune on the one hand and the world of nature that presents itself as real on the other. In both cases, we should resist the temptation to impose our own thoughts, experiences, and ideas onto the objects of our investigation, since these will "distort the objective reality we are attempting to conceptualize."[9] According to Molnar, Torrance was keen to keep apart the unique objects of inquiry that determine theology on the one hand and the sciences on the other. "His view of natural science affected his view of theological science, but always with a view toward *distinguishing* the unique objects of reflection that determine each."[10]

In line with this, Molnar is inclined to consider the "new natural theology" that Torrance developed on the basis of his engagement with the sciences as a kind of *Fremdkörper* in his theology.[11] This is strange, however, since it is precisely here—in the outline of a new natural theology—that the two main foci of Torrance's intellectual interest seem to converge. Now Torrance's specific reconstruction of natural theology has rightly been claimed to be "one of the most difficult aspects of his theology."[12] It is clear that, along with Barth, Torrance rejects the traditional kind of natural theology that become comprehensible."

7. Torrance, *The Ground and Grammar of Theology*, 158–59.

8. Molnar, *Thomas F. Torrance*, 2.

9. Molnar, *Thomas F. Torrance*, 23, with a general reference to T. F. Torrance, *Theological Science*.

10. Molnar, *Thomas F. Torrance*, 29. My italics.

11. Molnar, *Thomas F. Torrance*, 93–99 (cf. esp. Molnar's criticism from within Torrance's own theological premises on 98–99).

12. Colyer, *How to Read T. F. Torrance*, 192 (note the conjunction "Trinitarian and Scientific" in the subtitle, which leaves open how exactly the two are related).

considers itself as a source of knowledge of God *prior to* the actual knowledge of God that comes to us through faith in the God who reveals himself in Jesus Christ. It is also clear that Torrance interprets Barth in such a way that a natural theology that is *included within* revealed theology (rather than preceding it) is legitimate. This kind of natural theology would most naturally amount to what is usually called a theology of nature: a theological interpretation of the natural world in light of the gospel.[13] Instead, however, Torrance continued to speak of a natural theology here, albeit a "new" one, and suggested that the structure of the universe as such, i.e., *independent of God's self-revelation in Christ*, contains intimations of the existence of a Creator God. In particular, in his view it is the sheer comprehensibility of the natural order that "would seem to suggest that there is an active agency other than the inherent intelligibility and harmony of the universe, unifying and structuring it, and providing it with its ground of being."[14] Thus, whereas this is still a far cry from the claims of (some forms of) traditional natural theology that the existence of God can be established beyond doubt from the structure of the natural world, the direction of thought here is still the same: *from* the world as studied by the sciences *toward* God.

Molnar rightly notes that "one can easily observe that this reference to God is not a reference primarily to God the Father in his relation to the Son"—or, we might say, to the triune God.[15] Rather, a much bleaker notion of the deity is at play here; at best, this is the Creator God (and at its worst, as Karl Barth would say, it could have been the devil). Isn't this an example of a split Torrance elsewhere laments and criticizes, namely "the split of the knowledge of God into two parts, natural knowledge of the One God and revealed knowledge of the Triune God"?[16] Rodney Holder as well concludes that despite Torrance's official repudiation of traditional natural theology, his actual involvement with the sciences brings him quite close to it. For the connection Torrance makes, works both ways: from God to the world and from the world to God:

> Torrance argues that the rationality of the Creator, who reveals himself in Christ, grounds the rational order of the cosmos and its fundamental harmony with the working of the human mind. If that is so, then the rational harmony and order of the cosmos

---

13. Cf. Holder, *Heavens Declare*, 240: "Torrance's view of natural theology makes it more like a theology of nature than what has been traditionally considered to be natural theology."

14. Torrance, *Reality and Scientific Theology*, 56.

15. Molnar, *Thomas F. Torrance*, 97.

16. Torrance, *Ground and Grammar*, 90.

provide rational grounds for believing they are the product of a Creator God.[17]

The phrase "a Creator God" is appropriate here: this is not necessarily the Triune God as revealed in Jesus Christ. So it seems that Torrance did not really approach the sciences from a Trinitarian point of view—reflection on the nature of the scientific endeavor rather seems to have led him to a more monotheistic way of thinking. At least we have to say that there is a tension in Torrance's work here between his wish to put the doctrine of the Trinity center stage and his actual engagement with the sciences, where instead of the Trinity it is rather the deistic (or at best generally theistic) God of the philosophers who seems to raise his head.[18]

While this is certainly true, Torrance was definitely serious in his wish to build a bridge between his Trinitarian approach to the dogmatic task and his "theistic" interpretation of the scientific endeavor. Apparently, he did not by definition regard such an attempt as unduly dualistic; if anyone was aware of the dangers of dualism in this connection, it was Torrance himself. But how then could his wish to build a bridge between Trinitarian theology and the Christian interpretation of the natural world be fleshed out in a more detailed and, hopefully, compelling way? Let us examine the specific attempt in this direction which was undertaken by someone who, being both a physicist and a theologian, was perhaps more fit for this task than Torrance himself: John Polkinghorne.

3. Strong Parallelism: John Polkinghorne

A well-known voice in the contemporary science and religion dialogue is that of John Polkinghorne (born 1930), a theoretical physicist who in the course of his career left his university chair in order to enroll in a teaching program for the ministry and to become a priest in the Anglican Church.[19] One of Polkinghorne's many books bears a title which sounds very promising for our purposes: *Science and the Trinity*. The aim of this book—issuing from the Warfield Lectures given at Princeton Theological

---

17. Holder, *Heavens Declare*, 240–241.

18. Lamoureux, "Do the Heavens Declare," misses this subtlety (or incongruence) in Torrance's position when he contends that Torrance would answer his title question with an unambiguous "yes, but only to Christians" (21). This is true when we focus on Torrance's "official" view; it is not true, though, when we look at Torrance's actual treatment of the order in the natural world as something that "projects our thought beyond it" (Torrance, *Reality and Scientific Theology*, 53).

19. Knight, "John Polkinghorne," 622.

Seminary in 2003—is "to explore and defend the thesis that Christian belief is as illuminating and intellectually credible in the twenty-first century as it was in the century that gave it birth."[20] Polkinghorne sets about to do so from a robustly Trinitarian framework, and his book can be read as a brief introduction to Christian systematic theology, covering themes such as the doctrine of Scripture, theological epistemology, Christology and soteriology, the Eucharist, and eschatology.[21] The doctrine of the Trinity does not figure with equal prominence in each of these cases, but the heart of the book (chapters 3 and 4) contains a sustained reflection on the relationship between Trinitarian doctrine and contemporary science.

How does Polkinghorne use Trinitarian theology as an interpretive framework for understanding the modern scientific enterprise? The short answer is: by highlighting *strong parallels* between both, and by advocating their compatibility. Polkinghorne realizes that, at first sight, broad and general theological ideas, such as that of "a divine Mind behind the order of the universe" (xii) may seem more attractive as interpretive grids for understanding nature than such a complex and highly detailed theological notion as Trinitarian doctrine. Yet, he argues that just as in science some basic insight is often only a first step, followed up by much more complex elaborations, in theology as well bare theism need not be seen as the final stage of our reflections. "In science, it is well-articulated proposals that lead ultimately to conviction" (xii). Similarly, in theology more complex notions than the "simple recognition of the Mind of God behind the order of nature" (xiii) may be more persuasive. What is decisive here is what our collective experiences make us to believe. Drawing on the same critical-realist bottom-up approach as Torrance, Polkinghorne argues that both our scientific and our theological theoretical reconstructions should match the depth of experience and move from experience toward understanding (xiv). Given the fact that the object of theology is "the God who transcends humanity rather than the physical world we transcend" (xii), it is only to be expected that a highly complex and diversified account is needed in order to do justice to the way in which the divine subject presents himself to us in experience. Trinitarian doctrine offers such an account.

Tying in with what had been discovered during the "Trinitarian renaissance," Polkinghorne points out that the doctrine of the Trinity is rooted not in "ungrounded metaphysical speculation" but in the earliest Christian experience of salvation (100). The first Christians were "driven by their

---

20. Polkinghorne, *Science and the Trinity*, xiv; page numbers in parentheses in the body of this section refer to this book.

21. For a more extensive rendering of Polkinghorne's theological views, gleaned from his many small books, see Oord, *Polkinghorne Reader*, esp. parts 2 and 3 (79–232).

experience of the risen and exalted Christ to use divine language about him," and similarly they knew of "a divine Spirit at work in their hearts and lives." This is how talk about the triune God emerged in the first place. This is not to say that we should restrict talk of the Trinity to the realm of the divine economy, since we may hold our experience to be "a trustworthy guide to the way things are" (101). In this connection Polkinghorne cites "Rahner's rule"—the economic Trinity is the immanent Trinity and the immanent Trinity is the economic Trinity[22]—interpreting it in such a way that it safeguards theological realism. Still, like in science in theological analysis as well, it is unavoidable to go beyond the raw data of experience by reflecting on how it can be interpreted in a coherent way. It is this process that led the first generations of Christians "to the modification of relatively naïve first-order categorizations" of their salvific experiences (101) by developing the doctrine of the Trinity. Like in science, such a theoretical notion finds its support in the additional insight that it provides (e.g., by illuminating the biblical statement that "God is love" and shielding this notion from narcissistic interpretations) as well as in the way it coheres with what we know from other sources (102–3).

It is especially the latter notion of "collateral support" that Polkinghorne elaborates in a number of directions. For example, he explores the notions of relationality, holism, and interconnectivity that have emerged as characteristic of the physical world in contemporary science (73–75), arguing that these developments are "deeply congenial to Trinitarian ways of thought" (75). In particular, he has in mind here the relational or "social" doctrine of the Trinity, with its strong emphasis on the eternal perichoretic exchange between the divine Persons. Speaking more specifically of quantum theory, Polkinghorne points to its strong counterintuitiveness, which in his view resembles the counterintuitiveness of Trinitarian thinking. In both cases, however, the "novel pattern of thought is forced upon us by the reality encountered" (77). Both are examples of what happens when we try to interpret our experiences of reality in a critically realist way. Also, quantum theory (along with chaos theory) has opened our eyes to the openness and indeterminacy of the universe. In the physical process novelty emerges, but at a deep level there is also order and stability. Here, Polkinghorne sees "some resonance" (81) with Trinitarian theology, as the interplay between openness and order may be seen as a "pale reflection" (81) of the closely coordinated external operations of the divine Persons.

Apart from pointing out analogies, Polkinghorne also holds that science's description of the physical process is *compatible* with belief in a

---

22. Rahner, *Trinity*, 22.

triune God who is active in history. The openness and indeterminacy of the universe does not "condemn God to the non-interactive role of a deistic spectator" (84) but enables us to see God as actively involved in creation "by the input of information within its open history" (84). Whereas other specialists in the field of science and religion are critical of the notion of special divine action, Polkinghorne defends its conceivability given contemporary scientific parameters.[23] Just like we can consider human agency as operating freely and intentionally given the "causal openness" (83) of the physical process, we can also conceive of God as acting providentially in creation. At the same time, such divine actions will always be hidden and concealed to some extent; given the many factors bearing on the physical process and its (perhaps even principal) unpredictability, we cannot "filter out" God's involvement through some experiment. "What is going on cannot be analyzed exhaustively and itemized into components, so that one might assert that nature did this, human will did that, and divine providence did the third thing" (84). This compares well with the hidden nature of the working of God's Spirit as conceived of in Trinitarian theology: the Spirit guides and influences history from within in ways that are not unambiguously clear, but that are only recognizable by the eye of faith.

Along such lines, Polkinghorne attempts to show that there are many analogies and that Trinitarian theology is entirely compatible with the contemporary scientific worldview. It seems fair to say that in his own theological outlook Polkinghorne on the one hand adopts insights from the sphere of natural theology (though not taken in its traditional sense as aiming at proof of God's existence, but in the "revised" sense as showing theism's persuasiveness given "the way the world is")[24] and on the other hand he adds to this insights from the sphere of revealed theology. Whereas in Torrance we observed a tension between these two as a result of his Barthian leanings, in the more sacramental Anglicanism of Polkinghorne both go together more harmoniously.[25] We may ask, however, whether by highlighting the

---

23. Cf. the so-called "Divine Action Project," a multi-year series of volumes by scientists, theologians and philosophers, most of whom (e.g. Arthur Peacocke, Philip Clayton and others) are critical of an "interventionist" view of divine action. See Wildman, "The Divine Action Project," 31–75. For critical discussion see e.g. Plantinga, *Where the Conflict Really Lies*, 97–121.

24. Cf. Polkinghorne, *Reason and Reality*, 80. The phrase "the way the world is" refers to Polkinghorne's first book on the science-faith relationship, *The Way the World Is*.

25. Cf. Knight, "John Polkinghorne," 626. See also Polkinghorne, *Science and Creation*, 8–9, where he explicitly contradicts Barth in attributing a modest but important role to natural theology and considers the created world as "potentially a vehicle also for His [God's] self-disclosure" (something which Barth, by the way, did not necessarily deny).

analogies and pointing out the compatibility between science and Trinitarian thinking, as well as by adding up insights from both domains, Polkinghorne has indeed attained his goal. Remember that this goal was, in his own words, to show "that there are aspects of our scientific understanding of the universe that become more deeply intelligible to us if they are viewed in a Trinitarian perspective" (61). Though the parallels he adduces definitely bring with them some "analogical support" (112), it seems that this support works mostly to protect the doctrine of the Trinity from the suspicion of being an outworn piece of incomprehensible speculation. In other words: the analogies help us to develop an apologetic theology—not yet the much more constructive form of theology that is needed if we want to show that the universe, or at least certain aspects of our scientific understanding of it, can best be interpreted along Trinitarian lines. Thus, the question is whether Polkinghorne's "strong parallelism" is sufficient to reach his goal. Let us now see how McGrath's thinking on Trinity and science fares at this point.

4. Inference to the Best Explanation: Alister McGrath

One of the most prolific authors in the contemporary field of science and religion is no doubt Alister McGrath; despite his vast oeuvre, as far as I know his way of thinking has not yet received much scholarly attention in the secondary literature (apart, of course, from many reviews of his books). Yet, there is ample reason to subject his views to sustained scrutiny, since they are by no means as simple or easy to grasp as his more popular writings may lead one to suppose.

In many respects, McGrath is a pupil of T. F. Torrance. Like Torrance, he opts for a "new" natural theology (which is, therefore, no longer very new in his case) as being embedded in, rather than independent of and prior to, revealed theology. It even seems that whereas Polkinghorne resolves the tension in Torrance's thinking by rehabilitating natural theology unashamedly as a *preambulum* toward Christian Trinitarianism,[26] McGrath resolves the same tension the other way around, namely by taking his point of departure more consistently in the Christian revelation and faith tradition. Living in a postmodern age, McGrath is sensitive to the profound ways in which our personal view of life bears upon and shapes our experience of reality. He

---

26. As we saw, Polkinghorne as well speaks of a "revised" or "revived" natural theology; in his case, however, the revision mostly implies that the natural theologian is no longer aiming at conclusive proof for the existence of God but, less ambitiously, at persuasive (but noncoercive) arguments.

does not go so far as to suggest that each of us constructs his or her own reality, but he actually comes quite close to this in his discussion of the concept of nature. According to McGrath, the classical metaphor of nature as a book should also be taken to mean that, like any book, nature is "open to multiple interpretations on the part of its autonomous readers."[27] "Nature" as such, irrespective from any precommitment, does not exist. In particular, nature looks very different to someone who denies any transcendent dimensions to it than to someone who does not have such a precommitment.[28] According to Rodney Holder, McGrath verges on the border of relativism here, for example when he writes that "[t]here is no *right* interpretation of nature."[29] Similarly, McGrath questions the universality of the concept of rationality, drawing on Alasdair MacIntyre's critique of the Enlightenment ideal of a universal rationality. Though he concedes that there is a bare concept of rationality in terms of effectiveness in puzzle solving, one that is independent of time, he criticizes the "great myth of universal reason."[30] In fact, what we hold to be rational is culturally conditioned and historically contingent—and more specifically *tradition-mediated*.[31]

It is here that the Christian tradition comes in as one player alongside others. The challenge for Christian thinkers is to show that their faith tradition offers a more powerful explanation of empirical reality than alternative traditions (including naturalism), in that it illuminates the inner coherence of things and situates them in their true perspective. In that sense, nature is "an 'open secret'—a publicly accessible entity, whose true meaning is known only from the standpoint of the Christian faith."[32] Indeed, that this is so is the claim that McGrath makes and elaborates in his 2008 Riddell Memorial Lectures as published in *The Open Secret*. We may wonder, however, to what extent this claim can be substantiated if different religious and nonreligious traditions inhabit different concepts of rationality. For how then could we reasonably compare each of them? It seems that in practice McGrath falls back on a notion of rationality that at least allows for trans-traditional

---

27. McGrath, *Scientific Theology*, 1:104.
28. McGrath, *Open Secret*, 75.
29. McGrath, *Open Secret*, 138. Cf. Holder, *Heavens Declare*, 191, who comments: "This is a large claim, sounding dangerously postmodern. So, can we interpret nature any way we please?" But this is what McGrath explicitly denies a few lines later—his point being that there is no *self-evident* or "natural" interpretation of nature. Holder offers one of the few sustained investigations of McGrath's views on how exactly science and religion relate (169–231).
30. McGrath, *Scientific Theology*, 2:62, 57.
31. McGrath, *Scientific Theology*, 2:64.
32. McGrath, *Open Secret*, 11.

aspects and criteria. Following up on Polkinghorne, McGrath mentions economy, scope, elegance, and fruitfulness as four such (tradition-independent) criteria of excellence, and he contends that in the light of these criteria theism fares better than naturalism, whereas "Trinitarian theism is superior to a more generic theism in this respect."[33]

But how could this be established if it requires fully-fledged Trinitarian faith to see the point? How could we use McGrath's favorite method of abduction (Charles Peirce) or "inference to the best explanation" (Peter Lipton and others) if "the insight that nature has the capacity to disclose God is only given from the standpoint of knowing that God"?[34] I can only side with Rodney Holder here, who comments as follows:

> McGrath gives great weight to "inference to the best explanation" . . . where he names criteria that seem to be universal, even in line with the Enlightenment kind of rationality he wishes to reject. But only Christians are able to make the IBE [inference to the best explanation] from nature to God because they believe in God in the first place! So where is the inference if the conclusion is already the premise?[35]

At least we must observe that there seems to be an intriguing ambivalence in McGrath's thinking on these issues. In his sequel to *The Open Secret*, *A Fine-Tuned Universe* (the outcome of his 2009 Gifford Lectures), McGrath forcefully rearticulates his specific Trinitarian approach to natural theology, elaborating it in various directions, but he does not remove this ambiguity. On the one hand, we find the claim that the Trinitarian "way of looking at things is a consequence of the Christian tradition, and is not entailed by nature itself," and on the other hand one page further McGrath once again promises that "it will be argued that Christianity makes better sense of the empirical evidence than any of its alternatives or rivals."[36] If the latter is true then McGrath will have to concede that it works both ways, i.e., not only from the Christian worldview toward nature but also from nature toward the Christian worldview—as in more traditional accounts of natural theology. Of course, it is not incumbent upon him (or anyone else) to show that the Trinitarian perspective is *entailed* by nature itself (as in Enlightenment conceptions of natural theology), but at least he must point out that it is suggested, or hinted at, by nature, and more consonant with nature than any of its alternatives. The point is that McGrath at times acknowledges

33. McGrath, *Open Secret*, 17.
34. McGrath, *Open Secret*, 139.
35. Holder, *Heavens Declare*, 192.
36. McGrath, *Fine-Tuned Universe*, 36, 37.

this but then again seems to deny it. Even in such a relatively clear case as the finetuning of the universe, McGrath prefers to work from the Christian believer's Trinitarian perspective to the interpretation of nature rather than the other way around.[37]

We do not find in McGrath's work the kind of parallels and analogies between Trinitarian doctrine and contemporary science (e.g., quantum theory) that we came across in Polkinghorne. Presumably, this is because McGrath—without denying such analogies—is looking for something more than that. He is not content with showing the compatibility of Christian patterns of belief with scientific theories or highlighting the intellectual credibility of Trinitarian theism in light of contemporary science. He aims at something more than that. Perhaps the best way to grasp what exactly McGrath is after, is to examine his approach to the problem of theodicy. This is the final one of "four points of particular significance" characterizing "the specific form of natural theology that emerges from within a Trinitarian vision of reality."[38] Following up on reflections about God's self-revelation, the doctrine of *creatio ex nihilo* and the notion of humanity as created in the image of God, it is the only one that bears more directly upon the doctrine of the Trinity. Whereas a deistic or barely theistic approach has difficulties in doing justice to the existence of suffering and "evil" in nature, a Trinitarian approach that takes its point of departure in the economy of salvation takes this "groaning of creation" into account from the very start, acknowledging that we live in a fallen world.[39] Indeed, it is only a Trinitarian account of natural theology that "brings to the observation and interpretation of nature an understanding of God that is deeply shaped by the revelational and soteriological implications of the cross."[40] The God who created this world is the very same God who reaches out both his hands—the Son and the Spirit, according to the famous metaphor of Irenaeus—in order to save the fallen world from the powers of evil. In such a view, the natural world with all its sufferings is not seen as unambiguously pointing to a good and almighty creator—a theistic God—but to the triune God of the Christian

---

37. McGrath, *Fine-Tuned Universe*, 69. Cf. 79: "Nature must be 'seen' in the right way for it to act as a witness to, or conduit for, the Trinitarian God of the Christian tradition."

38. McGrath, *Fine-Tuned Universe*, 71.

39. On the extent to which we can indeed describe our world as "fallen" given a contemporary evolutionary perspective, see Van den Brink, *Reformed Theology*, § 6.4, 6.5.

40. McGrath, *Fine-Tuned Universe*, 80. "A Trinitarian engagement with nature is already marked with the sign of the cross and is thus especially attentive to the problem of suffering in nature."

faith. Trinitarian theology has a much greater "empirical fit" here than either deism or theism.

5. Evaluation

The problem of how to relate the natural world with its possible transcendent reverberations and revealed theology—or how to relate "science and the Trinity," for short—continues to haunt Protestant theology ever since Karl Barth. We see this reflected in the lines of thought stretching from Torrance to Polkinghorne and McGrath as sketched in this chapter. In all three of these Christian thinkers, there is certainly an awareness (stemming from Torrance) that the Christian revelation can explain how science is possible at all, and how there can be a correspondence between the human mind and the rationality of the cosmos (Einstein's source of wonder). Similarly, all three of them endorse the maxim that "ontology determines epistemology," i.e., the specific way a particular reality exists and appears to us determines how we can approach it in our attempts to make sense of it. It is not strange, therefore, that in theology we must proceed along methodical lines that differ from those that have to be followed in physics—and yet, the physical process may point to and suggest a divine origin in various ways, thus showing the interconnectedness or consonance (Polkinghorne) or resonance (McGrath) of the realms of science and theology.

As we saw, however, opinions differed as to how such transcendent intimations of reality (which none of our thinkers denies) should be interpreted. According to Polkinghorne, phenomena like the anthropic cosmological principle and the wonderful fact that the universe can (at least in part) be comprehended by our human minds, can best be interpreted as—persuasive though not conclusive—evidence for the existence of God, which is available for every reflective person independent of his or her view of life. Both Torrance and McGrath, on the other hand, are (most of the time) unwilling to follow this path, and insist that it is only from the perspective of Christian Trinitarian faith that we are enabled to fathom the significance of such phenomena. More than Torrance, McGrath has aimed at fleshing out a specifically Trinitarian natural theology along such lines. However, we have also seen that the way in which he proceeds raises important questions with regard to his methodical consistency. As Holder pointed out, McGrath seems to want to have his cake and eat it. That is, he both contends that the specific Trinitarian perspective is required to perceive nature in its full meaning and significance (so that only believers can grasp it) *and* that it is possible to corroborate this Trinitarian perspective by means of inference to the best explanation—which requires that it can be compared with other perspectives on the basis of commonly shared criteria of rationality.[41]

We are now in a position to return to Lamoureux's question with which we started: what does the Trinity have to do with science? Given the subtlety and professional acumen with which all three thinkers, but in particular McGrath, have argued for the development of a natural theology from a specific Trinitarian perspective, Lamoureux's suggestion that this is all "merely fashionable Christian rhetoric"[42] cannot be sustained. The various ways in which Torrance, Polkinghorne, and McGrath attempt to relate the Trinitarian faith to the scientific inquiry of the natural world and its philosophical presuppositions are deeply rooted in serious theological considerations. Among other things, these considerations have to do with the problems of more traditional ways of doing natural theology as undertaken during the Enlightenment period.[43] As a result of these problems, observers will seldom be enticed to move from deism, through bare theism, to Trinitarianism. It is therefore fully comprehensible that theologians such as Torrance and McGrath started to take more seriously Karl Barth's dictum that "whoever does not start with Jesus Christ, will never end up with him." Something similar could be claimed about fully-fledged Trinitarian Christian faith. Irrespective of whether or not we find such theological considerations compelling, it is clear that they are elaborated here (however tentatively) in detailed ways that invite careful analysis rather than being disparaged out of hand.

Yet, it seems that the attempt to interpret the natural world as investigated by the sciences from a Trinitarian perspective can also be overstretched. One way to modify McGrath's claims in a way that makes them more plausible and open to general discussion would be to acknowledge that one need not be a Christian (or "to know God") in order to see the point of a Trinitarian natural theology. The only thing required is that one is willing to imagine what it would be like to take the Trinitarian Christian perspective as a framework for making sense of the natural world as we know it through the sciences. Even so, there is still a long way to go before

---

41. The same ambiguity in McGrath's work has been spotted by Paul Molnar, but he criticizes McGrath from exactly the opposite direction, disapproving of the way in which McGrath, much more so than Torrance, still displays apologetic intentions (as in traditional natural theology) in parts of his discourse. See Molnar, *Thomas F. Torrance*, 95n106.

42. Lamoureux, "Do the Heavens Declare," 36.

43. McGrath, *Fine-Tuned Universe*, 65–66, rightly points to the seminal work of Eberhard Jüngel in this connection; he might also have mentioned a classic from the Roman Catholic side: Buckley, *At the Origins of Modern Atheism*.

one can plausibly infer that Trinitarian theology offers the best explanation for the amazing ways in which the manifold hidden secrets of the constitution of the natural world have gradually been (and are gradually being) opened up through scientific research. Nevertheless, though we should not aim at something like a "Trinitarian science," from a Christian perspective it is not at all strange to explore this way in more depth. For if God exists, and if he really revealed himself in the person of Jesus Christ and in the Spirit, then what we see in the world should make most sense in the light of the Christian faith, which is by definition Trinitarian in nature.

Bibliography

Buckley, Michael J. *At the Origins of Modern Atheism*. New Haven: Yale University Press, 1987.

Colyer, Elmer M. *How to Read T. F. Torrance: Understanding His Trinitarian and Scientific Theology*. Downers Grove, IL: InterVarsity, 2001.

Gunton, Colin E. *The One, the Three and the Many: Creation and the Culture of Modernity*. Cambridge: Cambridge University Press, 1993.

Holder, Rodney. *The Heavens Declare: Natural Theology and the Legacy of Karl Barth*. West Conshohocken, PA: Templeton, 2012.

Holmes, Stephen R. *The Quest for the Trinity: The Doctrine of God in Scripture, History and Modernity*. Downers Grove, IL: InterVarsity, 2012.

Knight, Christopher C. "John Polkinghorne." In *The Blackwell Companion to Science and Christianity*, edited by J.B. Stump & Alan G. Padgett, 622–31. Chichester, UK: Wiley-Blackwell, 2012.

Lamoureux, Denis O. "Do the Heavens Declare the Glory of God? Toward a Biblical Model of Intelligent Design." *Faith & Thought* 59 (October 2015) 18–38.

McGrath, Alister E. *A Fine-Tuned Universe: The Quest for God in Science and Theology*. Louisville, KT: Westminster John Knox, 2009.

———. *The Open Secret: A New Vision for Natural Theology*. Oxford: Blackwell, 2008.

———. *A Scientific Theology*. Vol. 1, *Nature*. Edinburgh: T. & T. Clark, 2001.

———. *A Scientific Theology*. Vol. 2, *Reality*. Edinburgh: T. & T. Clark, 2002.

Metzger, Paul Louis, ed. *Trinitarian Soundings in Systematic Theology*. London: T. & T. Clark, 2005.

Molnar, Paul D. *Thomas F. Torrance: Theologian of the Trinity*. Farnham, UK: Ashgate, 2009.

Oord, Thomas Jay, ed. *The Polkinghorne Reader*. London: SPCK, 2010.

Plantinga, Alvin. *Where the Conflict Really Lies: Science, Religion and Naturalism*. Oxford: Oxford University Press, 2011.

Polkinghorne, John. *Reason and Reality: The Relationship between Science and Theology*. London: SPCK, 1991.

———. *Science and the Trinity: The Christian Encounter with Reality*. London: SPCK, 2004.

———. *The Way the World Is: The Christian Perspective of a Scientist*. London: SPCK, 1983.

Rahner, Karl. *The Trinity*. New York: Crossroad, 2003 [1970].

Torrance, Thomas F. *The Ground and Grammar of Theology*. Belfast: Christian Journals, 1980.
———. *Reality and Scientific Theology*. Edinburgh: Scottish Academic, 1985.
———. *Theological Science*. New York: Oxford University Press, 1978.
Van den Brink, Gijsbert. *Reformed Theology and Evolutionary Theory*. Grand Rapids: Eerdmans, forthcoming.
Wildman, Wesley. "The Divine Action Project, 1988–2003." *Theology and Science* 2 (2004) 31–75.

CHAPTER 10

Trinitarian Prayer

*Praying from Slave-Narratives
to Son-Narratives*

JULIE CANLIS

Every day that we wake to a world at all should shock us. As Malcolm Guite begins in his poem, "Gratitude," "Thanksgiving starts with thanks for mere survival, just to have made it through another year with everyone still breathing."[1] Or as Jane Kenyon reminds us in her poem, "Otherwise," "I got out of bed on two strong legs. It might have been otherwise. I ate cereal, sweet milk, ripe flawless peach. It might have been otherwise. I took the dog uphill to the birch wood. All morning I did the work I love."[2] The very fact that we are here at all "might have been otherwise." And even more astonishing is the miracle that we are invited to pray.

The fact that we pray at all should continue to astonish us; so too that there is open and free communication between us and God; that the universe is *personal*; that time rushes over a bedrock of love. This is what the Psalmists were trying to communicate when they spoke of trees clapping and rocks shouting. They sang God's praises right alongside the universe. And they marveled that in the midst of this personal universe, they were the apple of God's eye (Ps 17:8). In this essay, I want to focus on the marvelous

---

1. Guite, "Gratitude," in *Sounding the Seasons*, 60.
2. Kenyon, "Otherwise," in *Otherwise*, 214.

nature of our prayer—and the marvelous nature of the God who underwrites it. I also want to examine the power of the different "stories of God" from which we live that shape our prayer lives and, conversely, the way prayer can function as a litmus test for those stories. Finally, I will look at the specifically Trinitarian shape of prayer which intersects with our anthropology, allowing us to both receive the Father-Son relation and ourselves in the process. But first, before we examine the inner workings of prayer, the stage for prayer needs to be set with an appropriate attitude of wonder. To begin, I propose that an awareness of three things can help us marvel that not only is prayer possible, but that it is written into the heart of the universe.

Three Contexts for Prayer

The first context for Trinitarian prayer is, as articulated above, that we live in a relational universe. God, who in himself is not "alone," has brought creatures into being. This God has spoken *to us*. The ground of our being is love.

The second constituent of Trinitarian prayer is that this same God desires a love-response from us. This is perhaps an even greater mystery. Do we ever stop to wonder why this should be the way things are?

> Long before he laid down the earth's foundations, he had us in mind, had settled on us as the focus of his love, to be made whole and holy by his love. Long, long ago he planned to adopt us into his family through Jesus Christ. What pleasure he took in planning this![3] (Eph 1:4, *The Message*)

We not only have a relational God, but he has settled on *us* as the focus of his love. He desires *us* as his covenant partner. Why the God of the universe should desire this we do not know—but we do know it is in his character. Thus, part of being human is to be responsive—to be prayerful—to be *imago Dei*. Although much has been written of late about *our* being in the image of God, it says as much about God as it does about humanity: the relational God who created the relational universe desires us. "What pleasure he took in planning this!" Paul writes in Ephesians. This God set about creating a universe in which prayer and relationship is possible. Again, a marvel that should render us speechless. This is the second context for prayer.

Of course, sin changed all this. (This is the third context for prayer.) Sin did not change God's desire for us. Nor the relational grain of the universe.

---

3. Unless otherwise indicated, all Scripture quotations are taken from the Holy Bible, New International Version.

But sin has changed the *character* of our response to God. As the narrative in Genesis puts it:

> Then the man and his wife heard the sound of the Lord God as he was walking in the garden in the cool of the day, and they hid from the Lord God among the trees of the garden. But the Lord God called to them and said, "Where are you?" The man answered, "I heard you in the garden, and I was afraid." (Gen 3:8–10)

With sin came fear or "terror at the sight of God,"[4] notes Calvin. It is not so much that sin brings on atheism (or disbelief in God). Sin brings on *wrong* belief in God—belief that God is not a God of love. Sin questions the relational universe that makes prayer possible at all. Instead, we "hide" from God by believing instead in an impersonal universe ruled by fate, requiring not prayer but fear and bargaining. Or (as is the case today) we can "hide" from God behind believed divine disinterest, requiring from us self-sufficiency and just getting on with it. Either way, the relational understanding of God that provides the right framework for prayer has been lost. We need divine revelation to once again reveal who God is, and how we are to respond to the God who is beyond our wildest hopes. We need divine revelation to pray aright. In other words, we need to hear the story afresh.

The Power of Stories to Shape the Posture of Prayer

The arch of the Bible is concerned with the loss of belief in God's goodness and with how to regain the metanarrative of trust in which true prayer is possible. This is not just a problem in our secular world. It has been the challenge for every generation as far back as the formation of God's people. Moses was faced with no more difficult a task than we are faced with today. Like us, Moses faced the monumental task of moving the Hebrew people from fear to trust—from a slave narrative to a son narrative. His people did not awaken each day to a story of family and their place in a universe of love. They instead heard Pharaoh's story. They woke up to a world of mud, bricks, and whips.

In the Ancient Near East (ANE), humans (and the cosmos itself) came into being as a benefit to the gods. These gods had needs—*lots* of needs. As the story goes, the minor gods were grumpy about being tasked with the chores for the major gods and it is only in this context that people enter the story at all. Humans came into being as a *slave-class* to do all the work of

---

4. Calvin, *Institutes* II.12.1.

waking, feeding, cleaning, entertaining, and tucking the gods back into bed on a daily routine in their temples. There might be a few privileged humans, but only because they directly served the gods.

Pharaoh, as the "father" of a people, was responsible for narrating a story in word and deed. His story would have sounded something like this:

> In the beginning there were no gods, but only darkness and chaos—and from this chaos the gods arose. They had no world to stand on, and so they created our world for themselves, as their footstool. By subdividing themselves they created other gods to help control the chaos. The heaven-god was born to regulate the things above, the earth-god was born to regulate life and fertility below. At the pinnacle of this cosmos stands the sun-god, who rises and dies daily to keep the heaven-god and the earth-god together.
>
> Yet the gods had no one to do the lower tasks on earth, and this made them very sad. So you, my dear son, are an accidental byproduct of a god's tears. You come in handy to perform these lower tasks of keeping the earth, and serving the gods' need for food and adoration. You, dear Egyptians, are the honored slave-class of the divine. Make sure you uphold this order, by serving them and me (the representation of god in front of you). Make sure you keep the images of the gods in their temples happy, otherwise they will leave the temple—and take with them fertility, prosperity, and justice. You must keep the gods happy, by meeting their (and my) continuing needs.

As a mother, I often imagine Moses—rescued from the basket of reeds—being tucked into bed by Pharaoh's sister, who entertained him night after night with different versions of this great Egyptian bedtime story in which humans are, quite simply, the slave-class for the divine. I also imagine that the Hebrew nation, being the literal slave-class for the Egyptians for centuries, might begin to believe Pharaoh's alluring story. Which story would you believe? Everything about their reality seemed to support the Egyptian story, as they labored to build these cities for the gods. Just as the priests and the ruling class existed to serve the gods and the ruling Pharaoh-god, so the slaves existed to keep this whole microcosmic cycle running smoothly by serving the priests and the ruling class. This tale was the ugly reality they inhabited.

Prayer, in this context, cannot be anything but appeasement. Sacrifices are required to keep the powerful gods in check. Success is being answered. Failure is not being answered. This is the pattern associated with all forms of paganism, but it arises from what is more primary: a slave-narrative, rather than a son-narrative. A slave-narrative exists wherever there is a belief in a cosmos not dominated by love but by power that must be appeased, checked, propitiated, and pacified. But, fortunately, the child Moses grew up. And he heard God's story direct.

One of the first things Moses needed to do was not only lead God's people into freedom, but give them a new story. After four hundred years of hearing themselves encased in Pharaoh's story, they needed a new narrative to tell them who they were and who God was, and it must have sounded like a manifesto for radicals. Here is my version of Moses's divinely given revolutionary manifesto:

> In the beginning, God creates, not by copulation or incest, but God speaks a beautiful world into being. This whole world is his temple—and it did not come about by accident but by loving intention. This is a world alive with beauty—a world not for him to stand on, or to meet his needs but for him to love. At the pinnacle of this world is . . . you.
>
> As this beautiful world-temple takes shape, God places his image in the temple. This image is not of stone or wood, it does not need to be woken up or fed or entertained. You are the image of God. For you and the creatures, God has created this world. For you, God has created food and he will feed you. You are set as the apple of his eye, in his temple, as the image of himself. Not one of you shall be a slave of the gods, not even one. Now rest my little one. For God who watcheth over you neither slumbers nor sleeps. Rest.

Genesis is a new story, deliberately retold to counter the destructive story told by Pharaoh. It will take years for God's people to really allow this story to seep into their bones, to unlearn the slave stories of four hundred years. But this God has chosen to form a people, to watch over a people, and lead them out from slavery. This God is making a family of nations.

As is now evident, this is no average story—it was dangerous. It was a dangerous challenge to Pharaoh's preferred story, with its tale of hierarchy, inequality, and fatalism. The Israelites knew that it was also dangerous because it is deceptively simple. Saint Jerome reported that in his era, Jewish men were not allowed to read Genesis by themselves (without a rabbi) until they reached the age of thirty. From Moses's story, one learns about who one is, who God is, and what the world is in the face of an Egyptian story that threatened to swallow humanity whole. Moses, through revelation, was able to speak of the God who declared himself to be "I AM"—existing not to have his needs met, but to meet those of his beloved people in the midst of their trials and tribulations.

For hundreds of years, this story was adequate for the task of loosening the bonds of a slave-narrative. Prayer, in this context, becomes the richness of the Psalms and of worshippers confident enough to bring both their joys and laments into the presence of this One who created them at the pinnacle of creation, and of the One who desires their response. David is famous for arguing with the Lord on the grounds of his ontology, "will the dust praise you, Lord?" (Ps 30:9). This God is the I AM, slow to anger—and abounding in love. As Brueggemann points out, even this God's wrath is a sign of his covenant-faithfulness and of his capacity to be moved by those he loves and from who he desires a response.[5]

Jesus's Story

Unfortunately, slave-narratives did not entirely disappear with Moses and his new story. It is hard for us to break free of the wounds of our past. Slave narratives keep weaving their way throughout the Old Testament, and it is the prophets who continue to rail against the Hebrew people for reverting to Pharaoh's story of a god who must be appeased, feared, "kept" in his temple. For even Moses's story, though correct, was not able to reveal the fullness of who God is—or of who we are. What was needed was a new storyteller to tell us who the Father is.

As salvation history has shown, the story and the storyteller are one: Jesus. Jesus came to replace the slave-narrative once and for all by showing us in his own person *who* the Father is and what it looks like to be a *son*. Jesus not only tells a new story, he *is* the new story. He invites us to enter into this story and for it to become our own.

This invitation is more often than not received with mistrust. Adam sums up the plight of humanity, "I heard you in the garden and I was afraid." T. F. Torrance tells a similar Adamic story from when he was a stretcher-bearer on the Italian front lines of World War II. His career as a theologian was born when he came upon a mortally wounded twenty-year-old soldier who clearly did not have much time to live. He cradled the head of the bleeding man named Philip who—with his last breath—asked, "Padre" (the name for a chaplain in WWII) "Padre, is God really like Jesus?"

For Torrance, this was the beginning of a lifelong theological journey: what had gone wrong in Christian theology that could lead someone to

---

5. Brueggemann, *Genesis*.

believe that there was a wedge driven between Jesus and God? What had happened that Pharaoh's story still held sway?

If we try and read Moses's story without Jesus's story, we will get it wrong. Even though Israel had Moses's story, they could not from it discern God as *Father*. In fact, over history, we have seen that Moses's story can at times begin to look like Pharaoh's with a powerful, dictator-type God. Karl Barth discerned that Moses's story, without the fuller story given by Jesus, could revert right back to Pharaoh's with an abstract "sovereign" with an unlimited amount of power. Right after World War II, Barth wrote:

> It is not "the Almighty" who is God; we cannot understand from the standpoint of a supreme concept of power, who God is. And the man who calls "the Almighty" God misses God in the most terrible way. For "the Almighty" is bad, as "absolute power" is bad. The "Almighty" means Chaos, Evil, the Devil. We could not better describe and define the Devil than by trying to think this idea of a self-based, free, sovereign ability.[6]

If we cannot understand God from the standpoint of a supreme concept of power, then what is it that we are to go by? The partial revelations in creation, in the law, and in the people of God are correct, but inadequate to reverse Adam's (and our own) primal mistrust. The only full revelation of God is in Jesus.

The Gospel of John tells us that Jesus has given us a new story, one that tells us who God is and who we are. John's gospel says that "No one has ever seen God, but the one and only Son, who is himself God and is in the bosom of the Father, *has made him known*" (John 1:18). The Greek for "making known" is *exejayomai* or exegete: Jesus exegetes God to us as *Father*. This is what caused the people of God to want to kill him (John 5:18). Jesus is not only revealing a new name for God, but he is revealing God's being to us—more than we had ever been able to glimpse in Moses's story of the "I AM." What this means is that the name "Father" reveals a different genre of God than any monotheistic interpretation can support.

In Moses's story, we begin with a generous God creating the world. But what was this God doing before the world began? What was his character? For this, we need a storyteller even greater than Moses. John drops this clue, when he reports Jesus's prayer to his Father: "Father, you loved me before the foundation of the world" (John 17:24). Being creator is not central to God's nature; being *Father* is. God was *Father* prior to creation, because he is Father to the Son. This is his eternal identity.

---

6. Barth, *Dogmatics in Outline*, 48.

What John reveals is that central to this "genre" of God is *being for the other*. This kind of God is neither solitary nor self-sufficient; this God places his being in the hands of another. For example, the Father determined that there is something greater to be gained by receiving his identity from the Son, than by possessing his "godness" rightfully on his own. There is no power struggle. There is no hierarchy. There is mutual love and self-giving. It is *this* that constitutes the persons of the Trinity and that characterizes the Trinitarian God. As Calvin, who immersed himself in the early church fathers, discerned, the only individually identifying characteristics of the members of the godhead are *the relations they have with one another*. That is how we can discern the Father from the Son and the Spirit: the different way each one is God—for and from the other two—is the only difference between them. This is why we can never contemplate one without the other two—for in so doing, we have removed all their identifying characteristics! Calvin was very fond of Gregory of Nazianzus's remark: "When I say God, I mean the Father, the Son and the Holy Spirit. . . . I cannot think of the One without immediately being surrounded by the radiance of the Three, nor discern the Three without being carried back to the One."[7] Reality, at its most fundamental level, is *personal*.

The Trinity is not an optional "upgrade" in the category of divinity that we Christians have. The Trinity is not just one option among many equals but is a whole other *kind of being*. It is only "Trinity" that differentiates our God from a Muslim approach to divinity or a Mormon approach to divinity. Only in Jesus can we begin to discover the character of this God. If we decide that "Fatherhood" is not essential to our God's being, then we undo the Christian God completely—for the Father cannot be Father without the Son, nor can the Son be the Son without the Father. This is their eternal identity. (This is not just a systematic theologian jumping on her high horse and splitting theological hairs in the horse's tail. This is about whether or not we pray to a God of legalism or communion. This is about whether or not we "deep down" believe we are caught up in a slave-narrative or a son-narrative. And this, of course, radically affects the way we pray.)

We Christians too need the prophets because even with Jesus, we can unknowingly revert to Pharaoh's story. This is the gravitational pull of sin. We can placate God with our devotional regimen, trying to get on with our life. We can mistrust God's heart toward us, and keep him screened behind a theology of propitiation and appeasement. These slave-narratives always appear when we forget that Jesus exegetes God to us as *Father*. Michael

---

7. Calvin, *Institutes* I.13.17.

Reeves has done a marvelous job in outlining a particular "Christian" slave-narrative that makes the rounds among churches today:

> If God's very identity is to be The Ruler, what kind of salvation can he offer me (if he's even prepared to offer such a thing)? If God is The Ruler and the problem is that I have broken the rules, the only salvation he can offer is to forgive me and treat me as if I had kept the rules.
>
> But if that is how God is, my relationship with him can be little better than my relationship with any traffic cop (meaning no offence to any readers in the police force). Let me put it like this: if, as never happens, some fine cop were to catch me speeding and so breaking the rules, I would be punished; if, as never happens, he failed to spot me or I managed to shake him off after an exciting car chase, I would be relieved. But in neither case would I love him. And even if, like God, he chose to let me off the consequences of my law-breaking, I still would not love him. I might feel grateful, and that gratitude might be deep, but that is not at all the same thing as love. And so it is with the divine policeman: if salvation simply means him letting me off and counting me as a law-abiding citizen, then gratitude (not love) is all I have. In other words, I can never really love the God who is essentially just The Ruler. And that, ironically, means I can never keep the greatest command: to love the Lord my God.[8]

When Jesus exegeted the Father to us, he did not do so by giving us information about the Father, but by living in perfect filial relationship with him. He showed us what it was to obey *this kind of God*. He had to show us that slave-obedience is not what this kind of God desires. Through his birth, life, death, and resurrection, he lived the freedom of a Son (in the loving embrace of a Father) in the perfect communion that we were intended for, but are never able to manage. He came to save us from slave-narratives by breaking the power of sin and uniting us to himself, *the Son*. This is what happens when we are baptized and find ourselves "in Christ": our identity is changed from a slave to a son.

Prayer: A Litmus Test for the Stories of Pharaoh, Moses, and Jesus

Many of us profess our faith in one story, but pray from another. Prayer is where the story that controls our spiritual life is revealed. Many Christians

---

8. Reeves, *Delighting in the Trinity*, 22.

(including myself) can pray from Pharaoh's story of fatalism, of responsibility to keep the gods appeased, of successful answers to prayer—or failed requests. We Christians have many variations of this kind of prayer, where we fast to get God's attention, where we doubt ourselves when our prayer is not answered. We turn to this God for help in times of desperation, knowing that something will be extracted from us later down the line. Praying from Pharaoh's story is still part and parcel of the impact of sin upon our lives, but one which we can attend to and confess.

Others of us, despite praying the "Our Father," continue to pray deep down from Moses's story of a good, loving God—but who is still impersonal. This God is the sovereign "I AM" but who cannot be counted on as *Father*. This God has high expectations of us, will discipline us when we are out of line, and can be counted on to get something done. This God is distant, but kindly. We can work for this God; we are servants of this God; but we wonder—when we are in times of distress—whether this God is vaguely disappointed with us. This is the traffic-cop God, to whom we are so grateful—but who we cannot love.

And sometimes we are freed to pray from Jesus's story, which narrates a Father who has his being in communion and has created us for communion. But why is this so seldom the place from which we pray? Karl Rahner wrote that "despite the orthodox confession of the Trinity, Christians are, in their practical life, almost 'mere' monotheists . . . should the doctrine of the Trinity have to be dropped as false, the major part of the Christian experience and literature could well remain virtually unchanged."[9] Despite Jesus revealing the Father to us, the gravitational pull of sin would have it otherwise. Sin has so marked us that we expect a dictator God. This is why, Calvin writes, that our salvation consists in being able to call God *Father*.

Renewing Prayer I: Receiving the Father-Son Relation

Having seen the stories from which we might pray, the first step in Trinitarian prayer (which is really the only form of Christian prayer there is) is an impossible leap. We cannot reverse the gravitational pull of sin that prevents us from seeing God as *Father*. "I heard you in the garden and I was afraid." So the Father sent the Son and the Spirit to fulfill in us his communion purposes.

When we are baptized, whether we know it or not, we are united to Christ. We begin living the mystery of being "in Christ," which means that

9. Rahner, *Trinity*, 10.

his narrative now encompasses us. His life, lived for us, is given to us as a gift—and the content of this life is Sonship. His life lived with God the Father is ours for the taking, since we are now *in him*. From birth, through his growth in obedience, to his baptism and ministry, death and resurrection, he not only shows us the Father—but he shows us what it looks like to respond to this God: how to be a *child*.

Through his life on earth, Jesus, by exegeting God as *Father*, came to overturn the slave narratives to which we turn. Before Pentecost, Jesus said something radical, "I no longer call you servants, but friends" (John 15:15). As if that weren't enough, Jesus said that not only was he asking the Father for particular things for his friends, but indicated a greater time was coming. "In that day, *you will ask in my name*. I will not ask the Father on your behalf. No, the Father himself loves you because you have loved me" (John 16:26–27). Jesus was praying for his friends to be freed from slave narratives, such that they could actually approach the Father candidly, assured of his love. With the sending of the Spirit (Acts 2), Paul says that something even greater happened, "Therefore you are no longer a servant but a son" (Gal 4:7).

In prayer, we enter this Father-Son relation. Jesus modeled this new way of being for us, when he taught us to pray "Our Father." Calling God "Abba—Father" is not just giving God a friendly nickname. It is entering into the same trusting, intimate, liberating relationship that Jesus had with his Father. Yet it is the Spirit who actually helps us claim the words as our own, crying for us, "*Abba*"—Jesus's very words. For those of us for whom slave-narratives come as second nature, we need help. "For we do not know how to pray as we ought, but the Spirit himself intercedes" (Rom 8:26). We need the Spirit to lift us up into Christ's prayer life (which is his relational life) to the Father. As Von Balthasar writes,

> Mysteries such as these . . . are thoroughly practical. It makes a great difference to the act of [prayer] whether I see myself as an isolated subject, who, albeit assisted by God's grace, endeavors to understand something of the mysteries of revelation; or whether, in faith, I have the conviction that my inadequate attempt to understand is supported by the wisdom of the Holy Spirit dwelling within me . . . that my [prayer] is borne along and remodeled by the Spirit's infinite and eternal acts, in that ineffable union by which all human doing and being has been lifted up and plunged into the river of eternal life and love.[10]

---

10. Balthasar, *Prayer*, 76.

So be encouraged: the Father has sent the Spirit of Sonship into our hearts, who articulates within us that first word that defines Christian prayer: *Father*. Even in prayer, we are not alone. The "Our Father" is a radical, defiant prayer against all slave-narratives.

Renewing Prayer II: Receiving Ourselves

The first step into Trinitarian prayer is praying from a new story—gathered up and folded into Jesus's relationship with the Father. Thus, Trinitarian prayer is first of all receiving the Father-Son relation as our own. The second step into Trinitarian prayer is receiving ourselves from the Father.

Trinitarian prayer requires radical trust that in God's sight we are the beloved. So in the case of prayer, it is abandoning our habituated formulas of prayer and allowing for new trust. Trinitarian prayer involves hearing our name once again. Whereas slave prayers involve praying to a powerful yet impersonal deity (who is more concerned with our right prayers, than our uniqueness before him), *Trinitarian* prayer is being named by the Lord. It is living our unique identity before him—without comparison to anyone else, any other form of prayer, any technique, style, or how-to. It is refusing to compare ourselves to the prayer lives of others (or some ideal standard we have for ourselves against which we are always failing) and instead saying, "Father, into your hands I commit my spirit" (and my prayer life, for that matter). It is being uniquely ourselves, in the presence of God.

If we feel prayer is a duty or a burden, we are probably praying as monotheists. We are aware of the "duty" to speak to God—who is separate from us—but we might lack the discipline, or the desire. Our prayer lives sit as a relic upon a shelf of a once-zealous past. We feel inadequate and mute. But if prayer is being borne along by the Spirit in the relationship of the Son and the Father, if prayer is the sacred space where the Father names himself to me, and also names me to him, then prayer is not about doing something—but being someone. Prayer is being caught up in this relationship and dwelling in our identity as children of a loving Father. Prayer is being content with this identity and no other. Even so, we cannot sustain this brave act of identity on our own; we can only do this in Christ who forged the way ahead as the first man to relate to God as a *Son*.[11] We can

---

11. Praying "in Christ" can be interpreted by one of two spiritualities: one emphasizes that I pray "in Christ" due to failure ("I will never pray properly. . . . I will always pray inadequately. . . . I will never be the pray-er God wants me to be, so Christ has to come and step in") while the other emphasizes anthropology ("I was created for this conversation . . . in Christ, I can become the 'home' where this ongoing conversation is happening all the time").

only do this with the "Spirit of sonship" (Rom 8:15) who unites us to the Son. When we pray in this way, we are not praying to get a job done but that slave-narratives might fade away. We pray as an entrance into this relationship over and over again.

And so, it just might be, that prayer is the only place where we can be authentically ourselves. There is a Hasidic story that gets at this, which recounts the last words of the Hasidic Rabbi Zusya.

> "When I am taken to heaven," Zusya told his disciples, "I shall not be asked, 'why were you not more like Moses?' No, I shall be asked, 'why were you not more like Zusya?'"[12]

In our prayer lives, we cannot seek to emulate others with heroic prayer efforts and disciplines. (Although prayer efforts and disciplines might be central to our growth in prayer.) In so doing, we miss the very gift and reality of prayer. In our prayer lives, we should seek to be named and known by the only one who can truly know us. Only in prayer can we be our truest selves—the selves the Father names. Not the generic selves we fabricate to fit into the slave narrative (the dutiful self, the disciplined self, the ideal Christian self, etc.). In Christian prayer, we receive our identity and are declared to be "children," created for communion. The greatest enemy of Christian prayer is not a lack of discipline, but a lack of being ourselves in prayer. The more we lean into techniques, the more unreality we can generate. As C. S. Lewis cries in *Letters to Malcolm*, "May it be the real I who speaks. May it be the real Thou that I speak to."[13]

Prayer is where anthropology and theology are most related—either most dissonant or most harmonious. The Trinity is not something we "believe" in; it is how we pray. Trinitarian prayer is never something we can "do" or be "good at," but rather it is a place to dwell richly. It is without ceasing, because it is inhabiting the eternal relationship of Father and Son, that is life in the Spirit. From this place we can act, minister, and be God's kingdom here on earth. But we never move from this primal place of prayer: entering the Trinitarian life that has been opened to us in Christ.

A Prayer of Francois Fénelon

> Lord, I do not know what I ought to be asking of you.
> You are the only One who knows what I need.
> You love me better than I know how to love myself.

---

12. Buber, *Tales of the Hasidim*, 251.
13. Lewis, *Letters to Malcolm* , 82.

Father!—give your child what I do not know how to ask for myself.
I do not dare ask for crosses or for consolation.
All I can do is present myself to you.

Lord, I open up my heart to you.
Observe my needs—the ones that I am not even aware of.
Look at them, and act according to your mercy.
Bring suffering on me or heal me,
Cast me down or raise me up.
I adore your will for me even when I do not know what it is.

I will remain silent,
Offering myself up and giving myself over completely to you.
I no longer have any desire other than to accomplish your will.

Teach me to pray.
May you pray yourself in me and through me.[14]

Bibliography

Balthasar, Hans Urs von. *Prayer.* San Francisco: Ignatius, 1986.
Barth, Karl. *Dogmatics in Outline.* Translated by G. T. Thompson. London: SCM, 1949.
Brueggemann, Walter. *Genesis.* Interpretation: A Bible Commentary for Teaching and Preaching. Atlanta: Westminster John Knox, 2010.
Buber, Martin. *Tales of the Hasidim: The Early Masters I.* New York: Schocken, 1968.
Calvin, John. *Institutes of the Christian Religion.* Edited by John T. McNeil. Translated by Ford Lewis Battles. Library of Christian Classics 20–21. Philadelphia: Westminster, 1960.
Fénelon, Francois. *The Complete Fenelon.* Translated and edited by Robert J. Edmonson and Hal M. Helms. Brewster, MS: Paraclete, 2008.
Guite, Malcolm. *Sounding the Seasons.* Norwich: Canterbury, 2012.
Kenyon, Jane. *Otherwise: New & Selected Poems.* Minneapolis: Graywolf, 1997.
Lewis, C. S. *Letters to Malcolm.* New York: Harcourt, 1992.
Rahner, Karl. *The Trinity.* London: Continuum, 2001.
Reeves, Michael. *Delighting in the Trinity: An Introduction to the Christian Faith.* Downers Grove, IL: InterVarsity, 2012.

---

14. Fénelon, *Complete Fenelon*, 62.

CHAPTER 11

The Trinity in Paul

From Confession to Ethics

Douglas A. Campbell

The "divine identity" debate has been one of the most important movements in recent New Testament scholarship, and we are indebted to Larry Hurtado and Richard Bauckham for the way they have changed the conversation. Supported now by the contributions of a second generation of scholars, like Chris Tilling's powerful *Paul's Divine Christology*, the evolutionary approach of previous scholarship has been overthrown, and the existence of an "early high Christology" in the early church has been, at least to my mind, convincingly established.[1] Of course, the debate continues. But it is not my intention to provide a further defense here of the new and refreshingly orthodox position. I want to presuppose it, and to ask about what comes next. For a scholar of Paul, a fascinating and important question lies here that has not to my knowledge yet been sufficiently explored.

As we do so, however, I will speak in terms of Trinitarianism and not merely in terms of an early high Christology. Accompanying the new emphasis on Jesus as Lord—at least to the modern academy—is a renewed emphasis from other quarters on the importance of the Holy Spirit.[2] Hold-

---

1. Bauckham, *Jesus and the God of Israel*; Hurtado, *One God, One Lord*; Hurtado, *Lord Jesus Christ*; Tilling, *Paul's Divine Christology*.

2. Important treatments of pneumatology in Paul include Fee, *God's Empowering Presence*; Fatehi, *Spirit's Relation*; Rabens, *Holy Spirit and Ethics*. Important yet

ing them together, we should, as a result, speak of a certain sort of Trinitarianism as operative in Paul. God the Father, the Lord Jesus, and the divine Spirit, are all part of the divine identity, and are all key elements within his thinking. But we immediately encounter challenges here concerning the reference and precision of this nomenclature. Does Trinitarianism refer to a triune God at work in Paul's life, and consequently in history as a whole, or merely to a mental construct on the part of a somewhat deluded apostle, who was echoed by an equally deluded church, suggesting in turn a very different construction of history? And how does this nomenclature relate to the key creedal formulations of subsequent centuries, which were so precise?

Suffice it to say that although it is important to attend constantly to the particularities of history, I find the claims of histor*icism* reductionist and unconvincing, and so will work with an open, rather than a closed, view of history, and will consequently refer Trinitarianism to something real, divine, and triune. Furthermore, if the living God is triune, it is fair to interpret Paul as if a triune God is influencing his categories and activity. Having said this, however, we must recognize the ways in which Paul's early articulations lack the precision of the later creeds. To insert their formulations into his thinking *tout court* would be anachronistic, and should be avoided. In Paul's day, in short, the Trinity was not mapped fully by the church's doctrine of the Trinity, and we should interpret accordingly. In what follows, then, I will assume that Paul's theology was informed by Trinitarian categories, but that these are less articulated than those developed later on by the creeds.[3]

With these opening clarifications we can turn to our detailed discussion. My suggestion here is that a fascinating Trinitarian implication lies hidden within the history of Paul's mission. Once uncovered this prompts us to recognize that the doctrine of the Trinity, even in this early form, can never be left at a merely confessional level, where some current debate might suggest. It is supposed to do work on the ground, forming the communities who confess it in virtue, and authenticating the surprising missional inclusions that the triune God effects.[4]

---

accessible treatments of the Spirit in broader theological terms include Heron, *Holy Spirit*; Smail, *Giving Gift*; and Holmes, *Holy Spirit*.

3. Yeago and Rowe treat the Trinitarian issues insightfully: see Yeago, "New Testament," 152–64; Rowe, "Biblical Pressure," 295–312; and Rowe, "For Future Generations," 186–209. The implications for history are sketched by Nathan (Nate) Kerr in *Christ, History, and Apocalyptic*; and probed in more depth, in critical conversation with N. T. Wright, by Samuel V. Adams, *Reality of God*; and more broadly by Murray Rae, *History and Hermeneutics*. The issues are also constantly in view in the mature work of the figure who underlies much of this: Karl Barth's *Church Dogmatics*.

4. See Curtis Freeman's comments about a moribund scholastic Trinitarianism

Explaining Paul's Mission

We are so familiar with what Paul did as a missionary that we tend to forget how innovative and even disruptive it was. In the first instance, he was called to be an apostle to the pagans. The comprehensive offer to pagans of eternal life by way of a place in the Age to Come was unusual, to put it mildly. Acts repeatedly notes the horror this aroused among Jews.[5] But, to make matters worse, in the second instance, the communities that Paul succeeded in founding did not convert to Judaism (which might have eased some of the horror), but lived as "Christians," as Acts puts it (11:26c).[6] They were clearly ethical, or they were supposed to be. Paul's letters—which were unusually long for missives to common folk—are little more than extended ethical admonitions. But his letters also attest to the way in which Christians were not ethical in a standard Jewish way, which is why they were first called Christians. Some Jewish practices, like endogamy and respect for parents, are apparent, but these are present alongside a puzzling disregard toward other key Jewish practices, like the observation of Jewish dietary and calendrical rules and the circumcision of males. In short, it is reasonably easy to see that Paul's Torah-free mission to the pagans was a shocking salvific *and* ethical innovation, something confirmed by its contestation within the early church. Nevertheless, Paul did succeed in justifying it, at least to some, and so pagans continued to convert and to become Christians, not Jews, with the result that Paul's theological rationale for his radical mission became the basis for the later Christian church. We need now to try to recover this rationale.

Unsurprisingly, in view of the stakes, Paul's theological justification of his Torah-free mission has been as contested as its original advent. But I suggest that "apocalyptic," suitably defined, maps some of its key dimensions, making this claim over against competing claims that it is best explained either by pagan religious categories, drawn especially from the Mystery religions, or by a "Lutheran" argument, using this last descriptor with strict reference to Stendahl's account.[7] Even the meaning of the term

---

within the Baptist tradition in his *Contesting Catholicity*, 143–90.

5. For variations on this narrative see Acts 11:1–2; 13:6–12, 44–52; 14:19; 15:1–29; 17:5; 21:21, 27–28; 22:21–22; and 26:23–29. Paul attests to this response as well in 1 Thess 2:14–16.

6. See my essay, "Beyond the Torah at Antioch," 187–214.

7. The definitions in Krister Stendahl's classic essay are important: "Apostle Paul," 199–215. However, his analysis can be made more precise: see my *Deliverance of God*, ch. 1, 11–35 (an outline of "justification theory"), and 172–76 (a clarification of Stendahl's concerns).

"apocalyptic" is contested, however (again, in part because the stakes are so high). So let me clarify that I am using it here to denote the importance to Paul of resurrection and eschatology, notions discussed at length in Jewish apocalyptic literature.[8] Paul appeals repeatedly to inaugurated eschatology, which is to say, to a resurrection operative in some sense within his converts already, in advance of the universal cosmic arrival of the Age to Come, to justify their nature, status, and behavior as Christians rather than as messianic Jews. It is this highly counterintuitive claim that leads to our first glimpse of the Trinity at work in Paul and his converts.

Trinitarian Participation

The present life of Christians as a new creation and hence resurrected is stated especially clearly in 2 Cor 5:17 and Gal 6:15. But important summaries of the transition to this resurrected life as enacted by the entry ritual of immersion can also be found in Gal 3:26–28; 1 Cor 12:13; and Col 3:11.[9]

> So then, if someone is in Christ, he is a new creation;
> the old has gone: behold, he has become new!
>
> (2 Cor 5:17)[10]

> For neither circumcision is anything, or uncircumcision,
> but only a new creation!

8. Martinus C. de Boer provides several excellent points of entry into this approach: see his important doctoral thesis published as *Defeat of Death*; along with his essays "Paul and Jewish Apocalyptic Eschatology," 169–90; and "Appropriation of Jewish Apocalyptic Eschatology," 17–29. Ordinarily, I do not emphasize this aspect of the apocalyptic approach to Paul immediately. It is critical, rather, to attend first to its epistemological emphasis on a christocentric revelation; see my studies "Apocalyptic Epistemology," 65–85; and "Apocalyptic Reading of Paul." However, space precludes moving through this sequence here and we must jump immediately to the second key emphasis in the apocalyptic approach, on resurrection and eschatology.

9. I challenge the cogency of the arguments that Ephesians, Colossians, and 2 Thessalonians were not authored by Paul in my *Framing Paul*. In the absence of convincing—and even vaguely probative—considerations proving their pseudonymity, their authorship by Paul, as suggested by their opening statements and closing signatures, can be trusted, along with their contributions to this discussion. (I am not so sanguine about the authenticity of the Pastorals.) To exclude the data of these letters on the grounds that they are disputed is in fact to decide the argument in favor of pseudonymity, and on overtly confused grounds; the data underlying other interpretative disputes in Paul is never *excluded* merely because it is disputed! What data in Paul would remain?

10. The gender is masculine singular although the meaning is generic. All translations are my own unless otherwise specified.

(Gal 6:15)

> For all of you who are in Christ Jesus are sons of God
> by means of the believing we have just been talking about.
> For you have been immersed into Christ,
> you have been clothed in Christ.
> There is no Jew or pagan;
> there is no slave or free person;
> there is no "male and female."
> For all of you who are in Christ Jesus are one and the same.

(Gal 3:26–28)

> . . .for through one Spirit we all have been immersed into one body,
> whether Jews or pagans,
> whether slaves or free people;
> and we have all been given one Spirit to drink.

(1 Cor 12:13)

> . . .so that there is no pagan or Jew,
> circumcised or uncircumcised,
> barbarian, Scythian,
> slave, or free person,
> but Christ is everything in every way.

(Col 3:11)[11]

Significantly, the claims of these short statements can be found writ large in Rom 5–8, as well as, to a lesser degree, in Eph 2. And they are presupposed whenever Paul exhorts his converts to act ethically and yet does not enforce full Torah observance, as he does, for example, throughout 1 and 2 Thessalonians and Philemon. The position is also referenced through all his letters, Paul's preferred summary for this, namely, being "in Christ" or its close equivalent, occurring upward of one hundred and sixty times.[12]

Paul's point in all these locations, counterintuitive but insistent, is that Christians live out of a resurrected location that *transcends* current visible locations structured by things like ethnicity, race, class, status, and even gender (there is no "male and female"!). These last categories are no longer determinative. He and his converts live from a new world, which is to say, from a new creation. Furthermore, this new location is dramatically

---

11. See my study "Unravelling Colossians 3.11b," 120–32.
12. Deissmann, *Saint Paul*; Campbell, *Paul and Union with Christ*.

superior to the old. This is clearest in his brief comparison in Phil 3, where he contrasts life as a zealous Jew with life in Christ.

> But whatever was gain to me,
> these things I considered loss because of Christ;
> furthermore, I also considered everything to be loss
> because of the sheer surpassing nature of the knowledge of
> Christ Jesus my Lord,
> because of whom everything has become a loss,
> and I consider them excrement
> that I might gain Christ
> and I might be found in him...
>
> (Phil 3:7–9)

Paul's point here can be muted by an overly polite translation. He looks back on his previous life, good in and of itself, or "gain" as he puts it, and then characterizes it in comparison to his present life within the resurrected Christ as σκύβαλα or "excrement." It is largely beyond doubt then that it is a resurrected location that justifies Paul's pagan converts *qua* Christians and not Jews. This location transcends current dynamics, including ethnicity, and does so *massively*—as much as a Christmas dinner surpasses what happens later in the toilet.

A minority tradition of scholars has long recognized and affirmed this important dimension within Paul's theology. Its most famous forbear is, as is often the case, a learned German, here Albert Schweitzer, although by his own admission he was not the origin of the view.[13] My teacher, Richard N. Longenecker, who also belongs to this tradition, looked back to the earlier work of G. Adolf Deissmann, and notes its transmission through key English-speaking scholars like James Stewart, W. D. Davies, C. F. D. Moule, and Morna Hooker. William Wrede's name could also be included here.[14] However, in a particularly important moment, the position has been

---

13. Schweitzer, *Paul and His Interpreters*; Schweitzer, *Mysticism of Paul*.

14. In addition to those figures already noted, see Wrede, *Paul*; Stewart, *Man in Christ*; and Hooker, "Interchange in Christ," 349–61; Hooker, "Interchange and Atonement," 462–81. Robert C. Tannehill provides an elegant summary in "Participation in Christ," 223–37. A recent important and prolific advocate of the importance of participation is Michael J. Gorman; see his *Cruciformity*; *Inhabiting the Cruciform God*; "Romans"; *Death of the Messiah*; and *Becoming the Gospel*. M. David Litwa has also made some significant recent contributions: "2 Corinthians 3:18," 117–34; and *We Are Being Transformed*; as has Ben C. Blackwell in his *Christosis*. An important recent summary volume is Thate, Vanhoozer, and Campbell, *"In Christ" in Paul*.

advocated more recently by E. P. Sanders in his epochal *Paul and Palestinian Judaism*.[15]

Sanders summarizes Paul's thinking in these terms with the rubric "Participationist Eschatology," nicely capturing the apocalyptic emphasis on future categories breaking into the present and concretely transforming Christians. His position has been developed still further by his pupil, Gregory Tatum, who introduces the faithfulness of Christ and a more extensive role for the Spirit into Paul's position, motifs that Sanders was uncomfortable with.[16] Tatum affirms correctly that Paul speaks of Jesus faithfully enduring death on the cross to rise again so that Christians might participate in his resurrected life by way of the life-giving Spirit. But at this moment, with Tatum's additional insights, we can see that Participationist Eschatology has an overtly Trinitarian dynamic and so might also be fairly summarized with the rubric "Trinitarian Participation." Christians participate concretely in the risen Christ, or eschatologically, because they have been raised in some sense by the Spirit, both these divine agents fulfilling the will of God the Father, who sent the Son and the Spirit into the cosmos to rescue a humanity corrupted and oppressed since Adam. In other words, Participationist Eschatology is undergirded by, and only really makes sense in terms of, Trinitarian action. But further questions now immediately arise concerning the *plausibility* and *purpose* of Paul's notion of Trinitarian Participation, as well as with the potentially destructive *dualism* implicit in its claims. Unless these are dealt with straightaway, the entire position collapses.

Defending Trinitarian Participation

Paul's claims that Christians are participating in the Age to Come, and so characterized by resurrection and a resulting new creation, are strongly counter-intuitive, to put the objection gently. But he is well aware of this. He does not deny that life in the present cosmos continues. The resurrection is only as yet partial, while what Christians continue to see is the world of the flesh, as he puts it. However, Paul is certain that Christians have a new mind, derived ultimately from Christ. They possess Christ's φρόνημα or thinking, which is sensitive to the realities of the Spirit, *and it is this reality that is determinative*. Moreover, his proclamation of this good news is accompanied by confirming signs and wonders by the Spirit, while Christian worship evidences more of the same. These warrants suffice to reassure his converts that the spiritual world that they are involved with is quite real, and that the

---

15. Sanders, *Paul and Palestinian Judaism*, esp. 431–56.
16. Tatum, "Participationist Eschatological Reading."

story Paul recounts about what has happened to them is an accurate one (and in any case, ancient people were presumably much less skeptical about the existence of this unseen world than modern western individuals[17]). So Christians presently live with a foot in two worlds, and the apparent reality of the one must not be allowed to occlude the underlying determinative reality of the other.[18]

Despite the tensions suggested by this location, those living out of the new mind of Christ experience peace, over against the conflict they experience if they step back into the miseries of the flesh and its enslaved and conflicted thinking. Moreover, the new resurrected mind clearly also possesses ethical *capacity*, which the mind of the flesh conspicuously lacks.[19] Christians can now do the good, whereas previously they could not, and were frequently unaware even of what the good was, not to mention, hostile to God. Formerly, they were slaves to lusts living within, and to evil powers oppressing from without (see esp. Rom 7:4–25). As a result of this, however, it is clear that the eschatological transformation currently unfolding within Christians is not merely salvific, although it is this (Rom 8:8, 11). It is *ethical*.

There is a danger lurking here, however, that some of Paul's later interpreters embraced, and possibly even some of his own converts at Corinth. The claim that the determinative and important part of the person is a hidden mind of spirit can easily be extended into a destructively disembodied dualism, the stance that basically gave rise later to Christian Gnosticism.[20] Surely, if Paul's position is the case, the body is redundant and can safely be ignored?, a view that could lead to a shameless libertinism—so 1 Cor 5:1–13 and 6:9–20! Alternatively, the body's material drag on the goodness of the mind should be ruthlessly disciplined, leading to an inappropriate

---

17. An overdependence on ocular metaphors is exposed and attacked by Richard Rorty in his famous study *Philosophy and the Mirror*. But Michael Polanyi had earlier done much the same, displacing visual with tactile metaphors; see *inter alia*, his short account, *Tacit Dimension*. The collapse of modern culture into atheism, in response, at least in large measure, to the failures of theological foundationalism, is documented superbly by Michael J. Buckley in *At the Origins of Modern Atheism*; and summarized and updated in *Denying and Disclosing God*; as well as by William C. Placher in *Domestication of Transcendence*.

18. It is best not to understand the relationship between these two dimensions in zero-sum and essentially quantitative terms, so that the more of one suggests the less of the other. Musical analogies here are helpful. These are developed with unparalleled expertise by Jeremy Begbie; see especially his essay "Room of One's Own? Music, Space, and Freedom," in *Music, Modernity and God*, 141–75.

19. Our new ethical capacity is presumably another warrant for this gospel's truth.

20. See a lively study by F. B. Watson that exposes some of these implications: "Resurrection and the Limits," 452–71.

asceticism, far from the freedom that Paul's gospel lays claim to—so 1 Cor 7:1–7 and Col 2:16–23.

But a careful reading of Paul reveals that he never made this extension and would doubtless have refused to do so if asked. Although the current body of flesh is contaminated and oppressed, it is still the locus for personhood and activity. Our lingering problems will only be solved when we receive a new body of spirit, "in the twinkling of an eye," when Christ returns in glory.[21] Paul does, admittedly, leave awkward questions here for his later students to struggle with concerning the nature and fate of Christians if they die before Jesus returns—what scholars tend to refer to as the intermediate state.[22] But Paul's basic position, affirming the full particulars of our present location, is well warranted. The Son entered our human condition, assuming a body made of flesh, so that he might terminate it and create a new ethical capacity for us.[23] And in doing so he also *affirmed* our current fleshly location fully and completely as both embodied and manageable.[24] As a result, every detail of our concrete existence, however evanescent—every hair on our heads, to slip for a moment into gospel idiom[25]—matters. Such details are neither permanent nor perfect, but they are important. They are the form through which the new mind acts. Consequently, any gnostic extension of Paul's emphasis on a resurrected mind of spirit within our present body of flesh into a destructive dualism should be firmly repudiated. Paul's mind of the spirit can be *distinguished* from its current body of flesh, but it cannot be *separated* from it until it receives its new body of spirit.[26]

With these immediate challenges addressed, we can continue on the assumption that what Paul is claiming is both true and defensible. We participate in the Trinity, in an eschatological albeit inaugurated sense, by virtue of the Trinity's action upon us. But why?

Herein lies the rub.

---

21. 1 Cor 15:50–54.

22. The issues are introduced tidily by Aune, "Anthropological Duality" 215–39. I provide a deeper defense of Paul's position, utilizing a particular view of space-time (as we have to) in "Defending Resurrection," ch. 7 in my *Pauline Dogmatics in Outline*.

23. Rom 8:3–4; Phil 2:7.

24. The Methodist emphasis on perfection captures this nicely, provided it is correctly understood. Randy Maddox treats the issues with accuracy and clarity in "Change of Affections," 3–31; "Shaping the Virtuous Heart," 27–28; and, with Paul Chilcote, "Introduction." (My thanks to Randy Maddox for these references.)

25. Matt 10:30; Luke 12:7.

26. Phil 4:21.

Trinitarian Communion

Up to this point, the *basis* of Paul's ethic has been described, along with our newfound *capacity*, by way of our participation in the resurrected Jesus through the work of the Spirit.[27] But we have yet to explain its *shape* or *content*. Moreover, in order to do so we must press beyond the categories of apocalyptic, and deeper into the reality that Paul's converts participated in. It is not enough, that is, to affirm that we have been raised in Christ. Apocalyptic helps us to understand this resurrection. We need now to ask what this partially inaugurated eschatological existence is like as we start to live it, beyond the event of resurrection, since this ongoing structure now supplies the all-important ethical dynamics that press upon the renewed minds of those who have been touched by the Spirit. But there is a reasonably simple although somewhat shocking answer to this query.

We live now *in* the Trinity, with the resurrected Son, and it follows from this that the nature of the Trinity *is* the content of Paul's ethic. Moreover, the Trinity is, precisely, a trinity of divine persons. So a Trinitarian ethic will inevitably be an *interpersonal* or *relational* ethic. Indeed, at this moment, the Trinity discloses to us the further critical insight that a person *is a fundamentally relational entity*, something we should pause to consider.

The Trinity discloses that the being of a person is essentially ecstatic. People exist, in marked opposition to most of the self-contained and individualistic conceptions dominating modernity, in relationship with one another, and therefore only as those relationships exist, and through those relationships, and so "outside of themselves." As a result of this, relationality could hardly be more important. It is constitutive of our personhood *and* of our ethics.[28]

Paul's account of God discloses these insights into personhood fairly obviously once one knows where to look. God *the Father* is characterized above all by his relationship *with his Son*. The Son is then clearly constituted in the reverse direction, by his relationship with his Father.[29] The Spirit is characterized in much the same way, by relationships with the Father and with the Son; the Spirit is the Spirit both *of God the Father* and *of Christ*

---

27. Rom 8:9–10.

28. The origin of much of the modern theological emphasis on the relationality of persons, although grounding that meticulously in the thought of the Cappadocians, is Zizioulas, *Being as Communion*. The point is developed superbly by Alan J. Torrance in his *Persons in Communion*. Also highly insightful is Luke Ben Tallon's dissertation, supervised by Alan Torrance: "Our Being Is in Becoming."

29. I treat Paul's use of "father" and "son" language in my essay, "Story of Jesus," 97–124.

Jesus. And it follows from this that familial metaphors are fundamental to Paul's account of Christian community.[30] His preferred nomenclature for Christians, by far, is ἀδέλφοι, best translated gender inclusively as "siblings."[31] Paul articulates these insights especially clearly in Rom 8:29, which is an especially important verse:

> ...those he foreknew he appointed beforehand
> to be conformed to the image of his Son
> so that he might be the firstborn among many siblings....

All of this might seem somewhat abstract, however, so it is worth taking a moment to bring these revelations home emotionally and concretely. In my case, I am the partner of Rachel and the parent of Emile and Grace. As a result of our covenantal relationships with one another over the years, these three people are now literally part of who I am, and I of them. Where I go, Rachel, Emile, and Grace go, and where they go I go too. Our personhood is intertwined together, which is why when trauma happens to one of them it happens to me, and vice versa, although the same applies to more positive experiences like excitement and joy as well. We *are primarily* constituted *by our relationships*, and especially by our key ones, whether these are within our families or with our deepest friends.[32]

If this relational notion of personhood is starting to bed down, then we need to consider next what the tenor or quality of these relationships is, since this will generate the specifics of our ethic. I have just mentioned in passing that our key relationships are covenantal, meaning by this that they are unconditional. These relationships never break and are never withdrawn. To speak concretely again, my children will always be my children and I will always be their parent. Nothing that they or I do can alter this.

---

30. James B. Torrance develops this point elegantly in two essays: "Covenant or Contract," 51–76; and "Contribution of McLeod Campbell," 295–311. Behind these insights lies the work of one of his teachers, John Macmurray, esp. as developed in his Gifford Lectures in 1952–54, published as *Self as Agent*; and *Persons in Relation*.

31. This data is provided in my essay, "Story of Jesus."

32. Friendship is treated as a theological practice by Stanley Hauerwas and Charles Pinches in "Companions on the Way: The Necessity of Friendship," and "Friendship and Fragility," in their *Christians among the Virtues*, 31–51 and 70–88, respectively. I am interested in the way this practice spills over into specific—and frequently highly compelling—narratives like Osha Gray Davidson, *Best of Enemies*. The missional implications are articulated nicely by Chris Heuertz and Christine Pohl in *Friendship at the Margins*; and by Samuel Wells and Marcia A. Owen in *Living without Enemies*. I draw some of this material together briefly, in a prison context, in "Strange Friendships," 4–9. An important feature of this practice is the connection that emerges with sociological research on network theory. This is introduced in a fascinating way by Rodney Stark in *Rise of Christianity*.

These relationships can be damaged, to be sure, and be the source of a great deal of pain. But they are *irrevocable*, and when they are operating as they should, they result in a great deal of joy.[33] But underlying the covenantal nature of these relationships is a more fundamental relational dynamic that Paul knows well.

The relationships within the Trinity, and the relationships that we are being drawn into, are relationships of love.[34] Their love should not be defined in terms of the sentimentality that modern culture frequently confuses it with.[35] Real love is revealed ultimately by Jesus's determined walk to the cross for us while we were still estranged, wicked, and hostile to him.[36] It is costly and powerful. It also operates in a specific way, shifting modalities as it encounters different circumstances. As Paul puts it, relationships informed by love can be, as they need to be, patient, kind, and affirming of others. They are joyful, enduring, hopeful, and persevering. They evidence, when it is appropriate, joy, peace, patience, generosity, gentleness, and self-control.[37]

This then is the heart of Paul's ethic (in brief!). The Trinitarian relationships within God, between Father, Son, and Holy Spirit, draw us into communion with them, thereby transforming us into their covenantal and loving way of relating—a priceless gift. And although Paul would not have put things in quite this way, this fundamentally relational ethic does explain most of what he enjoins on his converts ethically in his letters. First Corinthians is a useful quick test case for this claim.

Love is incarnational; it gets alongside people, irrespective of their status, so Christian leaders should evidence this. Moreover, it does not get involved in overzealous partisanship, aggressively promoting certain leaders at the expense of others (1:10—4:21). It undertakes sexual activity within certain boundaries, outside of which damage ensues (5:1–12; 6:12–20; 7:1–40).[38] It resolves communal disputes, like thefts, internally (6:1–11). When someone is offended by the breach of a Jewish dietary practice, it

---

33. Rom 11:29. Barth's development of this notion, especially in *CD* II/1, IV/3.1, and IV/3.2, is worth spending time on.

34. See esp. (of course) 1 Cor 13; but also Rom 13:8–10; Gal 5:13–14. See also Alan J. Torrance, "Is Love the Essence of God?," 114–37.

35. Stanley Hauerwas's concern in "Love's Not All You Need," 111–26; and Richard B. Hays, "Why Love and Liberation Are Not Sufficient," 200–204.

36. Rom 5:6, 8–9.

37. Gal 5:22–3; Phil 4:8.

38. There is more to be said here, but this is an important dynamic. See further in my *Paul: Apostle's Journey*, ch. 8 ("Navigating Sex and Gender"); and *Pauline Dogmatics*, chs. 24 and 25 ("Navigating Marriage & Sex," and "Navigating Gender").

prescinds from eating the offending article again, however theologically innocuous it might be, and if necessary indefinitely! (chs. 8–10). When people are worshipping in a way that shames their spouses, they modify their behavior accordingly (11:1–16). When people are being humiliated by the largesse some enjoy at the Christian communal meal, that ostentatious behavior is to cease (11:17–34). When people are crowding out the spiritually inspired voices of one another, they are to slow down and to take turns (chs. 12–14). Love recommends the involvement of others in a community selflessly (16:10-18), and gives money to those who need it (16:1–4). In short, attention to the quality of the relationships involved in each of these issues, with the goal of making them as loving as possible, explains most of what Paul is urging through this, his most complex ethical letter.[39] Indeed, the realization that it is the tenor of relationships that matters explains the bulk of Paul's ethical advice in all his letters. He is constantly exhorting his converts to relate to one another with the appropriate sensitivity and kindness, ultimately in love.[40]

If we appreciate that Trinitarian communion results in a fundamentally relational ethic, with loving and covenantal behavior issuing forth from our new location within the loving and covenantal relationships of the Triune God, then we are ready for the next step in our investigation. We need to explore how a relational ethic grounded in the Trinitarian God unfolds in practical terms, on the ground, in mission, and among any new communities that result from this.

---

39. Only chapter 15, the letter opening (1:1–9), and Paul's final travelogue and closing formulae are missing from this coverage (16:5–9, 19–24).

40. For further, more specific guidance about this ethic, we will find some help in virtue ethics, the ancient philosophical tradition, rooted in Greek thinkers, that was especially concerned to define and to foster good behavior. Most current exponents look back primarily to Aristotle. There is considerable overlap between Paul's ethic and ancient virtue ethics, although there are also significant differences, that much of church tradition subsequently parsed for us.

Helpful analyses of the insights and advances of the Fathers are Wetzel, *Augustine and the Limits of Virtue*; Colish, *Ambrose's Patriarchs*; Smith, *Christian Grace and Pagan Virtue*; and Boersma, *Embodiment and Virtue*. (My thanks to Warren Smith for these references.)

An important current exponent of a virtue ethic, combining it with the Barthian emphasis on revelation that also characterizes Paul, is Hauerwas. His key works are *Community of Character*; *Peaceable Kingdom*; and, with Pinches, *Christians among the Virtues*.

Helpful, more recent, treatments, include Herdt's superb *Putting on Virtue*; and Banner's Bampton Lectures published as *Ethics of Everyday Life*.

Methodological fountainheads for this tradition include MacIntyre, see esp. his *After Virtue*; and Hadot, see his *Philosophy as a Way of Life*. A powerful conversation between Paul and other ancient virtue thinkers is Rowe's *One True Life*.

Communal Diversification

We return here to our opening reference to the radical nature of Paul's mission to the pagans that resulted in Christians rather than in yet more messianic Jews. And what becomes apparent now, after our theological digression, is that this was not a process of erasure, with one form eliminating the other, but of legitimate and appropriate *diversification as justified by a relational Trinitarian ethic*. Given time I would want to show how the Trinity was *prompting* this diversifying inclusion, but our focus here is on ethics and the resulting theological justification of this diversity.[41]

The key to this sort of appropriate diversification is the recognition that a relational ethic is concerned above all with the tenor and dynamics of the relationships in a community rather than with their form. The easiest way to think about this, although it has some limitations, is to grasp that in this ethic the "how" matters more than the "what." All relationships operate within structures or forms that contain multiple dimensions providing options for individuated behavior.[42] But every specific action can be assessed in terms of its charity and its tenor. No details are irrelevant. Every act is particular and occupies a form and must do so in order to take place. But its interpersonal effects that unfold in a detailed way can always be evaluated relationally and this is what matters. Is it loving? If appropriate, is it covenantal? In the right circumstances, is it gentle, and/or kind, or self-controlled, or patient?, and so on.

If, in an act of kindness, I offer to get my coworker a free beverage, it does not matter if she asks for a cup of coffee, of cocoa, or of tea. The act can't take place without a concrete drink, but the what of the drink does not matter as much as the how of the offer and its delivery.[43] Just so, Paul is not very concerned about whether someone is eating meat that has been previously sacrificed to an idol and not drained of its blood.[44] But he knows that this "what" will scandalize anyone with Jewish commitments, so he counsels his converts not to cause offence—the "how" of the situation. If someone will be

---

41. As noted earlier, I locate the first pneumatological incursion into a radically different constituency in Syrian Antioch: see my "Beyond the Torah" (n. 6). A useful probabilistic rationale for this situation is supplied by Esler in "Glossolalia and the Admission of Gentiles," 37–51.

42. A useful—and deeply learned—conversation partner at this moment is Oliver O'Donovan, see *Self, World, and Time*; and *Finding and Seeking*.

43. Chancellor, "Everyday Prosociality," 1–11.

44. His principal navigation of this situation can be found in 1 Cor 8–10, but a more generic treatment also appears in Rom 14. A subtle analysis of Paul's navigation of these questions is supplied by Horrell, *Social Ethos*; and Barclay's treatment of Rom 14 is also typically probing in "Do We Undermine the Law?," 287–308.

upset, or perhaps even theologically thrown, by seeing Christians feasting on such meat, they should determine never to eat meat again.

> If your sibling is grieved because of food
> then you are no longer walking in love....
>
> For the kingdom of God is not a matter of food and drink
> but of goodness and peace and joy in the Holy Spirit.
>
> (Rom 14:15, 17)

With the "how" mattering more than the "what", the stage is set for a diversification of God's people over time into different forms—into a garden where a thousand flowers bloom. Forms may differ as long as the relationships operating within them are loving. It is important to appreciate that there is no trivialization of all these emerging differences. The embodied forms within which all relating takes place remain *important*, and for much the same reasons that led us earlier on to repudiate Gnosticism. God is fully engaged with every aspect of our lives, and with what we do through and with our bodies. God is deeply interested in all this. Every detail matters; without them we cannot relate at all. But the nature of God's interest also matters. Such details are expressions of particularity. They are part of the delightfully diverse relational play unfolding within our creation and our history. They are *interesting*, and even fun, and contribute to our *identities*. They are the *vehicles* for our relating. As the forms within which our relating and acting play out, they do matter. But they matter *to us*. There is no warrant, therefore, on the basis of these considerations, to universalize these forms and to mandate them for everyone. This would be a stunning *non sequitur*.

I myself like drinking a mug of hot tea in the morning, made with loose-leaf tea originally harvested in India. This is very much a part of who I am, and I am strongly committed to this practice (as are others). But it is not a universally applicable ethical form, to be applied in the name of God, to everyone living around me who drinks coffee, water, or orange juice for breakfast. It is just something I do, and I learned to do it from my culture and my forbears, who are (in part) British, and frequently do the same. Paul is deeply interested in the nature of the relationship playing out around my tea-drinking, as is God. Am I generous with my offers of tea? Do I make tea for my spouse, perhaps even unbidden? Am I loving and generous? (And eventually we should ask if the entire process by which the tea arrives on my bench is loving, or at least, considerate.)

The same concerns apply to every action I undertake. Its relational tenor is of profound importance. The "how" matters ethically. But the "what" is merely important to me. This is a rule of thumb or, stating things rather better, a generalized practice. It will need to be nuanced, and some qualifications will need to be introduced straightaway. But in the main it holds good, and as we might expect, since it flows from our involvement with the profoundly loving relationality of the triune God. And the result of this ethic at work is a fascinating diversification of God's people into different forms, all the while being guided, shaped, and informed, by a stringently relational ethic.

Hence, there is, on the one hand, no erasure of identities and various particularities in the name of one normative identity, and, on the other hand, no libertine endorsement of all actions and relationships as somehow equal and appropriate. There is simply a steady expansion and diversification, much as Paul says, in Rom 11, from a root in the specific form of Judaism, through its messianic variant in particular (although not in fact permanently erasing its rebellious, non-messianic forms), and then out through different, formerly pagan and now Christianized, branches, whether those are basically Greek, Roman, or a specific barbarian form, in Colossae probably Phrygian (perhaps with a dash of Scythian), elsewhere Galatian, and so on.

We need now to note two important qualifications of this basic position.

Qualification 1. We must appreciate that the forms and structures within which relationships are embedded and actions take place are seldom entirely neutral, while some particularly toxic structures may limit actions to a suite of entirely evil options. We must consequently allow a lovingrelationality to modify the structures within which it operates, pressing them toward ever more considerate and ultimately Trinitarian configurations. We can always ask if a form impedes loving behavior, or could be modified to do so more readily, and if the answer is "yes," we should reform accordingly.

Paul is a difficult example to cite in support of this phenomenon because it is patient, time-consuming work, and his focus was generally elsewhere, on community founding, while his time horizon was short. He was happy to let things "stay where they are."[45] But a careful reading suggests that he modified all sorts of cultural structures and forms subtly, and at times overtly. We see how in Corinth he ruled out visiting prostitutes, a standard male pagan practice, and prohibited ostentatious and humiliating feasting in the communal meal, this being another acceptable Hellenistic practice. He resisted the importation into the community of highly partisan rhetori-

---

45. See 1 Cor 7:17, 20, a maxim emphasized insightfully by Schweitzer in *Mysticism of Paul*, 193. I sketch out some of the difficulties this caused at Corinth in chapter 8 of my *Paul: An Apostle's Journey*.

cal and political practices from Hellenistic civic life, and the evaluation of leadership in terms of showy trained eloquence, and pressed almsgiving in cross-cultural and costly directions.[46] To the Romans, echoing Jesus, he even affirmed highly counter-intuitive practices of enemy-love (and so on).[47]

It is nevertheless crucial to continue this movement and to reshape even those forms Paul sometimes endorsed, when a loving relationality demands this. So, for example, Paul introduces a stunningly counter-cultural dynamic of care and love into the troubled relationship between Philemon and his thieving slave, Onesimus, but does not abolish their relationship of slavery itself,[48] a structure that is clearly not, in and of itself, facilitating unmitigated love and benevolence. The church later rectified this omission (although it took far too long to do so).[49]

Qualification 2. Having just said this, we must also appreciate that the modification of any structure or form *must itself possess relational integrity*. It is not the case that old structures can simply be judged, erased, and abandoned, and new forms introduced overnight, by fiat. People are embedded in forms and relate within them. So the movement toward their reform must possess relational integrity. Consequently, any endorsement of a new form of God's people will have to be *negotiated* with the rest of God's people. Diversification means differences, and people often find differences suspicious and even threatening (and not all differences should be accepted).[50] And this negotiation must itself participate in the relational integrity of the Trinity. To fail to behave as the Trinity calls us to behave during any such process—and they can be very difficult—clearly violates the very heart of Christian ethics. It follows from this, that is, that within a Trinitarian ethic, the end can never justify the means. Rather, as Aristotle correctly observed, the means *is* the end. Radically inclusive changes should never be imposed, or coerced, but must emerge from communal understanding, leading to

---

46. Respectively, 1 Cor 6:12–20; 11:17–34; 1:10–4:21; 2 Cor 8:1–9:15.

47. 12:17–21.

48. Phlm, esp. vv. 10, 12, 16.

49. A particularly powerful essay on the dynamics of slavery is Jennings, "Zurara's Tears," esp. 15–24. Willard M. Swartley selects a fascinating group of texts interpreting the Bible in relation to slavery, both *pro* and *contra*: see "Bible and Slavery," 31–64. Insightful essays on the hermeneutics of the situation are Meeks, "Polyphonic Ethics," 17–29; Meeks, "'Haustafeln' and American Slavery," 245–52; and Harrill, "Use of the New Testament," 149–86.

50. This story is a repeated one in the history of missions. It is particularly clear in missionary work in China. See Minamiki, *Chinese Rites*; and Walls, "Multiple Conversions," 271–94. I argue that Paul's life evidenced a similar dynamic; see ch. 21 in my *Pauline Dogmatics*, presaged in "Beyond the Torah," and *Paul: An Apostle's Journey*.

long, piecemeal, and specific shifts in forms through history. But there is a tension present here that must be navigated.

The one thing that cannot be compromised or patiently negotiated is the commitment of any participant within this process to the truths that underlie it as those flow from the Trinity. The truth must be spoken and defended in love, but the truth must still if necessary be defended.[51] If it is not, the very basis for navigating a challenging inclusion is lost, and we will be mispresenting God on a very fundamental level as well, a problem the Bible generally calls idolatry.[52]

Intriguingly, we see both these processes playing out in Paul's life. Scholars tend to emphasize the one or the other, but he clearly exercised essentially prudential judgments about which stance was appropriate in which situation. In Gal 2:11–14 we see Paul confronting no less a figure than Cephas, Jesus's right-hand man, and then standing up to Jesus's brother, James. In a similar vein, he trenchantly opposed a group he designates as "sneaking false brothers" in Jerusalem, who were presumably the cause of his troubles in Galatia, and potentially also in Philippi and Rome.[53] Here he clearly defended the truth. But even in Galatians we see Paul's diplomatic side at work as well. He comes with a collection of money from Antioch to Jerusalem, and promises to return with the same again—difficult labors and an extensive and inconvenient travel schedule.[54] While there, he *consults* with the Jerusalem leadership about his theological and ethical position, on an equal basis, to be sure, but he still consults, eventually winning them over.[55] And he engages in a similarly patient process to win back the loyalty of the Corinthians, after he has seriously upbraided and shamed many of them for various instances of inappropriate loyalty and behavior.[56] In short, he practiced what he preached, exemplifying how reform needs to be pursued charitably even as charitably diverse inclusions are made within God's

---

51. Eph 4:15.

52. The words of the famous maxim often attributed to Augustine but in fact coined in 1617 by the Archbishop of Split, Marco Antonio de Dominis, in his anti-Papal *De Republica Ecclesiastica*, are entirely apposite here: "in essentials unity, in non-essentials liberty, in all things charity. . . . *Unitatem in necessariis, in non necessariis liberatem, in omnibus caritatem.*" See Nellen, "De zinspreuk."

53. See Phil 3:2—4:4, treated in ch. 2 of my *Framing Paul*. Ch. 13 in my *Deliverance of God* provides a detailed analysis of the provenance of Romans in these terms.

54. 2:10; see also my *Framing Paul*, ch. 1.

55. 2:1–9.

56. Reconstructing the narrative largely from 2 Corinthians; see ch. 1 in my *Framing Paul*.

people, and structures are reformed so that people relating within them can do so more charitably as well.

This approach to communal change is profoundly counter-intuitive for a modern activist, accustomed to the categories of Liberal individualism, and to modern democracy, which effectively impose a pre-agreed coercion on its minorities.[57] But they are the way of the church, and we can see all the important dynamics playing out in Paul's life, at times dramatically.

Conclusion

Clearly the foregoing has been something of a programmatic sketch and not a detailed argument.[58] But hopefully enough has been said for the Trinitarian basis of Paul's ethic to become apparent, along with the way it informed and legitimized the first dramatic diversification of the community that took place through his mission.

The early church was originally a group of Jews who confessed Jesus to be their Lord and their Messiah. But Paul added converted pagans to this group, many of whom lived in a rather different, and unrecognizably Jewish, fashion. Some converted "God-worshippers" were presumably not far from orthopractic Judaism. Perhaps the only thing lacking was male circumcision, although this was important to most Jews. But other converts were not this orthopractic. They sat lightly to Jewish dietary and calendrical practices as well, and sometimes banqueted on pagan temple property and perhaps even feasted during pagan festivals ("because an idol is nothing"), although Paul thought that this last act was a step too far.[59] The important point to grasp here, however, is that this communal diversity is entirely legitimate in terms of Trinitarian participation and communion, as Paul seems to have argued. If our ethic, flowing from the nature of the Trinity, is fundamentally relational and interpersonal, it sits lightly, as a result, to forms located in our current cosmos of flesh. Forms still matter to those who occupy them, but they are not necessarily a key part of the evangelism of others or any resulting ethic, *and this is absolutely critical.*

If this is the case, Paul succeeded in providing an account of the church that does not erase Judaism, especially in its messianic form,[60] but coherently includes pagan converts within the community, without entirely erasing their pagan identities either. They become Christians. In this way,

---

57. See esp. Stanley Hauerwas's concerns as articulated in *After Christendom*.
58. My *Pauline Dogmatics* fills out much of this.
59. So 1 Cor 8–10, esp. 8:4 and 10:1–22.
60. A classic statement of this problem is Boyarin, *Radical Jew*.

Christian identity was not premised on the erasure of Judaism as a form prior to Christianity that is somehow inadequate and must now be superseded—as a religion of legalism now superseded by a religion of grace, or some such schema. (Ironically, Paul faced the mirror image of this threat in his day; militant Messianic Jews could not understand or accept Paul's mission, and attempted to reconvert his converts to a fully Torah-observant ethic in Galatia and elsewhere, erasing Christianity.) And at the heart of this rationale, and its attendant diversifying community, is the discovery that the Trinity is an *ethical*, and not merely a confessional and a salvific reality for Paul. Indeed, to fail to grasp this additional dimension is possibly to fail everywhere and most fundamentally.

Paul did not just confess the Trinity, although he did this. He did not just celebrate salvation by the Trinity, although he did this too, along with his converts. *He lived in and through the Trinity*. It structured his life and communities, and guided the diversification in his mission. And in doing so, it allows *us* to navigate differences in our communities as well, without lapsing either into some sort of supersessionism, and its implications of erasure, or into a symmetrical and destructive libertinism, or into some form of Gnosticism. Initially, the early church, with Paul's guidance, navigated Jew-pagan differences. Later, among other things, the church navigated differences of status and class like slavery. Now many of us are navigating gender roles, gender construction, and the appropriate relational location for sexual activity. The critical thing to grasp here and throughout, however, is that underlying all these navigations is the inclusive action of a Triune God, whom we "map" and follow, as best we can, guided by the doctrine of the Trinity.

A careful analysis of Paul reveals, in short, that the doctrine of the Trinity is an ethic, and it is a *live* ethic, although this should hardly surprise us. The Trinity is, after all, both alive and the source of all life. Hence Paul's famous blessing concerning "the gift of our Lord Jesus Christ, the love of God (the Father), and the society of the Holy Spirit" is not merely a wish on our behalf.[61] It is the reality in which we live and move and have our being.

Bibliography

Adams, Samuel V. *The Reality of God and Historical Method: Apocalyptic Theology in Conversation with N. T. Wright*. Downers Grove, IL: InterVarsity, 2015.

---

61. 2 Cor 13:13; and Acts 17:28.

Aune, David. "Anthropological Duality in the Eschatology of 2 Cor 4:16–5:10." In *Paul: Beyond the Judaism/Hellenism Divide*, edited by T. Engberg-Pedersen, 215–39. Louisville: Westminster/John Knox, 2001.

Banner, Michael. *The Ethics of Everyday Life: Moral Theology, Social Anthropology, and the Imagination of the Human*. Oxford: Oxford University Press, 2014.

Barclay, John. "Do We Undermine the Law? A Study of Romans 14:1—15:6." In *Paul and the Mosaic Law*, edited by J. D. G. Dunn, 287–308. Tübingen: Mohr Siebeck, 1996.

Barth, Karl. *Church Dogmatics*. Edited by T. F. Torrance and G. W. Bromiley. 4 vols. Edinburgh: T. & T. Clark, 1956–1996 [1932–67].

Bauckham, Richard. *Jesus and the God of Israel: God Crucified and Other Studies on the New Testament's Christology of Divine Identity*. Grand Rapids: Eerdmans, 2008.

Begbie, Jeremy. *Music, Modernity and God: Essays in Listening*. Oxford: Oxford University Press, 2013.

Blackwell, Ben C. *Christosis: Pauline Soteriology in Light of Deification in Irenaeus and Cyril of Alexandria*. WUNT 2/314. Tübingen: Mohr Siebeck, 2011.

Boersma, Hans. *Embodiment and Virtue in Gregory of Nyssa: An Anagogical Approach*. Oxford: Oxford University Press, 2013.

Boyarin, Daniel. *A Radical Jew: Paul and the Politics of Identity*. Los Angeles: University of California Press, 1994.

Buckley, Michael J. Buckley. *At the Origins of Modern Atheism*. New Haven, NJ: Yale University Press, 1987.

———. *Denying and Disclosing God: The Ambiguous Progress of Modern Atheism*. New Haven, NJ: Yale University Press, 2004.

Campbell, Constantine R. *Paul and Union with Christ: An Exegetical and Theological Study*. Grand Rapids: Zondervan, 2012.

Campbell, Douglas A. "Apocalyptic Epistemology: The *Sine Qua Non* of Valid Pauline Interpretation." In *Paul and the Apocalyptic Imagination*, edited by Ben C. Blackwell, John K. Goodrich, and Jason Maston, 65–85. Minneapolis: Fortress, 2016.

———. "The Apocalyptic Reading of Paul, and Its Road through Romans." In *Romans for the Pew*, edited by Scot McKnight and Joe Modica. Grand Rapids: Eerdmans, forthcoming 2018.

———. "Beyond the Torah at Antioch: The Probable Locus for Paul's Radical Transition." *Journal for the Study of Paul and His Letters* 4 (2014) 187–214.

———. *The Deliverance of God: An Apocalyptic Rereading of Justification in Paul*. Grand Rapids: Eerdmans, 2009.

———. *Framing Paul: An Epistolary Biography*. Grand Rapids: Eerdmans, 2014.

———. *Paul: An Apostle's Journey*. Grand Rapids: Eerdmans, 2018.

———. *Pauline Dogmatics in Outline*. Grand Rapids: Eerdmans, forthcoming.

———. "The Story of Jesus in Romans and Galatians." In *Narrative Dynamics in Paul: A Critical Assessment*, edited by B. W. Longenecker, 97–124. Louisville: Westminster John Knox, 2002.

———. "Strange Friendships." *Divinity* 14 (Fall 2014) 4–9.

———. "Unravelling Colossians 3.11b." *New Testament Studies* 42 (1996) 120–32.

Chancellor, Joseph, et al. "Everyday Prosociality in the Workplace: The Reinforcing Benefits of Giving, Getting, and Glimpsing." In *Emotion* (2017) 1–11. http://dx.doi.org/10.1037/emo000032.

Colish, Marcia. *Ambrose's Patriarchs: Ethics for the Common Man*. Notre Dame: University of Notre Dame Press, 2005.

Davidson, Osha Gray. *The Best of Enemies: Race and Redemption in the New South*. Chapel Hill: University of North Carolina Press, 1996.

De Boer, Martinus C. "The Appropriation of Jewish Apocalyptic Eschatology in the New Testament, Especially Paul." In *Hoffnung für die Zukunft: Modelle eschatologischen und apokalyptischen Denkens*, edited by Ed Noort and Mladen Popović, 17–29. Theologie zwischen Ost und West 2. Groningen: Groningen University Press, 2001.

———. *The Defeat of Death: Apocalyptic Eschatology in 1 Corinthians 15 and Romans 5*. Journal for the Study of the New Testament, Supplement Series 22. Sheffield: JSOT, 1988.

———. "Paul and Jewish Apocalyptic Eschatology." In *Apocalyptic and the New Testament: Essays in Honor of J. Louis Martyn*, edited by Joel Marcus and Marion Soards, 169–90. Journal for the Study of the New Testament, Supplement Series 24. Sheffield: Sheffield Academic, 1989.

Deissmann, G. A. *Saint Paul: A Study in Social and Religious History*. London: Hodder & Stoughton, 1912.

Esler, Philip F. "Glossolalia and the Admission of Gentiles Into the Early Christian Community." In *The First Christians in Their Social World: Social-Scientific Approaches to New Testament Interpretation*, 37–51. London: Routledge, 1994.

Fatehi, Mehrdad. *The Spirit's Relation to the Risen Lord in Paul: An Examination of Its Christological Implications*. Tübingen: Mohr Siebeck, 2000.

Fee, Gordon. *God's Empowering Presence: The Holy Spirit in the Letters of Paul*. Peabody, MA: Hendrickson, 1994.

Freeman, Curtis. *Contesting Catholicity: Theology for Other Baptists*. Waco, TX: Baylor University Press, 2014.

Gorman, Michael J. *Becoming the Gospel: Paul, Participation, and Mission*. Grand Rapids: Eerdmans, 2015.

———. *Cruciformity: Paul's Narrative Spirituality of the Cross*. Grand Rapids: Eerdmans, 2001.

———. *The Death of the Messiah and the Birth of the New Covenant: A (Not So) New Model of the Atonement*. Eugene, OR: Cascade, 2014.

———. *Inhabiting the Cruciform God: Kenosis, Justification, and Theosis in Paul's Narrative Soteriology*. Grand Rapids: Eerdmans, 2009.

———. "Romans: The First Christian Treaties on Theosis." In *Journal of Theological Interpretations* 5 (2011) 13–34.

Hadot, Pierre. *Philosophy as a Way of Life*. Translated by Michael Chase. Oxford: Blackwell, 1995.

Harrill, J. Albert. "The Use of the New Testament in the American Slave Controversy: A Case History in the Hermeneutical Tension between Biblical Criticism and Christian Moral Debate." *Religion and American Culture* 10 (2000) 149–86.

Hauerwas, Stanley. *After Christendom: How the Church Is to Behave if Freedom, Justice, and a Christian Nation Are Bad Ideas*. Nashville: Abingdon, 1991.

———. *A Community of Character: Toward a Constructive Christian Social Ethic*. Notre Dame: University of Notre Dame Press, 1981.

———. "Love's Not All You Need." In *Vision and Virtue: Essays in Christian Ethical Reflection*, 111–26. Notre Dame: University of Notre Dame Press, 1981 [1974].

———. *The Peaceable Kingdom: A Primer in Christian Ethics*. Notre Dame: University of Notre Dame Press, 1983.

Hauerwas, Stanley, and Charles Pinches. *Christians among the Virtues: Theological Conversations with Ancient and Modern Ethics*. Notre Dame: University of Notre Dame Press, 1997.

Hays, Richard B. "Why Love and Liberation Are Not Sufficient." In *The Moral Vision of the New Testament—Community, Cross, New Creation: A Contemporary Introduction to New Testament Ethics*, 200–204. New York: HarperCollins, 1996.

Herdt, Jennifer. *Putting On Virtue: The Legacy of the Splendid Vices*. Chicago: University of Chicago Press, 2008.

Heron, A. I. C. *The Holy Spirit: The Holy Spirit in the Bible, in the History of Christian Thought and in Recent Theology*. London: Marshall, Morgan & Scott, 1983.

Heuertz, Chris, and Christine Pohl. *Friendship at the Margins: Discovering Mutuality in Service and Mission*. Downers Grove, IL: InterVarsity, 2010.

Holmes, Christopher R. J. *The Holy Spirit*. Grand Rapids: Zondervan, 2015.

Hooker, M. "Interchange and Atonement." *Bullitan of the John Rylands Library* 60 (1978) 462–81.

———. "Interchange in Christ." *Journal of Theological Studies* 22 (1971) 349–61.

Horrell, David. *The Social Ethos of the Corinthian Correspondence: Interests and Ideology from 1 Corinthians to 1 Clement*. Edinburgh: T & T Clark, 1996.

Hurtado, Larry W. *Lord Jesus Christ. Devotion to Jesus in Earliest Christianity*. Grand Rapids: Eerdmans, 2003.

———. *One God, One Lord: Early Christian Devotion and Ancient Jewish Monotheism*. 2nd ed. London: T. & T. Clark International, 1998 [1988].

Jennings, Willie J. "Zurara's Tears." In *The Christian Imagination: Theology and the Origins of Race*, 15–64. New Haven: Yale University Press, 2010.

Kerr, Nathan R. *Christ, History, and Apocalyptic: The Politics of Christian Mission*. London: SCM, 2009.

Litwa, M. David. "2 Corinthians 3:18 and Its Implications for *Theosis*." *Journal of Theological Interpretation* 2 (2008) 117–34.

———. *We Are Being Transformed: Deification in Paul's Soteriology*. BZNW 187. Berlin: de Gruyter, 2012.

MacIntyre, Alasdair. *After Virtue: A Study in Moral Theory*. 3rd ed. Notre Dame: University of Notre Dame Press, 2007 [1981].

Macmurray, John. *Persons in Relation*. London: Faber & Faber, 1961.

———. *The Self as Agent*. New York: Humanity, n.d. [1957].

Maddox, Randy. "A Change of Affections: The Development, Dynamics, and Dethronement of John Wesley's 'Heart Religion.'" In *"Heart Religion" in the Methodist Tradition and Related Movements*, edited by Richard Steele, 3–31. Metuchen, NJ: Scarecrow, 2001.

———. "Shaping the Virtuous Heart: The Abiding Mission of the Wesleys." *Circuit Rider* 29 (July/August 2005) 27–28.

Maddox, Randy, and Paul Chilcote. "Introduction." In *A Plain Account of Christian Perfection*, by John Wesley. Kansas City, MO: Beacon Hill, 2015.

Meeks, Wayne A. "The 'Haustafeln' and American Slavery: A Hermeneutical Challenge." In *Theology and Ethics in Paul and His Interpreters: Essays in Honor of Victor Paul Furnish*, edited by Eugene H. Lovering Jr. and Jerry L. Sumney, 245–52. Nashville: Abingdon, 1996.

———. "The Polyphonic Ethics of the Apostle Paul." *Annual of the Society of Christian Ethics* (1988) 17–29.

Minamiki, George. *The Chinese Rites Controversy from Its Beginning to Modern Times.* Chicago: Loyola University Press, 1985.

Nellen, H. J. M. "De zinspreuk 'In necessariis unitas, in non necessariis libertas, in utrisque caritas.'" *Nederlands archief voor kerkgeschidenis* 79 (1999) 99–106.

O'Donovan, Oliver. *Finding and Seeking.* Ethics as Theology 2. Grand Rapids: Eerdmans, 2014.

———. *Self, World, and Time: An Induction.* Ethics as Theology 1. Grand Rapids: Eerdmans, 2013.

Placher, William C. *The Domestication of Transcendence: How Modern Thinking about God Went Wrong.* Louisville: Westminster John Knox, 1996.

Polanyi, Michael. *The Tacit Dimension.* New York: Doubleday, 1966.

Rabens, Volker. *The Holy Spirit and Ethics in Paul: Transformation and Empowering for Religious-Ethical Life.* 2nd rev. ed. Minneapolis: Fortress, 2014.

Rae, Murray Rae. *History and Hermeneutics.* London: T. & T. Clark [Bloomsbury], 2006.

Rorty, Richard. *Philosophy and the Mirror of Nature.* Princeton, NJ: Princeton University Press, 1979.

Rowe, C. Kavin. "Biblical Pressure and Trinitarian Hermeneutics." *Pro Ecclesia* 11 (2002) 295–312.

———. "For Future Generations: Worshipping Jesus and the Integration of the Theological Disciplines." In *Pro Ecclesia* 17 (2008) 186–209.

———. *One True Life: The Stoics and Early Christians as Rival Traditions.* New Haven: Yale University Press, 2016.

Sanders, E. P. *Paul and Palestinian Judaism: A Comparison of Patterns of Religion.* Philadelphia: Fortress, 1977.

Schweitzer, Albert. *The Mysticism of Paul the Apostle.* Translated by W. Montgomery. Baltimore, Maryland: Johns Hopkins University Press, 1998 [1931].

———. *Paul and His Interpreters.* Translated by. W. Montgomery. New York: Schocken, 1964 [1912].

Smail, Thomas A. *The Giving Gift: The Holy Spirit in Person.* Eugene, OR: Wipf & Stock, 2004 [1998].

Smith, J. Warren. *Christian Grace and Pagan Virtue: The Theological Foundation of Ambrose's Ethics.* Oxford: Oxford University Press, 2011.

Stark, Rodney. *The Rise of Christianity: A Sociologist Reconsiders History.* Princeton, NJ: Princeton University Press, 1996.

Stendahl, Krister. "The Apostle Paul and the Introspective Conscience of the West." *Harvard Theological Review* 56 (1963) 199–215 (reprinted in Stendahl, Krister, *Paul among Jews and Gentiles, and Other Essays*, 78–96. Philadelphia: Fortress, 1976).

Stewart, James. *A Man in Christ: The Vital Elements of St. Paul's Religion.* London: Hodder & Stoughton, 1935.

Swartley, Willard M. "The Bible and Slavery." In *Slavery, Sabbath, War, and Women: Case Issues in Biblical Interpretation,* 31–64. Scottdale, PA: Herald, 1983.

Tallon, Luke Ben. "Our Being Is in Becoming: The Nature of Human Transformation in the Theology of Karl Barth, Joseph Ratzinger, and John Zizioulas." PhD diss., University of St. Andrews, 2011.

Tannehill, Robert C. "Participation in Christ: A Central Theme in Pauline Soteriology." In *The Shape of the Gospel: New Testament Essays*, 223–37. Eugene, OR: Cascade, 2007.

Tatum, Gregory. "A Participationist Eschatological Reading of Justification in Galatians, Philippians, and Romans." Paper presented to International Society of Biblical Literature, Berlin, August 9, 2017.

Thate, Michael J., Kevin J. Vanhoozer, and Constantine R. Campbell, eds. *"In Christ" in Paul: Explorations in Paul's Theology of Union and Participation.* WUNT 2/384; Tübingen: Mohr/Siebeck, 2015.

Tilling, Chris. *Paul's Divine Christology*. Grand Rapids: Eerdmans, 2015 [2012].

Torrance, Alan J. "Is Love the Essence of God?" In *Nothing Greater, Nothing Better: Theological Essays on the Love of God*, edited by Kevin J. Vanhoozer, 114–37. Grand Rapids: Eerdmans, 2001.

———. *Persons in Communion: An Essay on Trinitarian Description and Human Participation with Special Reference to Volume One of Karl Barth's Church Dogmatics.* Edinburgh: T. & T. Clark, 1996.

Torrance, James B. "The Contribution of McLeod Campbell to Scottish Theology." In *Scottish Journal of Theology* 26 (1973) 295–311.

———. "Covenant or Contract?: A Study of the Theological Background of Worship in Seventeenth-Century Scotland." *Scottish Journal of Theology* 23 (1970) 51–76.

Walls, Andrew. "The Multiple Conversions of Timothy Richard: A Paradigm of Missionary Experience." In *The Gospel in the World: International Baptist Studies*, edited by David Bebbington, 271–94. Carlisle,UK: Paternoster, 2002.

Watson, F. B. "Resurrection and the Limits of Paulinism." In *The Word Leaps the Gap: Essays on Scripture and Theology in Honor of Richard B. Hays*, edited by J. Ross Wagner, C. Kavin Rowe, and A. Katherine Grieb, 452–71. Grand Rapids: Eerdmans, 2008.

Wells, Samuel, and Marcia A. Owen. *Living without Enemies: Being Present in the Midst of Violence.* Downers Grove, IL: InterVarsity, 2011.

Wetzel, James. *Augustine and the Limits of Virtue.* Cambridge: Cambridge University Press, 1992.

Wrede,W. *Paul.* Translated by E. Lummis. Eugene, OR: Wipf & Stock, 2001 [1908].

Yeago, David S. "The New Testament and the Nicene Dogma: A Contribution to the Recovery of Theological Exegesis." *Pro Ecclesia* 3 (1994) 152–64.

Zizioulas, John D. *Being as Communion: Studies in Personhood and the Church.* New York: St. Vladimir's Seminary Press, 1985.

CHAPTER 12

Bridging the Gap between Piety and the Theology of the Schools

A Working Sketch

Christoph Schwöbel

Fifty years ago, Karl Rahner famously deplored the isolation of the doctrine of the Trinity.[1] Though the doctrine could be found in the language of piety and in the theology of the schools, Rahner argued that it did not have any constitutive meaning for the exposition of Christian doctrine. Christians were merely monotheists in the way they led their lives and Rahner suspected that a large part of religious literature would be unaffected if the doctrine of the Trinity were recognized to be false and consequently eliminated from the corpus of Christian doctrine. In short, the religious literature could stay as it is, because it did not make significant reference to the doctrine of the Trinity in the first place.

Many things have changed since Rahner offered this critical view of the role of the doctrine of the Trinity in the life of the church. By the end of the century, the renaissance of Trinitarian theology had brought the doctrine of the Trinity to the forefront of theological discourse. More recently,

---

1. Rahner, *Trinity*, 10. Rahner's treatise was first published under the title "Der dreifaltige Gott als transzendenter Urgrund der Heilsgeschichte", in Feiner and Löhrer (eds.), *Mysterium Salutis*, 317–401. There, the relevant section heading reads: "Die Isolierung der Trinitätslehre in Frömmigkeit und Schultheologie" (319).

however, there has been widespread criticism of this Trinitarian revival, notably concerning the projection of aspects of created life onto the Trinity and with it being incommensurable with the doctrine of the simplicity of God hinted at by some patristic authors and—so it is claimed—systematically developed by Thomas Aquinas in *quaestio* 13 of the *Summa theologiae*. While this criticism has led to a wealth of philosophical literature on the conceptual problems presented by the doctrine of divine simplicity, the response by systematic theologians has so far been either controversial or relatively subdued, though it is still early days.[2]

In this situation, it might be useful for us to revisit Rahner's claim and look systematically at the connections between Christian piety in worship and the challenges of conceptually clarifying what Christians do when they worship the triune God. Is the alleged twofold isolation of the doctrine of the Trinity in the realms of worship and conceptual elucidation, which Rahner diagnosed, in fact an indication of a close relationship between Trinitarian discourse in worship and doctrinal exposition? If so, the fact that the middle ground of Christian living appears to be insufficiently shaped by attention to the Trinity could actually be due to an unsatisfactory grasp of the connection between worshipping the Triune God and attempting to clarify the conceptual intricacies of the doctrine of the Trinity. While the Trinity is primarily to be worshipped and adored, it is clear that the doctrine of the Trinity has played a very specific role in the history of Christian doctrine and theological reflection. The argument of this essay is that this role is best defined by the interaction between Christian worship and Christian doctrine, and it is therefore within *this* framework that the conceptuality of Christian doctrine must be developed and tested.

In other words, one of the most important tasks of the doctrine of the Trinity consists in offering possibilities for an adequate way of worshipping the Triune God. The old adage *lex orandi—lex credendi* points to this interaction. However, exactly *how* doctrinal formulation relates to the way in which worship is conducted seems to point to a number of specific links between worshipping the Triune God and the task of a doctrine of the Trinity. In the following I will try to spell out some of the links between elements of Christian worship and some of the questions the doctrine of the Trinity seeks to address, and to develop ways of response in conceptual form. The emphasis of this paper is not on the historical development of Christian worship nor on the historical development of the doctrine of the Trinity. Rather, it is an attempt to identify some of the constitutive elements

---

2. For an overview of the discussion in the last thirty years, see Schwöbel, "Where Do We Stand," 9–71.

in worship and in doctrinal exposition in order to explore their relationship. These elements could be seen as heuristic tools for analyzing the historical development of worship and the central questions addressed in the formulation, exposition, conceptual reflection, and justification of Trinitarian doctrine. In trying to trace some of the connections between worship and Trinitarian theology I do not follow a particular denominational setting of the liturgy nor a specific doctrine of the Trinity, let alone a particular Trinitarian theology. However, I have taken my orientation from the *Lutheran Book of Worship* and the *Evangelisches Gottesdienstbuch* with which I am most familiar.[3] Most churches in the West will be able to identify liturgical elements and patterns that also play an important role in their own worship. The result of this analysis—i.e., this attempt to trace the trajectories from the practice of worship to the conceptual questions of formulating doctrine—is something like an open list of correlations between elements of the liturgy and questions of Trinitarian theology, neither aimed at offering a comprehensive reconstruction of the liturgy nor at a systematically complete account of the doctrine of the Trinity. By pointing to the connections between celebrating worship and formulating doctrine, I am trying to overcome the twofold isolation of the doctrine of Trinity in piety and the theology of the schools by bridging the gap between them. The claim behind this attempt is, of course, that the connections I hope to point out are already there in the doctrinal implications and presuppositions of worship and in the liturgical consequences of doctrine.

Being Gathered in the Name of the Triune God

A Christian worship service begins with being gathered for worship by being called together out of the different contexts of our lives in the name of the Father, the Son, and the Holy Spirit. The element of being called out of something and being gathered for something is so central to worship that it has shaped the name of the Christian *ekklesia*, and corresponds to being sent out at the end of the service with the blessing of the Triune God. Being gathered "in the name" at once makes clear that we are not gathered in our own name and for our own purposes. Everything—the purpose,

---

3. All quotations from the liturgy are taken from the *Lutheran Book of Worship*, *Evangelisches Gottesdienstbuch*. To do theology as a theology of worship is, of course not new. Cf., the classics of such an approach: Wainwright, *Doxology*; Brunner, *Zur Lehre vom Gottesdienst der im Namen Jesu versammelten Gemeinde*. For an illuminating philosophical approach, see Wolterstorff, *God We Worship*. For a brief sketch of the theology of a Christian service as a relational communicative event presupposed here, see Schwöbel, "Was ist ein Gottesdienst?" 145–65.

the character, and the structure of the gathering—depends on who the one is who gathers us by *our* invocation of *his* name. In some liturgies, this Trinitarian invocation to which the assembled congregation responds with "Amen" is continued with Ps 124:8: "Our help is in the name of the Lord," and the congregation responds: "who made heaven and earth." This addition underlines an element of the gathering which is present even when this antiphon is not spoken. Being gathered in the name of the particular identity invoked by the triune name of God means being gathered in the name of the one who created heaven and earth and as such is radically distinguished from and related to everything created. In effect, the very particular and the most universal are brought together in the Trinitarian invocation. If our help is in the name of this Lord, it must cover everything that created beings could ever require. This includes, not least, to begin, maintain, and to end their existence.

This explains the specific structure of Christian worship. The particular identity of Father, Son, and Holy Spirit is also the Lord, the one God who as the maker of heaven and earth is the origin, meaning, and end of everything created. The gathering of persons is at the same time an act of focussing everything that is created in its relationship to this particular and universal creator. Everything is referred to its origin, its meaning, and its end. In this particular sense the Father, the Son, and the Holy Spirit is the one who alone is to be worshipped as the Lord. This contains the ultimate distinction between worshipping the true God and worshipping idols, i.e., other created beings. The triune identity and the predication of God as maker of heaven and earth make up the ultimate tension within which worship is conducted. In opening worship by this invocation it is asserted that God is personal, indeed tri-personal, and at the same time it is implied that the Father, the Son and the Holy Spirit is *the* One, since there can only be one who makes everything that is not God. Whatever else occurs in Christian worship is bracketed by what is asserted and implied in this invocation.

One of the very basic tasks of a doctrine of the Trinity generated by this Trinitarian invocation is that the church has to make clear that Christians are not worshipping three Gods, and this requires an understanding of the name of God that somehow can include reference to the Father, the Son and the Holy Spirit without breaking up the unity of the one who is to be worshipped. Citing Psalm 124:8 "Our help is in the Lord / who made heaven and earth" already gives an indication that if God really creates everything that is not God, then God must also constitute the possibility and actuality of invoking him and, furthermore, creates a particular commission to worship him in this way. This way of thinking about the God who is to be worshipped as the one who enables the relationship of worship is central to the biblical understanding of the relationship of God and humanity. Paul's argument in Rom 10 makes this abundantly clear. Quoting Joel 2:32, Paul starts from the premise: "Everyone who calls on the name of the Lord shall be saved" (Rom 10:13). He then constructs a series of rhetorical questions: How should they call on one, if they do not believe? How should they believe in one of whom they have not heard? How should one hear without those who proclaim him? (v. 14). And how should anyone preach if they have not been sent? (v. 15). Paul summarizes his argument: "So faith comes from what is heard, and what is heard comes through the word of Christ" (v. 17). By his account of the communicative constitution of faith, Paul has offered good reasons, each supported by scriptural warrants, for the assertion he started from: "Whoever calls upon the name of the Lord shall be saved" (Joel 3:5).

Calling on the Triune God and Speaking from the Triune God

Calling on the Triune God, which opens Christian worship, occurs throughout the liturgy. This presupposes that God can be addressed by his name. This, in turn, requires that God's name is known, and it can only be known by God making his name known. The revelation of God's name, as it is pictured in Exod 3:14, occurs expressly to enable the Israelites to call upon God. The self-identification of God is closely connected to his having noted the misery of Israel and his promise to lead Israel out of Egypt (Exod 3:16–17). The fulfillment of this promise then becomes an identifying description of God and is regularly combined with the name of God: "I am the Lord, your God, who led you out of the land of Egypt, the house of slavery" (Exod 20:2). Two requirements for calling upon God have been mentioned: The name of God must be known and the relationship of God to Israel is such that God can rightly be seen as the one from whom help can be expected. God must be known, able, and willing to help. In the book of Exodus, we therefore not only have God's self-identification but, closely connected with it, God's self-interpretation: "I will be gracious to whom I will be gracious and will show mercy on whom I will show mercy" (Exod 33: 19; cf., the more extended self-presentation of God in Exod 34: 6–7). If God is to be merciful and gracious we must be in need of grace and mercy. In fact, the need must be such that nobody else could help but God the creator, reconciler, and perfecter of the whole of creation. Calling upon God is a matter of ultimate importance because our misery is ultimate in the sense that it cannot be alleviated by any created entity.

The New Testament takes up all the conditions that make calling on God a meaningful activity. The name of God in Israel is retained but redefined through God's relationship to Jesus. God's self-identification is extended through his action in raising Jesus from the dead (Cf., Rom 4: 24). It is perhaps the most significant aspect of early Christianity that Christians retain the story of God's relationship with Israel, retain the identifying descriptions and the theology of the name, but extend it to include Jesus Christ so that in Jesus's name every knee shall bow (Phil 2:16) and all tongues shall confess that Jesus Christ is Lord to the glory of God the Father (Phil 2:11). In taking up and focussing the Spirit traditions in Israel's Bible, the Spirit of God becomes part of the way of talking about God's action and being, and of defining the potential of humans who are in God's Spirit: "Now the Lord is the Spirit, and where the Spirit of the Lord is, there is freedom" (2 Cor 3:17). It is the agency of God the Spirit that includes believers within the filial relationship of Jesus to God the Father (Rom 8:14). The extension of the way of talking about God to include Jesus Christ and the Spirit is correlated to a radicalized vision of human misery, indeed the misery of the whole creation. All have turned aside, as Paul explains by creating a pastiche of texts from Israel's Bible (Rom 3:10–18). Moreover, the whole of creation is in "bondage to decay" (Rom 8:20), eagerly waiting "to obtain the freedom of the glory of the children of God" (Rom 8:21). Humans can only be liberated to eternal life by participation in Christ's death and resurrection (Rom 6:4), an eternal life that is now anticipated in the gift of the Spirit (Rom 8:23).

In Christian worship, the misery of humans condemned to death is most drastically expressed in the order for confession and forgiveness. The Prayer of Preparation already makes this human situation transparent as one of estrangement from God in which humans are totally dependent on being redirected to love God perfectly. In the situation of utter helplessness, even the turning to God for forgiveness is a work of God the Spirit, made effective through Jesus Christ.

> Almighty God, to whom all hearts are open, all desires known, and from whom no secrets are hid: Cleanse the thoughts of our hearts by the inspiration of your Holy Spirit, that we may perfectly love you and worthily magnify your holy name, through Jesus Christ our Lord.

This requires the confession of sins as taking responsibility for our thoughts, words, and deeds as they receive their orientation from our heart. It is important to note that sin here covers sinful thoughts, words, and deeds as they are rooted in the dislocation of humans in their relationship to God in bondage to sin. Forgiveness of sin must therefore include a reconstitution of the human capacity to act, by relocating humans in the right relationship to God.

> Most merciful God, We confess that we are in bondage to sin and cannot free ourselves. We have sinned against you in thought, word, and deed, by what we have done and by what we have left undone. We have not loved you with our whole heart; we have not loved our neighbours as ourselves. For the sake of your Son, Jesus Christ, have mercy on us. Forgive us, renew us, that we may delight in your will and walk in your ways, to the glory of your holy name.

As we can see from this example, calling on God in Christian worship presupposes that God addresses us in the Trinitarian logic of the divine economy. The Father, the Son, and the Holy Spirit are both the name of the triune God and the way in which God relates to us. In order to enable us to call on him, God makes himself accessible in communicative relations through Jesus Christ and in the Holy Spirit. Our calling on the Triune God retraces the steps that God has taken to relate to us in his very being and so to enable our response to him. The way of God to the sinner, if we follow the witnesses of the New Testament, can only be described in a Trinitarian mode which in its most radical form is based on the notion of divine self-giving. In the absolution pronounced by the minister the calling upon God is turned into speaking in the name of God. This is made explicit in the form of address in which the minister speaks *in persona Christi*:

> Almighty God, in his mercy, has given his Son to die for us and, for his sake, forgives us all our sins. As a called and ordained minister of the Church of Christ, and by his authority, I therefore declare to you the entire forgiveness of all your sins, in the name of the Father, and of the Son and of the Holy Spirit.

What are the presuppositions of this practice of calling on God and speaking in the name of God? The one God must be conceived in such a way that it is God who overcomes our separation from God in which as created beings we are surrendered to nothingness and as sinners condemned to perdition. Moreover, it is God who appropriates to us this radical transposition from estrangement from God to communion with God. This momentous change of our position in relation to God, from dislocation to relocation in our relationship to God, must be one that is enacted in a communicative exchange that has ontological weight. It cannot simply be a declaration of what we have been and what we are now, but must be a creative transformation. The word of absolution must be an effective word, creating a new state of affairs by establishing a new ontological relationship. With regard to the understanding of God this requires that the different stages in the process of transformation are both distinguished and related, and so are both different and yet one. Offering forgiveness is not to be seen as a reaction of God to our sinfulness but as God's faithfulness in maintaining his primordial self-determination, an act of self-determination that is identical with his Trinitarian being. And it is precisely this dynamic of divine action, connecting God's creative, reconciling and perfecting agency, that must be rooted in the eternal being of God. God in his economic Trinitarian relations is the self-manifestation of the immanent Trinity. Liturgically, this is expressed by the way in which every communicative act of God comes from the Father through the Son in the Spirit. Every communicative act that we offer in response must be directed in the Spirit through the Son to the Father. If this is the structure of God's self-communication in his address to us, and if this is the order in which we respond to the self-communication, then the continuity in the different stages of this process must be rooted eternally in God, because God's agency is continuous with the Trinitarian being of God. The careful discussions that the early church conducted in order to show that giving glory to the Father through the Son and in the Spirit is ontologically identical with giving glory to the Father, the Son, and the Spirit make exactly this point. The differentiations in the one process of divine action are aspects of God's unitary action, which is one because it is rooted in the self-determination of God, which itself is the unity of act and being in God.

The connection between confession of sin and the promise of absolution is, of course, not the only aspect of Christian worship that shows the intrinsic relationship between calling on God and speaking from God. The most dramatic form of the interrelationship between calling on God, speaking of God, and speaking from God, is the recitation of the Psalms. The human situation is brought before God, and so God is addressed in praise, thanksgiving, petition, and lament. These speech acts always have ontological weight because the Psalms make it abundantly clear that God is not addressed as a being who in addition to having being has certain capacities and attributes of communicating, of speaking and of listening, of addressing and responding. God's being is consistently portrayed as communicative relational being. Similarly, because it owes its being and meaning to God's communicative action, created being is shaped by the way in which God addresses it. While the whole of creation speaks, telling the glory of God and proclaiming his handiwork (Ps 19:1), the response of creation is concentrated in humans, not exclusively but paradigmatically in the particular form of human language. The ultimate validation of human language as the medium of divine address and human response, and also the ultimate ontological ground to see being and speaking as one, is the incarnation: the divine Word that was in eternity with God becomes flesh and lives among us so that we can see the eternal attributes of God in his historical, bodily and communicative self-presentation: "And the Word became flesh and lived among us, full of grace and truth" (John 1:14).

The Trinitarian dimension of the recitation of the Psalms always becomes evident when the recitation is closed with "Glory be to the Father, the Son and the Holy Spirit." This suggests that all the different speech-acts preformed in the recitation of the Psalms find their place in giving glory to the Father, the Son and the Spirit, an act in which everything God is and everything humans can offer to him is comprised. In Christian worship the Psalms are included in the glorification of the eternal Trinity.

Being Located in the Story of the Triune God

In many denominations the order of worship contains three readings from Scripture, one from the Old Testament, one from the Epistles, followed by the reading of the Gospel. Used as Scripture, the pluralistic library of the Bible in its use in worship represents the canon of those biblical writings that have established themselves as suitable in worship. One has to keep in mind that it is this liturgical use that has for centuries been the main line of transmission of the biblical message for communal reading, long before the private reader played a significant role. When the patristic theologian, the scholastics, or the Reformers refer to Scripture, they presuppose this ecclesial use of the Bible as Scripture. The readings from the Lectionary conform to the liturgical year with its four seasons of (1) Advent, Christmas, and Epiphany, (2) Lent, Good Friday, Easter, (3) Ascension and Pentecost, and (4) the series of Sundays following Trinity Sunday. The sequence of the readings focuses on the Gospels and follows the life of Christ from his birth, through the commemoration of his suffering and death to the celebration of Easter. The Ascension and Pentecost point to the condition of the possibility that the church can live her life in the Spirit in continued communion with her Lord and through him with God the Father. In the Scripture readings of the liturgical year, all history is remembered, and the Bible is read as the book of the world, spanning its entire history from Alpha to Omega, from the beginning before all created beginnings to the end which is the world's absolute future.

The liturgical use of the Bible shows quite clearly that Christianity cannot easily be subsumed into the category of the "book religions." The focus of Christianity is not the book as the revelation, but the book of the

Bible used as Scripture as it is employed by God as a means for his self-presentation and for establishing community with believers. That is to say, the focus of worship is not the book but the person of Christ, and in this connection the book of Scripture is in its liturgical use to be seen as belonging to the means of grace, in connection with the word of proclamation and the celebration of the sacraments.

This way of reciting the Bible in worship makes the intertextual use of Old Testament and New Testament, of the Epistles and the Gospels, an established practice in the Christian church. That the Bible is its own interpreter may have been a critical rule for distinguishing God's word from human institutions and opinions in the Reformation, but in the church's liturgical use of the Bible as Scripture this was the established way of reading Scripture, and the typological interpretation that informs such an intertextual use could be developed from the liturgical use of Scripture. Similarly, the focusing of the Christian reading of the Bible on Christ was not a new discovery in the Reformation. Linking this christofocal reading to the literal sense of the Bible and connecting it to the other exclusive particles of the Reformation—only by grace and only in faith—shows continuity and discontinuity of the Reformation reading of the Bible with earlier periods in the history of the church. The most important change is certainly the connection established between the so-called Scripture Principle and the common priesthood of all believers. The believers can only exercise their common priesthood if their faith is constantly formed in the interpretation of Scripture. The way in which the connection between the common priesthood of believers and the emphasis on the constant conversation with Scripture has transformed worship is nowhere more significant than in the career of congregational singing that began with the Reformation.

This liturgical use of Scripture has the effect of locating the congregation of Christians in relation to the Gospel stories as presenting the person and work of Christ, and through Christ, as Israel's Messiah, as Christians believe, to the history of God with his people Israel. In this way, Christians are presented as being on the way to the Kingdom of God, inaugurated by Christ and already present in the witness of the church as the consummation of God's history with his creation. It is by looking back on the Christ event as the critical point of Israel's history that the Christian church looks forward to the future in the expectation of the coming of the Kingdom of God. The presence of the Spirit now, who is called to come and enlighten the minds of the worshippers, as it is sung in the *Veni Creator Spiritus*, is the intersection of the remembered history and the anticipated future.

The three coordinates in which the church is located are the person and work of Christ on earth, the way in which it relates back to God's relationship with Israel and opens it up even for Gentiles, and God's living presence in the Spirit with his church now as the first-fruits of the eschatological consummation. The liturgical use of the Bible always makes clear that in following Christ in the presence of Christ for his church, the church walks in the footsteps of Israel and is guided by the Holy Spirit on the way to the heavenly Jerusalem. Wherever Christian worship is celebrated with such a use of Scripture in worship, it always has a location in relation to the Exodus, to Galilee, and the earthly Jerusalem, and is oriented toward the heavenly Jerusalem. Whatever her concrete past may be, in worship she relates it to the past of the biblical narratives, and wherever she is headed, her future is defined by the coming of the Kingdom. Between these two horizons, memory and hope, the present of the church is defined. Through the liturgical use of Scripture in worship the church finds her location and her direction.

Being located and receiving orientation on her way through history presupposes for the church that the times that are presented in the readings from Scripture are part of one temporal sequence, so that the stories somehow fit in one plot. The liturgical use of Scripture presupposes that in the different notions of God and in the different literary representations we find in the biblical texts, there is nevertheless one referential subject to which all these texts refer. The liturgical use which places Scripture in the context of calling on God, responding to God, and speaking from God, does not place the different biblical texts in one historical time-line, defined by the continuity of history, but sees them coordinated by their reference to the communicative action of one God. If it is this referential identity that establishes the connection between the texts, there need not be continuity between their linguistic forms, their worlds of meaning, and their cultural contexts. The continuity between them is the continuity in their reference to the one God. However, reference to the one God is structured by the way Scripture speaks of God, as the God of Israel whom Jesus calls Father, as God's reconciling presence in Jesus, and as the Spirit, the promise of future consummation now at work in the present, granting freedom because he opens up possibilities that are not completely defined by the conditions of created existence alone.

It is here that we see the connection between the church's use of Scripture and the doctrine of the Trinity. The way in which the church uses Scripture requires an explication that can assert both the unity of the one referential subject of the story of which the church believes itself to be a part and its particular structure of the interconnection between God's presence in Israel, God's presence in Christ, and God's opening of the future now in the Spirit, who has his identity both in having his origin in the Father and in being sent by Jesus Christ. Just as calling on God and speaking from God requires a Trinitarian explication, so the use of Scripture in the different forms of reading from the Old Testament, expounding the Epistles, and communicating the promise of the gospel, needs to be coordinated by an understanding of God which can combine God's unity with the differentiation of God's agency and presence witnessed in Scripture.

It is important that the Scripture readings culminate in the proclamation of the gospel. The coordinates offered for the location of the church show its dynamic position as the recipient of a promise being guided on the way to the future. Its location is a location in a process of becoming, and the content, the direction, and the enactment of this process is offered as the promise of the gospel. If the church is the creature of the gospel, as the Reformers maintained, then its identity is precisely in the connection between receiving the promise and being set on the way toward its fulfilment. The church has this identity only by trusting in that promise.

Confessing the Triune God

The congregation responds to the proclamation of the gospel by the confession of faith, i.e., it recites the Creed. The Trinitarian doctrine contained and expressed in the Creed, be it the Nicene or the Apostles' Creed, explicates the theological presuppositions required for the practice of worship. The questions, "What are we doing when we worship the Triune God?" "What do we presuppose in such acts of worship and what follows from them?" are answered by the recitation of the Creed. In the recitation of the Creed, Trinitarian doctrine has an explicit place in Christian worship. Whereas in other forms of liturgical action it is implicitly presupposed for this action to be meaningful, it is here explicitly asserted—but stated not as doctrinal instruction but as a confession of faith.

A confession of faith is always self-involving. In this way it resembles the confession of sin. Whereas a confession of sin focuses on what we have done and what we are as sinners whose very existence depends on divine forgiveness, a confession of faith concentrates on who and what God is and what he has done, and so implicitly presents us with what we are as believers: creatures of promise and believing animals. Since Augustine, we have learned to distinguish between the content of faith, the beliefs expressed in a confession of faith (*fides quae creditur*), and the act of faith (*fides qua creditur*), the existential investment of who we are and what we are in trust.

In the Nicene Creed, we see in its overall structure and exposition of the material content of faith how believing in one God must be spelled out as believing in the Father, the Son, and the Holy Spirit. The fullness of God's work can only be expressed by pointing to the one divine essence of Father, Son and Spirit, and the identity of the triune being of God serves as the presupposition for the coordination, the unity in difference which we see in God's work.

If we look at the different clauses of the Creed we see that the introduction of the *personal name*, followed by *identifying descriptions*, form the beginning of each of the three articles. These identifying descriptions have the form of relational expressions that define the relation of the Son and the Spirit to the origin of all Trinitarian relations, God the Father. In the case of the Son and the Spirit, the expressions of the relations of origin are followed by *status descriptions*, either ontological specifications in the case of the Son, or a statement about the coequality with the Father and the Son in worship and glorification in the case of the Holy Spirit. Name and identity description—in the form of a statement of the relation of origin and status description—provide the background for the predications that attribute particular works to the three persons, *action terms* that either give a description of an agent ("maker"), or enumerate a series of activities ("came down," "became incarnate," "suffered," "rose," "ascended," "will come again to judge") or passive expressions ("was crucified," "was buried").

In characterizing the identity and the "nature" of God the Father, the phrase begins with the title-term one God and specifies it with the identifying name "the Father." "One God" states the ontological status of the one Christians believe in. The whole emphasis is on distinguishing this one from all other beings. The following description "maker of heaven and earth, of all that is, seen and unseen" emphasizes this categorical distinction. Later reflections have emphasized that this distinction establishes the most fundamental difference between God and everything that is not God. If one speaks of a categorical distinction, it denotes the difference between what can be grasped in categories and God, who does not fall into any category. The hotly debated issue in medieval philosophy and theology was the question whether this excludes any relation, because entities that are related were thought to have to belong to the same category. If God does not fall within a category, it was argued, there can be no relations in God. It has to be noted that this pertains only to contingent relations. That is because the Creed continues by talking of God as "the Father." This is clearly a relational term. The very first clause of the Creed claims in this way that the "one God" Christians believe in does not exclude relations. "The Father" is here used as the one term from which all other inner Trinitarian relations and status descriptions originate. One may wonder why this is immediately followed by the predicate "the Almighty." In whichever way one would specifically determine the content of "Almighty," it clearly implies that there is no other entity that could exercise *power over* God, and that the one God is the only one who has *power to* do anything. There are no external limits to God's power set by anything other than God. To speak of God is to speak of self-determination in the most radical sense. This does not exclude self-limitation because to deny this would mean to limit the power of God's self-determination. In connection with the phase "maker of heaven and earth, of all that is, seen and unseen" the attribute "Almighty" states a radical difference and relationship between God and what is not God. "All that is," from material beings to Platonic Ideas, or Popper's "World III," or the world of mathematical theorems, has its source and origin in God. The one God is the one actuality that makes everything else possible.

With regard to the Son, the set of descriptions must be richer. Jesus Christ is not spoken of as a second God but as "one Lord." This phrase, just as the reference to the Father, echoes Eph 4:5–6, "one Lord, one faith, one baptism, one God and Father of us all, who is above all and through all and in all." Although "Lord" may be the application of the Septuagint's rendering of the name of God to Jesus, we see here that it does not create a contradiction or conflict with the expression "one God." The next two expressions, "the only Son of God, eternally begotten of the Father" state expressions of the relation of origin. Jesus Christ is the only Son of God, and this is both an exclusive relation and one that obtains from eternity to eternity. The status descriptions that follow "God from God, Light from Light, true God from true God" affirm that the status of Jesus Christ is rooted in this exclusive and eternal relation to the Father. Jesus Christ is only "God" because he is "from God," he is "Light" because he is "from Light," and "true God" because he is "from true God." The Son and the Father are not members of the same class, "God," nor instantiations of the same category. Jesus Christ can only be God in virtue of the exclusive and eternal relation God the Father has to him, which characterizes Christ's being by the term "begotten." Whatever "begotten" means in detail, it must mean the transmission of and participation in the same "God-ness," which characterizes the Father as "one God." The famously contentious phrase "of one Being with the Father" in this way asserts a relationship where God the Father gives divine Being and the only Son receives divine Being without the Father losing it. The sameness of the divine being, expressed in the expression *homoousios*, implies that it cannot be given without being shared. The divine essence is in no way separate from the three persons and their relations, it is only in their personal communion. Otherwise it would become a mysterious "fourth," somehow lurking behind the persons of the Trinity. It is clear that the relation "from" is therefore neither an external relation both in the sense that it is not a relation from God to somebody who is not God, nor that it is a relation that can be accidental to the being of God, because it is precisely the communication of divine Being, which is expressed in the word "begotten." It is therefore an internal constitutive relation, both indicating a difference expressed in the names "Father" and "Son" and a sameness expressed in the "one Being." Both emphases, difference and sameness, the phrases of the Creed suggest, must be asserted together in order to avoid misunderstandings. Neither is the relation deniable in the sense that it would be possible to speak of the Father without the Son or the Son without the Father. This relation is not contingent, so it follows that one cannot speak of the one God or the being of God without speaking of the Father and of the Son and, as we shall see, of the Holy Spirit.

The next phrase, "Through him all things were made," includes Jesus Christ in the relationship of God the Father to everything that is not God. It also makes the additional point that the instrumentality through which something is created must be the instrumentality of God. If God the Father is the actuality that makes everything possible, God the Son is the divine instrumentality through whom everything that is possible becomes actual.

The specific christological phrases that follow have Jesus Christ as the subject of a series of activities. However, some of these activities are enabled or mediated by the power of the Holy Spirit so that they have to be spoken of in the passive voice, e.g., "was made man." In other expressions, the one who is the active subject of the incarnation is now spoken of as the object of another agency: "was crucified," "suffered death and was buried." How this relationship between activity and passivity is to be explained in detail would require a full Christology beyond the scope of this essay, but we can see that any account of Christology that tries to follow the statement in the Creed has to show how Christology fits in the Trinitarian framework that gives structure and content to the Creed. A number of points simply must be noted here. The assertion of Jesus Christ as the mediator of creation associates Christ with the beginning of all beginnings, the concluding statements about the Last Judgement and the coming of the Kingdom, "which will have no end" connects Christ to the end of all ends. The whole of the Trinitarian economy is also Christ's economy.

Within that comprehensive framework, the phrase "for us and for our salvation" introduces the section of the Creed concerned with incarnation, crucifixion, ascension, and Christ's sitting at the right hand of the Father. It concludes with Christ's coming again for the Last Judgement and for the coming of his never-ending Kingdom. These "states" of Christ have in this way a particular soteriological point that includes the worshipping community. Furthermore, the statement about the resurrection on the third day contains an explicit reference to the Scriptures (echoing 1 Cor 15:4) so that the first context in which the resurrection is to be understood is the context of Scripture. All these specifically christological points have to fit into the framework of the Trinitarian statements about the relationship of Jesus Christ as the only Son to God the Father.

The section about the Holy Spirit is introduced by a status description, "the Lord," and a particular activity description, "the giver of life." The identity description is, as in the case of the Son, provided by a relational description, relating the identity of the Spirit to the Father and the Son. Here is not the place to go into the intricacies of the *filioque* debate, but what seems to be excluded at the outset—because it would seriously question the statements made about the Father and the Son—is that the Spirit could proceed from two origins. Any claim that there are two *archai* would call the one *arche*, the Father, into question and would be a dangerous step in the direction of polytheism. If this cannot be meant here, because it would be self-contradictory, what is it that the Western church wanted to safeguard by the *filioque* clause? And what would be theologically acceptable to the East if it could be stated in such a way that their theological concerns could be fully taken into account? At least one of the questions that would have to be discussed in detail is: What difference does the *filioque* clause make to the way Western Christianity celebrates worship in relation to the patterns of worship in the Divine Liturgy of the East?

It seems that the phrase "who with the Father and the Son is worshipped and glorified" follows immediately from the statement of the procession of the Spirit. Proceeding, like begetting must be interpreted as the form of constitutive relation in which the divine Being is transmitted to the Spirit. That this is so is safeguarded by the reference to worship. If the Spirit were not of one with the Being of the Father and the Son (who is of one Being with the Father), worshipping and glorifying the Spirit would be idolatry. It seems that the explicit reference to the communicative relationship of God with Israel before the incarnation in the phrase "He has spoken through the prophets" explicitly makes the work of the Spirit coextensive with the whole divine economy. Everything that God does in relation to creation is done through the Spirit. The history of prophetic communication in this way becomes an introduction to the incarnation of the divine Word who "by the power of the Holy Spirit" becomes incarnate. The frequent emphasis on the sending of the Spirit by Christ, which in Western theology is based on a Johannine pneumatology, is thereby balanced by an account of the activity of the Spirit where the Spirit is not only consequent upon the Christ event but also constitutive for it.

That the Holy Spirit has spoken through the prophets becomes in this way an introduction to the statements about the church and baptism. The pattern of divine communication through human means of communication is continued, expanded, and modified in the one, holy, catholic, and apostolic church. Just as God addresses the community by the speech of the Holy Spirit through the human means of prophetic proclamation, so the church is witness and instrument of God's communication to creation. The attributes of the church as one, holy, catholic, and apostolic must be interpreted in a similar way. The oneness of the church is rooted in the oneness of the one God. The way in which this oneness relates to the historical reality of creation must be based on a christological mediation which through the Holy Spirit is directed toward the life of the world to come. In a similar way, holiness and catholicity would have to be interpreted as the witness to the divine constitution of the church which, on the basis of the scriptural witness, would always include reference to the being of the church as the form of being "in Christ" and to the outpouring of the Holy Spirit as the Spirit of that particular community. The apostolicity of the church contains a specific reference to the mission of the Apostles and thereby establishes a link to Jesus Christ. The combination of these attributes calls for a Trinitarian explication.

Baptism in the name of the Father, the Son, and the Spirit, already mentioned in Matt 28:19 and in Didache 17:1, asserts a link between the identity of the God Christians confess in their confession of faith and the forgiveness of sins as the establishment of communion with that God. Establishing communion with God is the hallmark of this particular community. On the basis of the Pauline statement that the "wages of sin is death, but the free gift of God is the eternal life in Christ Jesus our Lord" (Rom 6:23), the transition from acknowledging baptism for the forgiveness of sin to eschatological expectation is evident.

Looking for the resurrection of the dead and the life of the world to come combines the distinguishing mark of the work of the Spirit as the "giver of life" with the participation of believers in the death and resurrection of Christ. The closing statements of the Creed almost read like a commentary on one of the most concise statements of the prototrinitarian grammar of theological discourse in the New Testament: "If the Spirit of him who raised Jesus from the dead dwells in you, he who raised Christ Jesus from the dead will give life to your mortal bodies also through his Spirit which dwells in you. (Rom 8:11).[4]

---

4. I have used the expression "prototrinitarian grammar of theological discourse" in order to make quite clear that the doctrine of the Trinity is not stated in the New Testament in the form of doctrinal statements as we have them in the fourth century.

In our brief exegesis of some of the key phrase of the Creed, as it is confessed in worship we have concentrated on the content of the faith (*fides quae creditur*) and its Trinitarian assertions, presuppositions, and implications. What about the "we believe . . ." that introduces these contents? What about the act of faith, the faith through which one believes (*fides qua creditur*)? The connection between act and content can be expressed in the following way. If we understand faith as the act of ultimate existential trust in that upon which we "hang our heart," then the content of faith has to present the one in whom we can trust in this ultimate sense. It is one of the core convictions of Christian faith that only God who is the maker of heaven and earth, who secures our salvation and grants us eternal life in communion with himself can be the "object" of such ultimate trust. And conversely, if there is a God, who as the creator of everything that exists is the giver of salvation and the source of everlasting life, it would make no sense not to trust in him unconditionally. There is a relationship of strict correlation or even of mutual implication between the *act of faith* as ultimate existential trust and the *content of faith* as it is expressed in the Creed. It is precisely this correlation that calls for a Trinitarian explication. On the one hand, it is clear that the action of God in creation is continued in the reconciling work of Christ in such a sense that God's faithfulness to his original self-determination is maintained against the contradiction of his human creature and perfected in the work of God the Spirit by constituting a communion with God in a believing community that does not end with time but is continued in the eternity of God's eternal life. On the other hand, believing now in the power of the Holy Spirit, points to God's reconciling work in the Son as the access of God's estranged human creatures to communion with God the Father. According to the *ordo essendi*, the order of being, the direction goes from the Father, to the Son, to the Spirit. In the order of knowing, the *ordo cognoscendi*, we are directed by the certainty concerning the truth of the Gospel, which the Spirit grants, to the gospel of Christ as the true disclosure of the being and will of God the Father. This leads directly to the question: How is such a certainty of faith constituted?

Nevertheless, the grammatical rules for speaking of the Father, of Christ, and of the Spirit already anticipate ways of speaking about God that were then conceptually refined in the fourth century. This grammar is already adumbrated in Israel's Bible. In Second Temple Judaism we have a highly developed form of a differentiated understanding of God, which shows many analogies and parallels to the later Trinitarian formulations of Christian doctrine. For a recent provocative account shattering easy assumptions about Jewish monotheism, see Schäfer, *Zwei Götter im Himmel*. For a theological account of the roots of the prototrinitarian grammar of theological discourse, see Schwöbel, "Trinity between Athens and Jerusalem," 22–41.

The Promise of the Triune God

The Augsburg Confession seems to answer this question directly, when it states in Article V "Concerning the Office of Preaching":

> To obtain such faith God instituted the office of preaching, giving the gospel and the sacraments. Through these as through means, he gives the Holy Spirit who produces faith, where and when he wills, in those who hear the gospel. It teaches that we have a gracious God, not through our merit but through Christ's merit, when we believe.[5]

The constitution of the act of faith that invests ultimate trust in God is throughout history connected with the practice of preaching of which we already find echoes in the traditions of the New Testament. In the early church, preaching was closely related to the exposition of biblical texts, first the Old Testament, then increasingly focused on the Jesus traditions, and—in a further step—the Christian canon. It is perhaps no accident that the great theologians who shaped the doctrine of the Trinity, Basil of Caesarea, Gregory of Nazianzus, and Gregory of Nyssa, as well as Augustine, were all regarded as great preachers, combining intellectual subtlety, rhetorical brilliance, and a deep sense of Christian piety. In the early Middle Ages preaching had a predominantly doctrinal character or was employed for moral exhortation. The highly sophisticated sermons that were fashioned in the context of the cathedral schools and earliest universities found their counterpart in the popular preachers of the mendicant orders who made preaching one of the most popular events in the communicative life of medieval cities. In Reformation theology preaching was elevated to a place among the means of salvation since it was seen together with the administration of the sacraments as one of the instruments instituted by God to create faith. If one looks closely at the quotation from the Augsburg Confession one can grasp the Trinitarian structure of preaching. Instituted by God, preaching and the sacraments are the instruments employed by the Holy Spirit to create faith that has as its content the true treasure of the church, the Gospel of the grace, and glory of Christ. If faith shall be created through the instrumentality of preaching, then its content must be the Gospel of Christ that we have a gracious God.

The relationship of preaching and faith is often expressed in the correlation between the promise of the Gospel and faith. On such an account, preaching does not consist in providing information about what God has done in Christ. Rather, preaching continues Christ's work by witnessing

---

5. Kolb and Wengert, *Book of Concord*, 40.

to it in such a way that this testimony can be used as an instrument for creating faith. In order to witness to God's promise preaching must communicate this promise. The concept of witness is central for preaching because in preaching the preacher points away from herself to the event that is being witnessed to in the confidence that this event is continued and made effective by God in creating faith, employing the human witness to the event as the instrument of its communicative efficacy. It is important to restrict preaching neither to offering propositions about the truth of the events of God's saving history in Israel, in Christ, and in the church, nor to a performative speech-act that addresses the listener with Christ's promise. The performative dimension of preaching remains bound to the assertorical dimension making specific truth claims, since the effect of the performance is not based on uttering the right words in the right context, but on the illuminating experience in which the listeners find that the truth asserted and promised creates a correspondence in their personal experience.

The relationship between the external word of preaching and the inward testimony of the Holy Spirit follows the Trinitarian logic in which the Spirit authenticates and ascertains the truth of the Gospel of Christ as a true account of God's gracious will toward creation as it is rooted in God's being. The practice of preaching in Christian worship is in this way made an element in the self-presentation of the triune God in the Spirit and through Christ. Preaching becomes an instrument of the self-presentation of the triune God and so waits on the event of the disclosure of the presence of God.

The Presence of the Triune God

The presence of God in the communion of his people is the focus of Holy Communion in Christian worship. The mode of this presence is also one of the most contentious issues in the doctrinal debates between the different Christian churches. Can it be characterized as real presence or is it a form of presence mediated in the signifying acts of liturgical action? Does it require a transubstantiation of the elements in order to be authentic presence? Who effects this transubstantiation? In our reflections so far we have tried to point to the Trinitarian elements embedded in Christian worship and we have tried to point to the way in which the practice of Christian worship requires conceptual explication in a Christian doctrine of the Trinity. Does this approach also help to expose the Trinitarian logic implicit in the practice of celebrating Holy Communion? In this way it would point to the tasks of an adequate conceptual explication.[6]

6. For the particularities of a Lutheran understanding of Holy Communion, see

Many forms of celebrating Holy Communion in the Western churches contain the following elements: the Offertory, the Great Thanksgiving, beginning with an opening dialogue and the so-called Preface, followed by the Sanctus. The Narrative of the Institution is at the heart of celebrating communion followed by the Epiclesis, the sharing of bread and wine as body and blood of Christ, followed by a prayer of thanksgiving. If one looks carefully at the words, gestures, and liturgical actions, we see that the presence of the triune God in Holy Communion is asked for, celebrated, enjoyed, and given thanks for in the modes of prayers to the Father, the Son and the Holy Spirit. In the Preface, the minister offers thanksgiving to the Father for the sending of his Son for our salvation, and this thanksgiving leads into praise of God in which the whole cosmos is involved. The presence of God is here the cosmic presence which comprises the whole cosmos. The Sanctus, which is usually sung at this point, expresses this pointedly: "Heaven and earth are full of your glory." The presence of God is here not to be understood as God's presence in the world but rather as the pervasive presence of the glory of God in all the world so that the world becomes present before God. When the Sanctus continues with the Hosanna, "Blessed is he who comes in the name of the Lord," we hear a clear echo of the Creed's phrase: "For us and our salvation he came down from heaven." The cosmic presence of God is in this way related to the coming of the Incarnate Son. The presence of the glory of God which envelops and pervades the whole created world becomes a historical presence in creation. The act of praise that is sometimes inserted here usually connects the comprehensive presence of God to the historical presence of God in creation and in Israel, concluding with the presence of God in Jesus Christ, the incarnate Son. Christ is the incarnation of the plenitude of God in creation, precisely in the way in which he receives everything from the Father and refers everything to the Father.

When we now hear the narrative of the Institution it has one point from which all other aspects are illuminated. Jesus Christ, in the night when he was betrayed, gives himself to his people in the form of a continued practice of celebrating communion with him and through him with the triune God and in the form of the preaching of the gospel, which is intrinsically connected to the celebration of the Eucharist. Our remembrance of him is the form of his self-presentation to us. The Anamnesis makes that clear. Our remembering of Jesus Christ's self-giving can have no other form then the petition: "Amen. Come Lord Jesus." Just as our remembering is the mode of Christ's self-presentation, so is our reception of the presence of Christ

---

Schwöbel, "Zum Verständnis des Abendmahls nach evangelisch-lutherischer Lehre," 382–423.

in the gifts of his body and his blood, not something that we could receive appropriately by ourselves. Therefore, in the Epiclesis we ask for the coming of the Holy Spirit to enable us to receive the presence of Christ. This, too, is the gift of the Triune God in the Holy Spirit. This has a number of crucial implications. If it is the self-presentation of Christ in the Spirit that gives continuity to the life of the Christian church, the church cannot be seen as the extension of the incarnation, as Johann Adam Möhler maintained in a phrase widely repeated in Roman Catholicism and Anglicanism. There is no change of subject here. There is only one hypostatic union. Christ's own continuing presence in word and sacraments is the extension of the incarnation and nothing else. Christ's continuing presence in the church is the essence of the church as Christ's body.

The presence of God in Holy Communion is the event of his Trinitarian self-presentation in which the modes of his presence are related in such a way that they are focussed in the presence of Christ with the communion of his people in the act of celebrating this communion in a shared meal. If we follow the different speech-acts and communicative actions that make up the celebration of the Eucharist, it seems clear that the task of conceptual explication must take its starting point from these liturgical acts and one cannot fit them into the scheme of a preconceived metaphysics. Rather, the direction of conceptual exploration must take the other direction of enquiring how our concepts must be reformed in order to be able to express and explicate adequately the reality of the presence of the Triune God that is celebrated in Holy Communion.

Being Sent

After the thanksgiving, the service continues with intercessions, usually consisting of prayers for the church, both world-wide and local, including ourselves as members of the church in all the different scenes of life, and of prayers for the world. The self-giving of Christ in Holy Communion is but one aspect in which Christ exercises his priesthood. The other closely connected aspect is that he intercedes for us before God the Father when we direct our prayer in the Spirit to God the Father. The one who gives his life for us, and so establishes in his communion with us our communion with God the Father, is also the one who makes our intercessions his own intercessions before God the Father. When intercessions follow the celebration of Holy Communion, they have a particular poignancy in bringing all the concerns for the church, globally and locally, and for ourselves as members of this church, into the presence of the triune God, which has just been celebrated in Holy Communion. This is the appropriate overture for the sending of the gathered community into the world, which is now no longer seen as the counterpart of the church, an independent realm that appears as enemy territory from within the church. Those who have just sung "Heaven and earth are full of your glory" cannot regard themselves as resident aliens in a foreign land. They will see themselves as those who follow the rays of God's creative, transforming, and perfecting glory into the darkest corner of the world, strengthened by the promise of God's Trinitarian presence.

The blessing, "The Lord bless you and keep you. The Lord make his face to shine on you and be gracious to you. The Lord look upon you with favor and give you peace," echoes the agency of the Trinitarian God as creator, reconciler, and consummator of his creation and reflects the threefold mode of God's presence as the enveloping presence for every place, the illuminating presence of his grace and truth, and the presence that accompanies us on our way to God's eschatological peace.

A Working Sketch for a Continuing Task

In this brief working sketch, we have tried to break up the twofold isolation of the doctrine of the Trinity in piety and in the theology of the schools, which Rahner lamented fifty years ago by bringing the two closer into contact by trying to elucidate the conceptual assertions, presuppositions, and implications embedded in the practice of Christian worship. We have tried to show that Trinitarian theology, asserting real personal relations within the unity of the divine Being, actually helps Christians to understand better what they do when the worship the Father, the Son, and the Holy Spirit.

There are two sets of questions that are generated by such an attempt. On the one hand, there are constructive questions regarding the way in which a Trinitarian conceptuality can be developed if one explores the implicit conceptuality embedded in worship and its explicit form in the Creed that is part of the liturgy. On the other hand, there are critical questions with regard to some forms of school theology that do seem to be less able to offer an account of what Christians do when they worship the triune God. The further task would be to bring the two sets of questions, the constructive explorations and the critical modifications, closer together and to analyze the specific concepts of the doctrine of the Trinity by employing the practice of worship as a provocation to reform the concepts of school theology. Christian worship is also a form of faith seeking understanding. Could it be that the blessing offered in the name of the triune God also holds a promise for such continuing work?

Bibliography

Brunner, Peter. *Zur Lehre vom Gottesdienst der im Namen Jesu versammelten Gemeinde.* In Leiturgia Bd. 1, 84–361. Kassel: Johannes Stauda Verlag, 1954.

Evangelisches Gottesdienstbuch. Agende für die Evangelische Kirche der Union und für die Vereinigte Evangelisch-Lutherische Kirche Deutschlands. Berlin: Verlagsgemeinschaft "Evangelisches Gottesdienstbuch," 2000.

Feiner, Johannes, and Magnus Löhrer, eds. *Mysterium Salutis: Grundriss heilgeschichtlicher Dogmatik.* Einsiedeln: Benziger, 1967.

Kolb, Robert, and Timothy J. Wengert, eds. *The Book of Concord. The Confessions of the Evangelical Lutheran Church.* Minneapolis: Fortress, 2000.

Lutheran Book of Worship. Minneapolis: Augsburg, 1978.

Rahner, Karl. *The Trinity.* Translated by Joseph Donceel. New York: Crossroad, 2004.

Schäfer, Peter. *Zwei Götter im Himmel? Gottesvorstellungen in der jüdischen Antike.* Munich: C. H. Beck, 2017.

Schwöbel, Christoph. "The Trinity between Athens and Jerusalem." *Journal of Reformed Theology* 3 (2009) 22–41.

———. "Was ist ein Gottesdienst? Theologische Kriterien zur Angemessenheit der gottesdienstlichen Feier." In *Kompendium Gottesdienst: der evangelische Gottesdienst in Geschichte und Gegenwart,* edited by H.-J. Eckstein, U. Heckel, and B. Weyel, 145–65. Tübingen, 2011.

———. "Where Do We Stand in Trinitarian Theology? Resources, Revisions, and Reappraisals." In *Recent Developments in Trinitarian Theology: An International Symposium,* edited by Christophe Chalamet and Marc Vial, 9–71. Minneapolis: Fortress Press, 2014.

———. "Zum Verständnis des Abendmahls nach evangelisch-lutherischer Lehre." In *Taufe und Abendmahl im Grund und Gegenstand des Glaubens,* edited by E. Herms and L. Zak, 382–423. Tübingen: Mohr Siebeck, 2017.

Wainwright, Geoffrey. *Doxology. The Praise of God in Worship, Doctrine and Life.* New York: Oxford University Press, 1984 [1980].

Wolterstorff, Nicholas. *The God We Worship: An Exploration of Liturgical Theology.* Grand Rapids, MI: Eerdmans, 2015.

www.ingramcontent.com/pod-product-compliance
Lightning Source LLC
Chambersburg PA
CBHW031808220426
43662CB00007B/567